ULTIMATE

BOOK OF

CARD GAMES

ULTIMATE

BOOK OF

CARD GAMES

The Comprehensive Guide

TO MORE THAN 350 GAMES

BY SCOTT McNEELY
ILLUSTRATIONS BY ARTHUR MOUNT

CHRONICLE BOOKS
SAN FRANCISCO

Text copyright © 2009 by Scott McNeely.
Illustrations copyright © 2009 by Arthur Mount.

Library of Congress Cataloging-in-Publication Data available.
ISBN: 978-0-8118-6642-2
Manufactured in China.

Designed by Allison Weiner.

10 9 8 7 6 5 4 3

Chronicle Books LLC
680 Second Street
San Francisco, California 94107

www.chroniclebooks.com

TABLE OF CONTENTS

- -

- -

Introduction

You could make the argument that "playing cards" sounds mighty old fashioned—not unlike bingo, croquet, or sword fighting. In the age of the Internet, can any game played with mere cards be anything but outdated?

Find out for yourself by hosting a poker or card night and watch what happens. No phones, no television, no computers—just everybody having a good time together. And that's the key word: *together*.

Playing cards is a massively social activity, whether you're bluffing your way out of a bad Texas Hold'em hand or going toe-to-toe with friends in a heated game of Hearts. Cards are a catalyst, and their real power is their ability to draw friends, families, and even strangers together.

It's a safe bet you've never heard of half the games covered in this book, and that's half the joy of perusing the *Ultimate Book of Card Games*. Certainly cards can be a dull diversion used to pass the time when there's nothing much better to do. But this is the rare exception to an otherwise inspired pantheon of such card games as Poker, Euchre, Bridge, Spades, Pinochle, Rummy, Blackjack, Spite & Malice, Brag, Klaberjass, Hearts, Canasta—the list of great games goes on and on.

While there is no single definition for what makes a game "great," I've used two simple guidelines to select what games to include in the *Ultimate Book of Card Games*. The games in this book have withstood the test of time and are guaranteed to satisfy the card player's most basic desire: to have a bit of fun.

—Scott McNeely

.OI

Let the Games Begin

CHAPTER ONE

Let the Games Begin

A VERY BRIEF HISTORY OF CARDS

The earliest "cards"—actually domino tiles, played like cards—came from China around AD 960. Playing cards made their first appearance in Europe in the 1370s. Remarkably, these ancient European cards would be instantly recognizable today. They contained four suits, each headed by a king and two "marshals," plus ten other cards, for a total of fifty-two cards. By 1480, the French had introduced the modern system of suits based on hearts, spades, clubs, and diamonds.

From the earliest times, cards have been associated with European aristocracy—they could afford hand-painted decks of cards and had leisure time to spare—as well as gamblers and lowlifes. Neither association is quite fair, because cards permeated all levels of society, with equal numbers of gambling and non-gambling games. The world of cards has always been diverse, from trick taking to melding, from Solitaire to multiplayer games, from massively complex games like Contract Bridge to absurdly simply ones like Indian Poker.

Poker and Panguingue were the first games to make serious inroads in the United States, along with Solitaire and its many variants. Poker and Panguingue were popular gambling games in the California goldfields from 1850 onward; Solitaire was an import from Victorian Britain.

By the early 1900s, in both the United States and Britain, the previously popular game of Whist was supplanted by various forms of Bridge. Bridge remained the most popular game in America well into the 1960s, followed by Rummy, Canasta, Solitaire, and Poker.

Poker has always been popular in the United States, but it wasn't until the 1990s that the game truly took off. That's largely due to Texas Hold'em and the invention of the in-table television camera. The camera (which lets a home audience see all the players' cards in real time) transformed a slow and—let's be honest—dull game for observers into an adrenaline-filled battle with millions of dollars at stake.

The Internet has breathed fresh life into many card games, with online forums dedicated to Hearts, Spades, Bridge, Solitaire, Poker—you name it. In a strange way, given the social nature of most games, cards are well suited to the Web 2.0's social networks, and to dispersed groups of friends who crave an interpersonal activity to bring them together. If nothing else, cards have proven to be highly adaptable over the past eight hundred years. There's no reason to believe the end of the card-playing era is anywhere in sight.

HOW TO USE THIS BOOK

The *Ultimate Book of Card Games* is a great resource. It contains hundreds of fascinating games to keep you entertained for months on end, and it makes a handsome addition to your gaming library.

What this book is *not* is a definitive guide to the games it covers. Do not follow this book zealously or take it too seriously. To do so would mean swimming upstream against the entire history of card games.

Card games are not pieces of legislation passed by a congress. They are not messages from on high. Card games are more like Darwin's finches. They evolve. They mutate. Take your eye off a card game and—presto!—new rules are added and old ones discarded.

> **If you've heard of Edmond Hoyle, you might think he literally "wrote the book" on card games and their rules. Nothing of the sort. Hoyle did publish a book called *A Short Treatise on the Game of Whist* in 1742. However, his focus was on how to play—that is, how to win—not on documenting the rules, which he assumed readers already knew. More than 250 years after his death, Hoyle would be surprised— unpleasantly so—by the dozens of books bearing his name and pretending to be a definitive guide to cards.**

The reality is that ninety-nine percent of the world's card games have no definitive rules. Bridge is the one exception: formal committees approve its rules. Every other game is in a continual state of flux and is played with variations from region to region, state to state, and country to country. And there's absolutely nothing wrong with this.

Disputes, when they arise, are the result of players relying on unspoken assumptions or following contradictory sets of rules. So use this book to discover new games and learn how to play them, but don't panic if you, your parents, grandparents, or friends use different rules or favor variations not covered in this book. That's OK. It's in the very nature of cards to be variable.

All we really ask is that you follow one basic piece of advice: Always review the rules of play before you deal a single card. Everybody at a table must follow the same set of rules, and everybody should know in advance what those rules are.

A note on terminology, too. We've included the most common gaming and card-playing terms in this book's glossary. So when you see a word or phrase in bold italics—**blind bet**, for example—flip to the glossary for a definition.

CARD BASICS FOR FIRST-TIME PLAYERS

Here are the most important things you need to know if you're new to card games. You can safely skip this section if you've played cards before.

☞ **SUITS & RANKS** A standard deck has fifty-two cards, divided equally into four suits called hearts (♥), spades (♠), diamonds (♦), and clubs (♣). The two jokers are not typically used. In each suit there are thirteen card rankings or ranks, from 2 to 10, plus a jack, queen, king, and ace. In most games, 2 is the lowest in rank, ace the highest (although in many games the ace also can be played as the lowest card, as in 5-4-3-2-A). Some games have their own peculiar ranking systems—for example, when 2s through 6s are removed from the deck, or when jacks rank higher than kings. Those ranking variances are outlined in the rules of play that are given for each game.

☞ **DEALING** Cards are usually dealt clockwise, starting with the person to the left of the dealer. Cards are always dealt face down, one at a time, unless otherwise stated in the rules.

☞ **GAMES, HANDS, ROUNDS & TURNS** Games are often made up of *hands* (sometimes called *deals*), in which all players compete. Points or scores earned in a hand typically count toward an overall game score. Hands are often broken into *rounds*, in which each active player is usually required to perform some action (play a card, discard, make a bet, etc.). Within each round, each player has his own specific *turn*, and it is considered rude for one player to perform an action (e.g., make a bet, fold, etc.) when it is not his turn.

☞ **TRICKS** Some games—such as Hearts, Spades, Bridge, etc.—are played in tricks. A *trick* comprises all the cards played in a single round (one card from each player). So in a Hearts game with five players, a single trick contains five cards. In Bridge, a trick typically contains four cards.

☞ **TRUMP & NO TRUMP**   Many trick-taking games also rely on ***trump***. A trump is a suit (e.g., hearts, spades, diamonds, clubs) that outranks all the other suits for the duration of that hand. For example, if spades are trump, it means that a spade will beat any other card, even if that other card is of a higher rank—a lowly 2♠ will beat A♥ or any other high card that isn't a spade. If two trumps are played in the same trick, the higher-ranking trump wins. *No trump* means that for the duration of the hand, no suit is trump.

☞ **BIDDING**   In games that include bidding, players must estimate how many total tricks they think they can win. Whoever bids the highest amount typically wins the bid and therefore earns the right to score points, determine the trump, play the first card, etc. Keep in mind that table talk (communicating with your partner about strategy, about your cards, or about anything remotely related to the current hand) is universally outlawed in games that feature bidding.

TIPS FOR HOSTING YOUR OWN POKER NIGHT OR CARD NIGHT

Here are five of the most important things to consider when hosting a home poker or card game. Ignore them at your peril!

1. **YOU NEED A TABLE**. At the risk of stating the obvious, you need a flat, uncluttered, reasonably large table in order to play the games described in this book.

2. **YOU NEED PLAYERS**. Seven or eight players are ideal for Poker, Blackjack, Texas Hold'em, and most of the betting games covered in this book. For Bridge, you need four players. For other games, you need from two to ten players—unless you're playing Solitaire, in which case one is the perfect number.

3. **YOU NEED A BANKER**. Many of the betting games in this book require somebody to play the role of banker/dealer. In Blackjack, players typically take turns serving as banker/dealer for a predetermined period (usually five to ten deals). If you're playing Bridge or another game where points are worth money, you don't need a banker so much as you need one person who can review the scores and verify everybody's math.

4. **"BUT OFFICER, WE WEREN'T PLAYING WITH *REAL* MONEY…"** Gambling is generally not endorsed by law enforcement agencies. Rest easy, though, because "social gaming" is legal in many U.S. states, as long as the event is held in a private home, is not advertised, has no minors present, and does not take a *rake* (it makes no money by hosting the game).

5. **STOCK UP ON CHIPS & CHANGE**. Chip values vary from game to game, depending on the **table stakes**. In "friendly" games, chips might be worth something like $5 (black), $1 (blue), 50 cents (red), 25 cents (white). At the end of the night, you'll also want plenty of $1 and $5 bills to make change.

THE MIND GAME: HOW TO THINK LIKE A WINNER IN CARDS

Whether you've been playing cards for five minutes or fifty years, the following commonsense rules will help you get the most from any card game.

☞ **THINK BEFORE YOU DRINK**. Excessive drinking—getting loaded, liquored, trollied, mashed, or hammered—is one of the main culprits contributing to a card player's bad decisions. Remember that casino drinks are free for a reason, so steer clear of alcohol, especially when you're playing Poker.

☞ **YOU NEED AN OBJECTIVE**. We're not talking about a war game or a performance review. We're talking about having a reason to play each time you sit at a table. Whatever your reason to play, stick with it. If you start playing to have fun, but then get agitated and start playing simply to win (or even worse, to win money), you're unlikely to do either very well.

☞ **DON'T BE IN A HURRY**. Each game has its own rhythm and subtleties, so take time to learn the basics from other players (or from experienced players at a casino). Even thirty minutes spent observing a table of skilled players is sure to be fruitful.

☞ **TRUST YOUR INSTINCTS**. Don't be afraid to bid or bet aggressively when you're on a hot streak, and conversely, if you think you've been beaten, you're probably right.

☞ **STAY IN CONTROL**. Don't play new games for high stakes; don't stay in games played for money with opponents who are clearly better than you; don't be afraid to ask about rules; don't be afraid to fold in gambling games; and don't play cards with money you can't afford to lose.

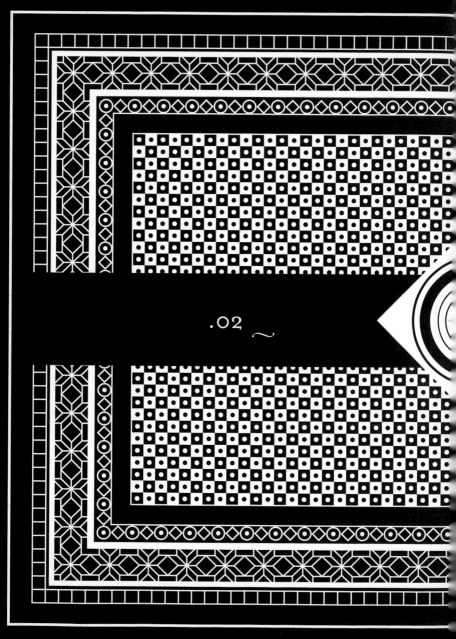

.02 ~

Games for One Player

CHAPTER TWO

Games for One Player

SOLITAIRE IS NOT A SINGLE GAME. The name refers to a family of games that use a *tableau* of cards laid out on a playing surface, plus a *stock pile* of cards from which to draw, in order to build piles of cards that are matched in some way (typically by suit and rank). There are hundreds of Solitaire variations, often known by different names, depending on where or how you first learned the game.

> **Is Solitaire a game or a puzzle? The answer is—it's a game! Puzzles have just one solution. And once you discover the solution, the puzzle is solved. Solitaire, on the other hand, is almost infinitely variable. There is no single solution to any hand. And it often requires a strong dollop of skill to win.**

In England this family of games is known as *Patience*, and in many respects the name Patience is better suited, since many of the games below can be played by two or more players and are not strictly solitary pursuits. Universally, the games also require plenty of patience to play.

A BRIEF HISTORY

Modern Solitaire was probably invented in Scandinavia or Germany in the 1700s. The first reference—a one-player game played head to head by two people, for a wager—dates from 1783. From the beginning, it seems, Solitaire was both a solo pursuit and a competitive game.

The British did not embrace Solitaire until the 1850s, but once they did, it was a huge hit. Charles Dickens's *Great Expectations* mentions the game (Magwitch was a Patience player!). In the United States, the game was never aggressively commercialized, and there is no single "official" compendium of rules or regulations. Hence the profusion of games, often played with major rule differences from region to region.

THE BASICS

At its most fundamental, Solitaire is a game in which players attempt to organize a deck of cards into a specific order, depending on the rules of the game being played. Most Solitaire games feature ***foundations*** (typically, but not always, the four aces), on top of which cards of matching suit are piled. You typically end a successful game of Solitaire with four piles, each containing thirteen cards organized by suit and rank.

Most games also feature a ***tableau***, which is a layout or workspace for cards organized into specific shapes, sequences, or even fanciful arrangements. Skip below to Archway or Clock for examples of tableaus gone wild.

Lastly, Solitaire games generally come in two varieties: *play out* (building up four foundation piles from ace to king, by suit) and *elimination* (removing cards from the game in pairs or in some specific pattern).

POPULAR SOLITAIRE VARIATIONS

ACCORDION

DIFFICULTY *high*	TIME LENGTH *short*	DECKS 1

This is a devilishly difficult Solitaire game. Hoyle's estimates the odds of winning Accordion at 1 in 100 (I think these odds are generous: I was unable to win a single hand after more—many more—than a hundred deals).

Like chess, Accordion rewards players who can visualize a handful of different options and mentally play each out over three, four, or even five plays, in order to select the best option. This game is all about thinking ahead.

∾ **HOW TO DEAL** Start with a standard fifty-two-card deck, and, moving left to right, deal cards face-up in a row. At any point, you may pause to build or move cards, and then continue dealing cards out in an ever-expanding row. There is no minimum or maximum number of cards you may deal, though players typically deal out four or five cards at a time.

∾ **WINNING** In Accordion, the goal is to build all fifty-two cards into a single pile.

∾ **HOW TO PLAY** You may build cards of matching rank (queen on queen) *or* of matching suit (club on club). However you may only build a card one position to its left *or* three positions to its left. For example, you may build 7♣ on top of Q♣ in the sample below because both are clubs and because Q♣ is one position to the left of 7♣.

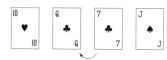

Things get complicated when you have more than one option, as in the deal 10♥-Q♣-7♣-2♦-Q♠. It is legal to build 7♣ on Q♣ (both are clubs) *or* to build Q♠ on Q♣ (both are queens). It's a bit easier contemplating the deal 5♥-7♣-Q♦-5♣. Move 5♣ to 5♥, then move 7♣ to 5♣. This consolidates your piles and gets you one small step closer to victory. The game ends when you deal out the deck and run out of moves.

ACES UP

DIFFICULTY *low*	TIME LENGTH *short*	DECKS 1

Here's a simple Solitaire game that is easy to learn. And because the odds of winning are around 1 in 10 hands, there's a decent chance you might actually win a few games.

∾ **HOW TO DEAL** Start with a standard fifty-two-card deck, and deal four cards, face up, in a square pattern. This is your tableau. Leave space in the middle for a discard pile.

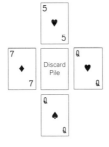

∾ **WINNING** The goal is to finish with all cards—except the four aces—in the discard pile. You have won if only the four aces are left facing up—hence the name, Aces Up.

HOW TO PLAY Deal one card to each tableau pile, then discard the lower-ranking card (or cards) of any cards in the same suit. In the example above, discard 5♥, since it is of the same suit as and of lower rank than Q♥. Deal four more cards when you can no longer move. Aces are ranked high, so once you deal an ace onto the table, it must stay on the table.

When a slot is empty, you must move the topmost card (and only the top-most card!) from another pile onto the empty slot. You are not allowed to deal directly from the deck onto an empty tableau slot.

ALHAMBRA

DIFFICULTY *medium*	TIME LENGTH *medium*	DECKS 2

Alhambra is just hard enough to provide a challenge, but not so hard as to be discouraging (you should win one in every seven games). Luck plays a starring role here, as it does in most Solitaire games. But with two decks of cards and eight foundation piles in play, Alhambra is rarely dull.

HOW TO DEAL Shuffle together two fifty-two-card decks (104 cards total). At the start of the hand, promote a random king and ace to the foundations. Deal eight tableau piles below, face down, with four cards per pile and the top-most cards face up. The remaining cards are your stock pile.

WINNING It's a two-step process. First, promote all kings and aces to the foundations (kings to the left, aces to the right). On kings, you build down in suit (K-Q-J . . . 3-2-A), while on aces you build up in suit (A-2-3 . . . J-Q-K). The goal is to end the game with eight piles of cards, each organized by suit.

HOW TO PLAY After the initial deal, move exposed kings and aces to the foundations, then build any cards of matching suit to the foundations. There is no other building in Alhambra—either you move a card from the tableau to the foundations or you move nothing at all. After moving a tableau card to the foundations, turn up the next card in that same tableau pile.

If you have no moves on the board, expose the top stock-pile card. You may play stock cards directly onto the foundations or the tableau. If there is no valid play for the stock card, turn it face down in a waste pile and then turn up the next stock card. Shuffle the waste pile and create a new stock pile once you've exhausted all stock cards. You are allowed to shuffle the waste pile twice. After that, the game is over.

AMAZONS

DIFFICULTY low	TIME LENGTH short	DECKS 1

This is named after a mythical all-female tribe of warriors. In honor of the Amazon women, the hand in this game is won when queens appear on all four foundations. The game is easy to learn, easy to play, and moderately easy to win (odds of winning are 1 in every 5 hands).

∾ **HOW TO DEAL** Start with a fifty-two-card deck, and remove the 2, 3, 4, 5, 6, K, A of each suit, leaving twenty-four cards. Deal four tableau cards, face up.

∾ **WINNING** The object is to build four foundations by suit and in ascending rank (7-8-9-10-J-Q). The game is won when each of the four queens is successfully played onto its appropriate foundation pile.

∾ **HOW TO PLAY** The starting layout is as basic as it gets: four tableau cards dealt face up. If you turn up a 7, move it to the foundation directly above (unless this slot is already filled, in which case you may move the 7 to any other vacant foundation).

In Amazons, you may not move or play cards from one tableau pile to another, nor may you play a tableau card on any other foundation pile except the one directly above it. In the example on the following page, you may promote 7♦ from the tableau to the foundation, but you *may not* play 8♦ on 7♦ because the diamond foundation pile is not directly above the 8♦. Instead, you must exhaust your stock pile and hope that the 8♦ is later turned up in the diamonds column.

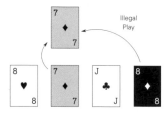

After completing your moves, deal four more cards from the stock to the tableau, and make as many moves as your cards allow. In the example below, 7♣ is turned up in the second tableau pile; since its foundation slot is already occupied, move 7♣ to any other vacant foundation slot. (This is the only time you are allowed to ignore the rule about playing tableau cards only to the foundation piles directly above them.) In this case the obvious move is above 8♣, which you may now move up to the foundation directly above it.

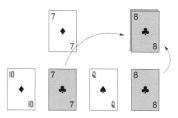

Note that you may only ever play the topmost tableau card. If a card you need becomes buried in a tableau pile, all you can do is wait and hope it will turn up.

Once you exhaust the stock, create a new pile by taking up the four tableau piles from left to right and turning them face down. Do not reshuffle. You may deal and redeal as many times as necessary until the game is either won or lost.

ARCHWAY

DIFFICULTY *high*	TIME LENGTH *long*	DECKS 2

The odds of winning Archway are less than 1 in 100 games. For some, this is reason enough to skip this two-deck monster. For the rest of you, Archway is a true Solitaire challenge requiring an equal mix of both skill and luck.

∾ **HOW TO DEAL** Start with two fifty-two-card decks (104 cards total). Take one ace from each suit and one king from each suit—these will become part of your eight foundations—and place them at the bottom of your tableau.

Next, deal four piles (twelve cards per pile) face down in the center of the table, and turn up the top card of each pile. This is your tableau.

Finally, deal the remaining cards into thirteen piles organized by rank. For example, deal all aces into a pile, all 2s, all 3s, etc. These thirteen piles are your ***reserve*** and should be arranged in the shape of an arch around your tableau, like so:

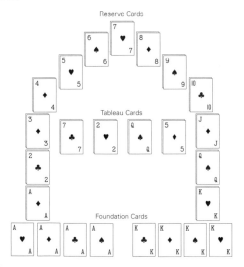

∾ **WINNING** The object is to move all tableau and reserve cards onto the eight foundation piles, organized by suit and by rank. On the aces, build in ascending rank (A♥-2♥-3♥ . . . J♥-Q♥-K♥), while on the kings, build in descending rank (K♣-Q♣-J♣ . . . 3♣-2♣-A♣).

∾ **HOW TO PLAY** Once dealt, Archway is simple to play. Move tableau and reserve cards onto your foundations as appropriate. There are only a few restrictions.

Only the top tableau and reserve cards may be played. If a card you need is buried deeply in a tableau or reserve pile, you must wait until all those suffocating cards on top are played.

There is no building. You may not, for example, move a card from a reserve pile onto another reserve pile or onto a tableau pile. Cards may be moved only onto the foundations.

The lone exception to this rule is if there's a vacant spot on the tableau or reserves, in which case you may move the top card from any other tableau or reserve pile into the vacant spot. Tableau cards can be dealt to a vacant reserve spot, and vice versa.

The game ends when you successfully build all eight foundations or exhaust your reserves and run out of moves.

AULD LANG SYNE

DIFFICULTY *high*	TIME LENGTH *short*	DECKS 1

Many of the best Solitaire games follow a similar recipe: 99 percent luck, 1 percent skill. Auld Lang Syne is a textbook example of this style. It's all luck, precious little skill, and devilishly hard to win. Odds of winning are 1 in every 300 games.

∾ **HOW TO DEAL** Start with a fifty-two-card deck, and place all four aces on the table, face up. These are your foundations. Next, deal four cards from the stock, face up, immediately below the foundations.

∾ **WINNING** The object is to build each of the four foundations from ace to king in ascending rank but regardless of suit (A♥-2♣-3♦ . . . J♠-Q♠-K♦).

∾ **HOW TO PLAY** Auld Lang Syne, unlike most other Solitaire games, lets you build the four foundations from ace up to king regardless of suit. You also may play the top card from any tableau pile. The only restriction is that you may not move a card from one tableau pile to another; cards may be moved only from the tableau piles to the foundation piles. Once you can no longer move, deal four more cards from the stock onto your tableau piles.

There is no redeal of the stock pile. Once you exhaust the stock, the game is over, simple as that.

- -
VARIATION 1: TAM O'SHANTER
Tam O'Shanter takes a game that is already very hard to win and makes it even harder (the odds of winning are now 1 in 10,000 games). It does so with one simple rule change: Do not deal the four aces at the start of the game. Instead, leave the foundations vacant until the aces are exposed during the normal course of play.

- -
VARIATION 2: SIR TOMMY
If Tam O'Shanter makes the basic game harder to win, Sir Tommy adds a bit of skill to the basic game. The odds of winning are the same (about 1 in 300). It's just that you now exert more control over how and where cards are played. Follow the basic rules of Auld Lang Syne, with one exception: rather than automatically dealing four cards at a time to the tableau piles, you may choose the pile onto which you place each card.

BABETTE

| DIFFICULTY *medium* | TIME LENGTH *short* | DECKS 2 |

Though Babette is not well known or widely played in the United States, it is challenging (odds of winning are 1 in 12 hands) and fast-moving, and well worth learning. The only drawback is that you need a large playing surface to arrange the thirteen rows of cards you'll eventually need to manage.

∾ **HOW TO DEAL** Start with two fifty-two-card decks (104 cards total), and deal eight cards in a row, face up. This is your first set of tableau cards.

∾ **WINNING** The object is to build eight total foundation piles by suit: four piles up in rank from ace to king (A♥-2♥-3♥ . . . Q♥-K♥) and four piles down in rank from king to ace (K♦-Q♦-J♦ . . . 2♦-A♦).

∾ **HOW TO PLAY** After the initial deal, move exposed aces or kings to the foundations.

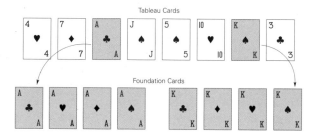

Tableau Cards

Foundation Cards

Once all eight foundation piles are started, deal a new row of eight tableau piles below the previous ones. It's important to overlap the cards, because you may only play cards that are not touching another card on the bottom edge. For example, you may play 2♣ on A♣ in the hand on the facing page, but you may not play 3♣ on the A♣-2♣ foundation pile until the 8♦ is played. Similarly, you may not play J♠ on Q♠ until 10♠ is played.

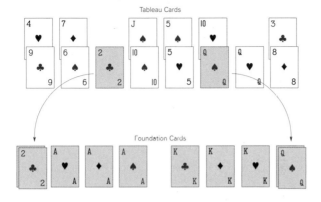

Tableau Cards

Foundation Cards

Keep in mind that you may not build within or among tableau piles—you may build only from the tableau to the foundations.

Your stock will be exhausted after you deal twelve tableau rows. Fortunately, you are allowed one—and only one—redeal. Collect the tableau cards one column at a time, moving left to right. Then simply turn the stack over (do not shuffle), and deal a new row of tableau cards. You win the game by completely building all eight foundation piles before your second deal of stock cards is exhausted.

BAKER'S DOZEN

DIFFICULTY *low*	TIME LENGTH *medium*	DECKS 1

Here's a game that is easy to play but requires enough concentration to keep things interesting. Best of all, it offers a good chance of winning (about 1 in 3 hands should win). The name refers to the thirteen columns—a baker's dozen—used to build the foundations.

∾ **HOW TO DEAL** Start with a fifty-two-card deck, and deal thirteen columns, each with four cards overlapping. Move any kings to the tops of their columns, so that no other cards start the game buried beneath a king:

2♥	A♣	2♣	K♣	J♥	2♠	J♠	K♦	8♦	K♠	J♣	K♥	10♣
5♦	A♦	3♥	3♣	6♦	4♥	5♥	Q♣	5♠	Q♥	8♠	9♥	2♦
A♥	9♦	4♣	7♥	Q♦	8♥	5♣	6♥	6♣	10♠	3♦	8♣	9♠
3♠	6♠	J♦	A♠	7♦	4♠	10♥	4♦	7♠	Q♠	7♣	10♦	9♣
3	6	J	A	7	4	10	4	7	Q	7	10	9

∾ **WINNING** The object is to build four foundations, each from ace to king by suit in ascending rank.

∾ **HOW TO PLAY** You may build the bottom (exposed) card from any column. When an ace is exposed, move it below the board to start a foundation pile. The interesting thing about Baker's Dozen is that you may build on both the foundations and the tableau. Tableau builds are always in *descending* rank and you are *not* required to match the suit. In the sample deal above, here are some moves you can make:

Move A♠ to foundation
Build 3♠ on 4♠
Move A♥ to foundation
Build 6♠ on 7♠
Build 8♣ on 9♥

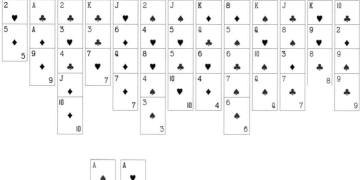

The resulting layout is shown above, and there are still many more moves to play (the 7♣-8♣-9♣ build looks promising), which is why Baker's Dozen is such a great game. Plenty of cards, plenty of action.

BARONESS

DIFFICULTY *medium*	TIME LENGTH *short*	DECKS 1

Baroness is good one-deck Solitaire. It's not easy to win (the odds of doing so are 1 in every 25 hands), but what really sets it apart from other Solitaire games is that there is no building.

∾ **HOW TO DEAL**   Start with a fifty-two-card deck, and deal five cards, face up. This is your tableau. All other cards are set aside as your reserve.

∾ **WINNING**   In Baroness, you may remove kings and any two cards from the tableau that add up to 13 points. You win by discarding the entire deck of cards in this manner.

∾ **HOW TO PLAY** All kings and any two cards that add up to 13 points may immediately be removed. In Baroness, cards are assigned the following values: aces count as 1, kings 13, queens 12, and jacks 11. All other cards are worth their **index value**. As a result, you may remove the following pairs from the table, as long as both are top cards on one of your five piles: Q-A, J-2, 10-3, 9-4, 8-5, 7-6.

After discarding all kings and pairs that add up to 13, deal five more reserve cards onto your five tableau piles and continue the discarding process. Note that you may not move cards from one tableau pile to another unless you first discard all the cards from one of your five piles. Then you may fill the empty slot with the top card from any other pile. If your other piles have no spare cards, deal a card from the reserve.

The final two cards in your reserve are treated a bit differently: don't deal them to the tableau. Instead, lay them face up on the table, and discard either (or both) cards in combination with each other or in combination with the top card from any of your tableau piles.

The game is over when all cards are discarded or you exhaust the reserve. There is no redeal.

BELVEDERE

DIFFICULTY *low*	TIME LENGTH *short*	DECKS 1

The odds of winning Belvedere are about 1 in every 3 hands. It will do quite nicely when you need a morale boost.

∾ **HOW TO DEAL** Start with a fifty-two-card deck, and deal eight piles (three cards per pile), all face up. This is your tableau. Next, deal three cards side-by-side, face up. These are the beginnings of your reserve.

∾ **WINNING** The game is won by building four foundations in ascending rank (not by suit—just rank) from ace to king. Belvedere is unique in that suits are not taken into consideration at all.

∾ **HOW TO PLAY**   After the initial deal, move any kings in your eight tableau piles to the bottoms of their respective piles. Now you may play any top card from your tableau or reserve piles. Start by promoting any playable aces to the foundations.

In addition to building your foundations *up* in rank from ace to king, you are allowed to build your tableau and reserve piles *down* in rank from king to ace. Again, suits do not matter and you may move or build only one card at a time.

Deal three more reserve cards when all moves are exhausted. And note that when a reserve pile becomes empty, it is not filled until the next group of three cards is dealt. There is no redeal in Belvedere.

BIG BEN

DIFFICULTY *medium*	TIME LENGTH *medium*	DECKS 2

This game is named in honor of London's most famous clock—the clock that towers proudly above Westminster and the River Thames. This game is challenging and moderately hard to win (odds say you'll win 1 in 15 hands). The goal is to build and reverse-build cards to replicate an accurate clock face (chimes not included).

∾ **HOW TO DEAL**   Start with two fifty-two-card decks (104 cards total), and set aside the following: 2♣, 3♥, 4♠, 5♦, 6♣, 7♥, 8♠, 9♦, 10♣, J♥, Q♠, K♦. These are your foundations, also called the "inner circle." Arrange these cards in a circle—meant to resemble a clock face—like so:

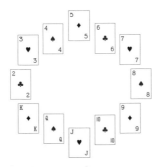

Next, deal twelve piles (three cards per pile) around the inner circle. These are your tableau piles, called the "outer circle":

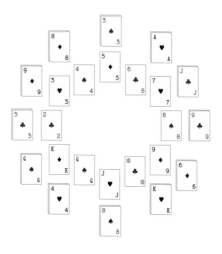

All other cards are set aside as the reserve.

∾ **WINNING** The goal is to transform the inner circle of foundation cards into a replica clock face, with each foundation card reflecting its true position on a clock dial. In this example, you need to build the 8♠ foundation up to 3♠ (it's in the 3:00 position), the 9♦ foundation up to 4♦ (in the 4:00 position), etc., all the way up to a J♠ in the 11:00 position, Q♦ in the 12:00, and A♣ in the 1:00 position.

∾ **HOW TO PLAY** The goal is to build the inner circle of cards up by suit, in ascending rank, until the appropriate clock position is displayed. So, to build the 8♠ foundation to 3♠ (its clock position), simply build up in suit until 3♠ is on top (8♠-9♠-10♠-J♠-Q♠-K♠-A♠-2♠-3♠).

In the outer circle, use the topmost tableau cards to build in the inner circle *or* to build on another tableau pile around the outer circle. Note that building on the outer circle is by suit in descending rank. Also note that, in order to build on it, an outer circle pile must contain a minimum of three cards. With fewer than three cards, it may not be built on.

Whenever a pile in the outer circle has fewer than three cards, it is said to have "gaps," one gap for each card below three. For example, an outer circle pile is said to have one gap if it contains two cards, two gaps if it contains one card, three gaps if the pile is completely empty.

Your reserve cards are used to fill these "gaps" according to specific rules. First you must fill all gaps at the same time. In other words, gaps will develop around the outer circle as you build and play cards. These gaps will continue to build until you decide to fill all gaps at once. Second, when you decide to fill gaps, start with the 12:00 pile and move clockwise. Deal as many cards as required to fill all gaps in a pile before moving to the next pile. Finally, you are not allowed to play or build cards in either the outer or inner circles until all your gaps are filled.

The last rule of Big Ben? It's an easy one. Deal a card from the reserve on the rare occasion that you cannot build, move, or fill any gaps. If the reserve card itself cannot be played, deal another. The game is over when the reserve pile is exhausted. There is no redeal.

BLACK HOLE

DIFFICULTY *medium*	TIME LENGTH *medium*	DECKS 1

Black Hole is a mathematically perfect game. It theoretically is possible to study the tableau before touching a single card, and map in advance how to build all fifty-one tableau cards onto the single foundation. Of course, if you can pull this off, you're probably a professional card counter and graduated a long time ago from Solitaire to Poker or Blackjack. The odds of winning Black Hole are about 1 in every 20 hands.

∾ **HOW TO DEAL** Start with a fifty-two-card deck, remove A♠, and place it face up at the center of the tableau. Shuffle and deal the remaining cards in face-up groups of three. You'll end up with seventeen three-card groups, or *fans*.

∾ **WINNING** Your goal is to move all cards onto A♠, so that you end the game with a single pile of cards.

∾ **HOW TO PLAY** Use the top or uncovered card from each of your three-card piles to build up or down on the A♠, regardless of suit. For example, place any 2 on the A♠, then any 3, etc. You may also change direction at any time (e.g., A-2-3-4-3-2-3-4-5 . . .). As you play the topmost cards from your three-card piles, the cards beneath become available for play. The game ends when you no longer can build cards. There is no redeal or shuffle.

CALCULATION

DIFFICULTY *low*	TIME LENGTH *short*	DECKS 1

Here's another fun—and dead easy—Solitaire game with decent odds of winning (about 1 in 5 games).

40

∾ **HOW TO DEAL** Start with a fifty-two-card deck, and remove one ace, 2, 3, and 4. Arrange these four cards in a column with the ace on top, the 4 at bottom. These are your four foundations.

∾ **WINNING** The goal is to build four foundation piles—regardless of suit—like so:

A-2-3-4-5-6-7-8-9-10-J-Q-K

2-4-6-8-10-Q-A-3-5-7-9-J-K

3-6-9-Q-2-5-8-J-A-4-7-10-K

4-8-Q-3-7-J-2-6-10-A-5-9-K

HOW TO PLAY Turn up cards from the stock, one at a time, and play any valid cards on your four foundations. And remember: suits do not matter!

If a stock card can't be played on a foundation, place it face up on a waste pile. You may create up to four waste piles; however, you may play only the top card from each pile (e.g., the most recently added). And you may use the trash cards only to build on a foundation pile; you may not move them among trash piles. Experienced players will tell you to reserve one of your trash piles for kings, since these may be played only at the end of a game. There is no redeal in Calculation.

CANFIELD

| DIFFICULTY *high* | TIME LENGTH *medium* | DECKS 1 |

Canfield began life as a gambling game, invented by Richard Canfield and made famous at his Saratoga Clubhouse (casino) in Saratoga, New York. The game seems easy enough, though the actual odds of winning are just 1 in 35 hands. No doubt that's why Mr. Canfield excelled at separating suckers from their money.

HOW TO DEAL Start with a fifty-two-card deck, and deal thirteen cards, face up, into a single pile. This is your stock. Turn up the next card and place it on the table. This is your first foundation (out of four).

Just below the first foundation card, deal four cards side by side and face up. These are your four tableau piles. The remaining thirty-four cards are called your "hand."

WINNING The goal is to build four foundations so that each pile contains thirteen cards organized by suit in ascending rank. The trick to Canfield is that the foundation cards vary from game to game. They also have a nasty habit of becoming buried beneath cards in your stock pile. Canfield is not an easy game to win.

HOW TO PLAY The rank of that first foundation card determines the starting rank of your other three foundation piles. So if you turned up J♦, for example, the other three foundations will be J♣, J♥, J♠. Once the foundations are established, build each pile by suit and rank (J♥-Q♥-K♥-A♥-2♥...), up to thirteen cards.

The top card of each tableau pile may be played on a foundation. You also may move cards among tableau piles, building *down* by suit and rank in alternating red-black or black-red sequences. If your tableau cards are 4♥, Q♣, 5♠, K♦, for example, you may build 4♥ on 5♠ and Q♣ on K♦. It's completely kosher to move groups of tableau cards, as long as you follow these matching rules.

When a tableau pile is empty, fill it first with a card from your stock pile—not from your hand, at least not until your stock pile is also exhausted. The top card of the stock pile can be played on a tableau card or the foundations.

When you're out of cards to build or move, deal three cards from your hand, face up. Play the top card on either a foundation or tableau pile. When your moves are once again exhausted, deal three more cards, and keep dealing until you run out. Pick up the unplayed cards, turn them over (do not shuffle), and start dealing again from the top. You may redeal as often as you like—it doesn't make this game any easier, however.

CARPET

DIFFICULTY *low*	TIME LENGTH *short*	DECKS 1

After getting roughed up by the really difficult Solitaire variations, players sometimes need an easy win. Carpet is part of that great Solitaire tradition of games that are intentionally easy (you can expect to win every 1 in 2 games).

HOW TO DEAL Start with a fifty-two-card deck, and remove the four aces. Place these face-up on the board; these are your four foundations. Next, deal twenty cards in four rows of five cards each. This is your tableau (called *carpet cards*). Set aside the remaining cards as your reserve.

∾ **WINNING** The goal is to build each of your foundation aces by suit in ascending rank.

∾ **HOW TO PLAY** You may play any card from the tableau (carpet cards) onto the foundations. You may not build or move carpet cards onto each other. And whenever a carpet card is played, deal a replacement card from the reserve (or from the waste pile, if the reserve is exhausted).

Deal one card from the reserve once you've exhausted all moves. If you can't play it, place it face up in a waste pile. The top card of your waste pile may always be played on a foundation pile. There is no redeal in Carpet, otherwise this easy-to-win game would become an impossible-to-lose game!

CLOCK

DIFFICULTY *high*	TIME LENGTH *long*	DECKS 1

Feeling obstinate? This quirky game has "I am stubborn, you shall not easily win me" written all over its smug clock face (the odds of winning are less than 1 in 100 games). If you enjoy the game play of Clock but are frustrated by its long odds, try the similar but easier game called Grandfather's Clock.

∾ **HOW TO DEAL** Start with a fifty-two-card deck, and deal thirteen piles, face down, with four cards per pile. Arrange twelve piles into a circle, mimicking a clock face, and set the thirteenth pile in the center of the circle.

∾ **WINNING** The goal is to create thirteen piles sorted by rank—for example, a pile of 4s, a pile of 5s, a pile of 6s, etc. The game is lost as soon as all four kings are turned up.

∾ **HOW TO PLAY** Turn up the top card of your thirteenth pile (the one in the circle's center) and place it face up *at the bottom* of the pile that corresponds to its position on the clock face. Turn up a 3, for example, and place it face up at the bottom of the pile in the 3:00 position; turn up a 9 and move it to the 9:00 position, etc. In Clock, jacks count as 11, queens as 12, kings as 13 (center pile), and aces as 1.

After moving a card, turn up that pile's top card and repeat. If you start by turning up an ace, for example, move it to the bottom of the pile in the 1:00 position. Then turn up the top card of the 1:00 pile and move it as appropriate. The game continues in this way until all thirteen piles are sorted by rank, or until you have turned up the fourth king.

If the final card in any pile belongs to that pile (e.g., if the last card in the 3:00 pile is a 3), turn up the topmost *face-down* card in the next pile moving clockwise (e.g., the topmost face-down card in the 4:00 pile).

CONGRESS

DIFFICULTY *medium*	TIME LENGTH *medium*	DECKS 2

Congress has no frills, no fancy tableau, and no needlessly complicated rules. This simplicity—and the fact that luck plays almost no role in winning—is the root of Congress's ongoing popularity. Few modern Solitaire games can boast Congress's loyal following of players. You should win 1 in every 8 hands.

∿ **HOW TO DEAL**   Start with two fifty-two-card decks (104 cards total), and deal eight cards, face up, in two rows of four. This is your tableau. Set aside all other cards as a reserve.

∿ **WINNING**   Build eight foundation piles up from ace to king, organized by suit and in ascending rank.

∿ **HOW TO PLAY**   All foundations must start with an ace, so promote aces as they become available. Then play the top card of each tableau pile on a foundation, or build it onto another tableau pile, one at a time in *descending* rank. Suits do not matter when building cards on the tableau.

Once your initial moves are exhausted, turn up the top card of your reserve and play it either on a foundation (matching suit in ascending rank) or on a tableau pile (regardless of suit, but in descending rank). If you cannot play a card, dump it onto a waste pile; the topmost waste card may always be played on a foundation or tableau pile.

When a tableau pile is empty, fill the vacant slot with the top card from any tableau pile or with the topmost card on the waste pile. There is no redeal in Congress.

CRAZY QUILT

DIFFICULTY *medium*	TIME LENGTH *medium*	DECKS 2

Crazy Quilt is so much fun you almost forget to ask, "Who invented such a strange game?" To win, you need solid Solitaire strategy (the odds of winning are 1 in every 9 hands, and luck is not much of a factor), plus a large enough table to accommodate the game's unique tableau.

∾ **HOW TO DEAL** Start with two fifty-two-card decks (104 cards total), and remove one ace and one king from each suit. Place the four removed aces in a column on one side of your board, the four removed kings in a column on the other side. These are your foundations.

Next, deal an 8 by 8 tableau (sixty-four cards total) in the following manner: eight rows of eight, with cards alternating in vertical and horizontal positions. The first card is dealt vertically, the second horizontally, like so:

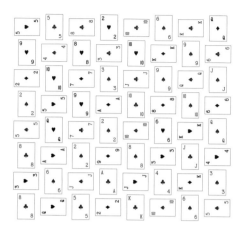

∾ **WINNING** Build the foundation aces by suit in ascending rank (A♠-2♠-3♠ ... Q♠-K♠) and the foundation kings by suit in descending rank (K♠-Q♠-J♠ ... 2♠-A♠).

∾ **HOW TO PLAY** Cards may be played from the tableau onto a foundation if at least one of the card's short (or "skinny") edges is not immediately bordering another tableau card. In the example above, you may play the Q♦ in the first row to the king foundations, since it has one "skinny" edge that does not border another tableau card. You may also play the 2♦ in the third row to the ace foundations. You may not move cards among the tableaus, nor may you fill an empty tableau slot with a replacement card.

If it's any consolation, you may build cards from the tableaus to a single waste pile (once established) by suit and either up or down in rank (your choice, and you may alternate direction at any time, e.g., 5♥-6♥-5♥-4♥). And you may play the topmost waste card onto the foundations at any time.

When you can make no additional moves, turn up a card from the reserve and play it to the foundations. If that's not possible, you must move the card to the top of your waste pile, even if it does not match the suit and/or rank of the card beneath it.

There's an ongoing debate over how many times you may recycle the waste pile to create a new reserve. The correct answer is either "just once" or "as many times as you like." Either way, don't shuffle the waste pile, just turn the cards over and deal as needed.

CRESCENT

DIFFICULTY *medium*	TIME LENGTH *short*	DECKS 2

This game moves fast. The challenge is to keep track of all the cards (Crescent has no fewer than sixteen tableau piles) while not missing an obvious opportunity to build your foundations. The name comes from the shape of the tableau, which forms a semicircle or rough crescent. Odds of winning are 1 in every 6 hands.

∾ **HOW TO DEAL** Start with two fifty-two-card decks (104 cards total), and remove one ace and one king from each suit. Place the removed aces in a row directly above the kings, all face up. These are your foundations. Next, deal sixteen tableau piles (six cards per pile, all face up) in a semicircle around your foundations. Leave room for a row of four reserve cards either directly above or below the foundations.

∾ **WINNING** Build the eight foundation piles like so: aces in ascending rank to kings, and kings in descending rank to aces. Suits and colors do not matter in Crescent, only rank.

∾ **HOW TO PLAY** You may play only the topmost tableau cards, and you may play them only to the foundations. In Crescent there is no building or moving cards within the tableau. Empty tableau spaces are not refilled.

Suits do not matter in Crescent. So your 5♥ tableau card may be played, for example, on any foundation of 4 (all suits) or 6 (all suits), depending on whether you're building up or down in rank.

Occasionally a card may be played both to the ace-up foundation and to the king-down foundation. If this happens, you are allowed (but not required) to move this card temporarily to the reserve. The card may stay in the reserve until a card of matching rank is turned up (for example 9♥ may stay in the reserve until another 9 turns up).

There's no redeal in Crescent. However, you may reshuffle the tableau by moving the bottom card of each pile to the top of the same pile (you must do this for every pile; you cannot skip some). You are allowed a maximum of three tableau reshuffles.

CRIBBAGE SOLITAIRE

DIFFICULTY *medium*	TIME LENGTH *short*	DECKS 1

If practice makes perfect, then hardcore Cribbage players will rejoice. This one-player Cribbage variant gives you ample opportunity to practice your fifteen once, fifteen twice, and run for three to make seven. Plus one for His Heels.

Huh? If this isn't making sense, you're probably not a Cribbage player, in which case you can safely skip this game and move on. Or, if your interest is piqued, turn to the description of Cribbage on page 144.

∽ **HOW TO DEAL**   Start with a fifty-two-card deck, and deal three cards to your hand, three to the crib, and three more to your hand.

∽ **WINNING**   The goal is to score 121 points before dealing the entire deck. Scoring is identical to Cribbage.

∽ **HOW TO PLAY**   Look at your six-card hand, place two cards in the crib, then turn up the first card from the deck as a starter. Score your hand, score your crib, then place the nine used cards (eight from your hand plus the starter) on the bottom of the deck, and deal again from the top. Continue until the entire deck is exhausted. The last hand will have only four cards—score them as a hand, with no crib and no bonus for His Heels or His Nobs.

CRUEL

DIFFICULTY *medium*	TIME LENGTH *medium*	DECKS 1

The odds of winning Cruel are 1 in 7 games. The pain here comes from having to concentrate so hard. Luck plays almost no role in the game.

∽ **HOW TO DEAL** Start with a fifty-two-card deck, and set aside the four aces, face up, as your foundations. Shuffle and deal the remaining cards into twelve piles (four cards per pile), all face up and fanned out so that all cards are visible. This is your tableau, and it's traditional to lay them out in four rows of three piles.

∽ **WINNING** Build the foundations by suit in ascending rank from ace to king.

∽ **HOW TO PLAY** Only the topmost tableau cards may be played, either on a foundation or to build (by suit in descending rank) on another tableau pile.

One of the game's cruel twists is that you may not fill vacant tableau piles. Another twist is the method of redealing whenever you run out of valid moves. Starting with the last tableau pile (the bottom right, assuming you began dealing at the top left), pick up all the cards and turn them over, then stack them on top of the next pile of cards until all tableau piles are picked up. Do not shuffle. Simply deal a new tableau, creating as many four-card piles as possible before you run out of cards.

You may redeal as many times as you like. However, the fact that you can predict (with a little practice) the results of redealing means there's no room for mindless play in Cruel. To succeed in this game, you must pay attention and concentrate. Undoubtedly this is the cruelest twist of all.

DECADE

| DIFFICULTY *high* | TIME LENGTH *short* | DECKS 1 |

Decade is the ultimate Solitaire-to-go game. On a bus, on a plane, on a train—you can play anywhere, because Decade does not require a playing surface. Instead, everything you need fits comfortably into the palm of one hand. This game's motto is "have cards, will travel." The odds of winning are 1 in every 25 hands.

> **If you like Decade, be sure to try Hand, another one-handed Solitaire game.**

∾ **HOW TO DEAL** Shuffle a fifty-two-card deck, and, dealing one card at a time from the bottom, turn up three cards and move them to the top of the deck.

∾ **WINNING** The goal is to discard every single card in the deck, according to the rules below.

∾ **HOW TO PLAY** In Decade, all cards are worth their face value (7♥ is worth 7, 8♦ is worth 8, etc.) and face cards are each worth 10.

The rules for discarding are straightforward: whenever two or more adjoining cards total 10, 20, or 30 points, discard them. So, all three cards in the hand 3♦, 7♦, 10♥ would be discarded, because they add up to 20 points (3♦-7♦ could also be discarded as a pair, since they add up to 10). If you're playing the literal one-handed version of the game, it's traditional to place discards face up at the bottom of the deck.

Once you run out of moves, deal a single face-down card from the bottom of the deck and place it, face up, on top of the deck. Keep looking for discards, and if none are available, deal another card from the deck. In Decade, there is no redeal; the game ends when all cards are dealt.

DEUCES

DIFFICULTY *low*	TIME LENGTH *medium*	DECKS 2

Deuces is neither too hard nor too easy (the odds of winning are 1 in every 5 hands), and you will typically be spared the regret inherent in the more strategic Solitaire games. Your job is simply to not overlook obvious moves, and to keep the waste pile as small as possible.

∾ **HOW TO DEAL** Start with two fifty-two-card decks (104 cards total), and remove all 2s. Place them on the table, face up, in two rows of four cards each. These are your foundations. Next, deal four cards in a row below the foundations, plus three cards on each side of the foundations, all face up. These are your ten tableau piles.

∾ **WINNING** Build the eight foundations by suit in ascending rank from 2 to ace.

∾ **HOW TO PLAY** You may play the topmost card of any tableau pile to the foundations or another tableau pile. Just remember to build foundations by suit in ascending rank and tableau piles by suit in descending rank. You also may move entire tableau piles onto other tableau piles, as long as the suit-matching and ranking rules are followed. What's unusual is that aces always and only rank high in Deuces (Q-K-A but never A-2-3).

Play a card from the reserve at any time to the foundations or tableau. Failing that, place it face up in a waste pile (the topmost waste card may always be played to the foundations or tableau). Whenever a tableau slot is vacant, immediately fill it with the top card from your waste pile. If the waste pile is empty, play a card from your reserve. There is no redeal in Deuces.

DIPLOMAT

DIFFICULTY *high*	TIME LENGTH *short*	DECKS 2

Diplomat poses a 1-in-100 game challenge. And while it is easy to learn, it's very hard to win.

☙ **HOW TO DEAL**   Start with two fifty-two-card decks (104 cards total), and deal eight tableau piles, topmost cards face up, each with five cards. All other cards form your reserve.

☙ **WINNING**   Aces are the foundation cards in Diplomat, and the goal is to build the eight foundations by suit in ascending rank from ace to king.

☙ **HOW TO PLAY**   The game starts with eight empty foundation piles, to be filled by aces as they become available. The topmost tableau cards may be played to the foundations by suit in ascending rank, or to another tableau pile in descending rank (suits and colors do not matter). When a tableau slot is vacant, you may (but are not required to) fill it with another tableau card or the topmost card from the waste pile.

At any time, you may turn up a card from the reserve and play it to the foundations or tableau. Otherwise, move it to the waste pile. The topmost card on the waste pile may always be played to the foundations and tableau. There is no redeal in Diplomat.

DUCHESS

DIFFICULTY *high*	TIME LENGTH *medium*	DECKS 1

If you like Canfield, you'll love Duchess. The two games share many features and are equally difficult to win. The difference is that in Canfield it often feels like you're going to lose from the get-go. In Duchess, it often feels like you might actually win—until those dastardly last few cards are played. The actual odds of winning are 1 in every 40 hands.

∾ **HOW TO DEAL** Start with a fifty-two-card deck, and deal four cards, face up, in a row. This is your tableau. Next, deal four reserve piles (three cards per pile) face up and fanned out, so that all cards are visible. Set aside the remaining cards as your stock. Your cards should look like this:

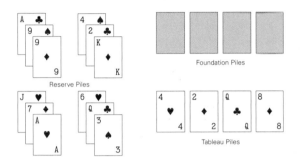

Reserve Piles

Foundation Piles

Tableau Piles

∾ **WINNING** Build four foundation piles, each with thirteen cards organized by suit and in ascending rank. The trick is that the starting foundation cards vary from game to game.

∾ **HOW TO PLAY** Your first job is to nominate foundation cards. Select one of your exposed reserve cards (either 9♠, K♦, A♥, or 3♠ in the example above), and move it to an empty foundation pile. The rank of this first foundation card determines the starting rank of your other three foundation piles. If you select 9♦, for example, the other foundation piles must start with 9♣, 9♥, and 9♠. Once the foundations are established, build each pile by suit in ascending rank (9♥-10♥-J♥-Q♥-K♥-A♥-2♥ . . . 8♥), using up to thirteen cards.

Build tableau piles in descending rank and in alternating color. In the example above, you may play J♥ or J♦ on Q♣; 7♠ or 7♣ on 8♦; etc. You may also move groups of cards among the tableau piles as long as you meet the color and ranking requirements.

When a tableau slot is empty, fill it with a card from the reserve or (if the reserve is empty) with a stock card. There's no rush to fill a vacant slot immediately, so take your time and choose wisely.

When you run out of legal moves, turn up a card from the stock and play it either to the foundations or tableau, or place it face up in a waste pile. You're always allowed to play the topmost waste card to the foundations or tableau.

In Duchess, you are allowed to redeal just once, by picking up the waste pile and turning it over (do not shuffle).

EIGHT OFF

DIFFICULTY *low*	TIME LENGTH *short*	DECKS 1

Eight Off moves quickly and has very high odds of winning (about 2 in every 3 games). This makes it an excellent antidote to this chapter's more bruising and difficult Solitaire games.

∾ **HOW TO DEAL** Start with a fifty-two-card deck, and deal eight tableau piles (six cards each), all face up so that all cards are visible from the start. The remaining four cards are set aside, face up, as the first four of eight total reserve piles.

∾ **WINNING** Build four foundation piles by suit in ascending rank from ace to king.

∾ **HOW TO PLAY** The topmost tableau cards may always be played. You may build on tableau piles by suit, in descending rank. Otherwise, move aces to the foundations as they become available. You also may move the topmost tableau cards to a reserve slot, as long as you never have more than eight cards total in reserve.

Play reserve cards to a foundation or tableau pile whenever you see fit. However, each reserve pile may contain only one card at a time. Eight Off has neither stock cards nor redeals. If you can't move, call it quits and deal a new hand.

FLOWER GARDEN

DIFFICULTY *medium*	TIME LENGTH *short*	DECKS 1

Flower Garden is not as easy as it looks. Although you may play any of the sixteen reserve cards at any time, this does not mean you'll win frequently (more like 1 in 20 games, if you're lucky).

∾ **HOW TO DEAL** Start with a fifty-two-card deck, and deal six tableau piles of six cards each, all face up and visible. The remaining sixteen cards are your reserve; lay them out in a single horizontal row, all face up and visible.

∾ **WINNING** Build four foundation piles by suit, in ascending rank from ace to king.

∾ **HOW TO PLAY** Flower Garden is unique in Solitaire because you may play any card in the reserve at any time. The trick is that you may not move cards from the tableau to the reserve; you may play cards only from the reserve to the tableau or foundations.

All other rules are straightforward. Build tableau piles in descending rank (suits and colors do not matter), and play the topmost tableau cards either to the foundations or another tableau pile. There is no stock and no redeal. The game is over once you're out of moves.

FORTRESS

DIFFICULTY *medium*	TIME LENGTH *short*	DECKS 1

Fortress is the ultimate WYSIWYG game—what you see is what you get. All cards are dealt to the tableau, leaving little room for error. Fortress is related to games like Forty Thieves and Chessboard, so if Fortress is your kind of game, now you know where to turn for your next Solitaire fix. The odds of winning are 1 in every 11 hands.

∾ **HOW TO DEAL** Start with a fifty-two-card deck, and deal two piles with six cards each (all face up), then eight more piles of five cards each (also face up). These are your ten tableau piles. There is no stock or reserve in Fortress.

∾ **WINNING** Build four foundations by suit in ascending rank from ace to king.

∾ **HOW TO PLAY** Move aces up to the foundations as they become available. The topmost tableau cards may always be played to the foundations or another tableau pile.

Fortress's unique feature is the ability to build tableau piles either up or down by suit. And it is OK if adjacent piles are built in different directions. The only limitation is that just one card at a time may be moved from pile to pile; you *may not* move cards in groups or sets. Whenever a tableau slot is vacant, fill it with the top card from any other tableau pile.

- -

VARIATION: CHESSBOARD

Start with a fifty-two-card deck, and deal two piles with six cards each and eight piles with five cards each (ten total piles).

As in Fortress, you may play the topmost tableau cards at any time. However, your first move is to nominate the rank of your foundations—unlike other Solitaire games where this is fixed, in Chessboard you select a foundation "starter card" from any of the ten face-up cards in your tableau. Go ahead and move your card of choice up to the foundation area. Do the same with the other three cards of equal rank as they become available (e.g., if you select 7♥ as the first foundation card, move up the 7♦, 7♣, and 7♠ as they become available).

Build your tableau piles by suit, either in ascending or descending rank (it's up to you, both are allowed). The only restriction is that cards may be moved only one at a time, not in groups or sets. When a tableau slot is vacant, fill it with the top card from any other tableau pile.

FORTY THIEVES

DIFFICULTY *high*	TIME LENGTH *long*	DECKS 2

This is a difficult two-deck game, requiring both patience (a single hand may last twenty to thirty minutes) and stamina (your odds of winning are less than 1 in 15 games). If you don't enjoy a serious challenge, don't play this game!

∾ **HOW TO DEAL**   Start with two fifty-two-card decks (104 cards total), and deal ten tableau piles with four cards per pile, all face up and visible. The remaining sixty-four cards are your stock.

∾ **WINNING**   Build eight foundation piles by suit, in ascending rank from ace to king.

∾ **HOW TO PLAY**   The topmost tableau cards may always be played, either to the foundations or to another tableau pile (within the tableau, build by suit in descending rank; you may move cards in a group as long as you follow these building rules). Move aces up to the foundations as they become available.

As needed, turn over the topmost stock card and play it to either the foundations or tableau, otherwise to the waste pile. The topmost waste card in the waste pile may always be played. You may not redeal in Forty Thieves, so don't rush to play your stock cards.

FOUR SEASONS

DIFFICULTY *medium*	TIME LENGTH *short*	DECKS 1

Whether it's a change of season or a change of your foundation starter cards, it's good to mix things up. Each hand in this game delivers a new foundation card, which keeps Four Seasons interesting. The odds of winning are a daunting 1 in every 15 games.

∾ **HOW TO DEAL** Start with a fifty-two-card deck, and deal one face-up card to the upper-left foundation pile and five cards (also face up) to the tableau piles, as shown. The remaining cards are your stock. The remaining three foundation piles start the game empty.

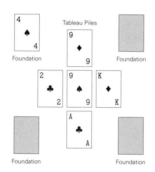

∾ **WINNING** Build four foundation piles by suit, in ascending rank, so that each pile ends with thirteen cards total. This game allows ***continuous ranking***.

∾ **HOW TO PLAY** The first card dealt to the upper-left foundation determines the starting rank for the three other foundation piles. In the example above, all foundations must start with 4 because 4♠ was dealt to the upper-left foundation.

The top tableau cards may be played to the foundations or another tableau pile. Build tableau piles in descending rank (suit and color do not matter, just rank). Fill empty tableau spaces with any available card.

Turn up a stock card at any time, and play it either to the foundations or tableau, or to the waste pile. The topmost card in the waste pile may always be played. There is no redeal in Four Seasons.

GATE

DIFFICULTY *low*	TIME LENGTH *short*	DECKS 1

Gate is very easy to win, so try to squeeze more excitement from it. Try to win every game you play, or three games in a row —or maybe play with one eye closed and one hand tied behind your back. With just a little luck, you really should win every hand.

∾ **HOW TO DEAL**   Start with a fifty-two-card deck, and deal eight cards, face up. This is your tableau. Next, deal two piles of five cards each, all face up. These are your reserve piles. Set aside the remaining thirty-four cards as your stock.

∾ **WINNING**   Build four foundation piles by suit, in ascending rank from ace to king.

∾ **HOW TO PLAY**   The topmost tableau and reserve cards may always be played, either to the foundations or another tableau pile. You may not play cards between or onto reserve piles.

Build tableau piles by alternating color in descending rank (e.g., play 7♥ on either 8♠ or 8♣). As long as you follow the color-matching rules, it is OK to move tableau cards in groups. When a tableau slot is vacant, fill it with a card from the reserve (or, if that is empty, from the waste pile).

Turn over stock cards one at a time, and play them either to the foundations or tableau, or to the waste pile. The top card in the waste pile may be played at any time. There is no redeal in Gate.

GAPS

DIFFICULTY *medium*	TIME LENGTH *medium*	DECKS 1

Gaps is a blast once you master its unique method of dealing cards and building foundations. The game is fast-paced and requires more concentration than strategy. Your odds of winning are about 1 in every 20 games.

∾ **HOW TO DEAL** Shuffle a fifty-two-card deck, and remove the 2s. Place the removed 2s face-up in a column, then deal twelve face-up cards in a row next to each 2. After dealing, remove the four aces to create four "gaps." Your final tableau will look something like this:

2♥—4♥—8♦—9♣—J♣—6♥—Q♠—Q♦—K♦—3♣—7♣—6♦—K♠

2♠—**gap**—4♦—8♥—5♣—7♠—3♠—J♠—6♠—9♠—5♠—9♦—Q♥

2♣—10♥—4♠—10♦—3♦—8♠—K♥—7♦—5♦—J♥—9♥—**gap**—10♣

2♦—8♣—4♣—5♥—**gap**—3♥—**gap**—J♦—6♣—10♠—K♣—7♥—Q♣

∾ **WINNING** The goal is to create four rows organized by suit, in ascending rank from 2 to king.

∾ **HOW TO PLAY** Start by filling gaps. The card to the left of a gap determines what card may be used to fill it—and it's always the next-highest card of the same suit. So, in the example above, move 3♠ into the gap next to 2♠, 10♥ into the gap next to 9♥, 6♥ into the gap next to 5♥, and 4♥ into the gap next to 3♥.

The only limitation is that if the card immediately to the right of a gap is a king, you may not fill that gap. Continue until all four gaps are blocked by kings. Once this happens, pick up all cards that are not in proper suit and sequence with the 2 at the beginning of their respective rows. Add back in the four aces, shuffle the cards, and deal into the gaps left in the existing four rows, so each row once again contains thirteen cards. Remove the aces to create four new gaps, and continue as before. In the row below, for example, you would pick up 8♦, 9♣, J♣, 6♥, 7♥ (these two hearts are not in proper sequence), Q♦, K♦, K♠, leaving 2♥, 3♥, J♥, Q♥ exactly as they are.

2♥—3♥—8♦—9♣—J♣—6♥—7♥—Q♦—K♦—J♥—Q♥—**gap**—K♠

You are allowed two redeals.

GERMAN PATIENCE

DIFFICULTY *high*	TIME LENGTH *long*	DECKS 2

This game (originally from Bavaria) is childishly simple to play and fiendishly difficult to win (the odds of doing so are 1 in every 50 hands). Luck plays almost no role. Instead you need skill, stamina, and more than a little patience.

∾ **HOW TO DEAL** Start with two fifty-two-card decks (104 cards total), and deal eight cards face up. These are your tableau *and* foundation piles—in German Patience there is no distinction.

∾ **WINNING** Build the eight tableau/foundation piles in ascending rank (suit and color do not matter) so that each pile contains thirteen cards total. This game allows ***continuous ranking***

∾ **HOW TO PLAY** Suit and color do not matter in German Patience, only a card's rank (so you may build eight on any seven, any seven on any six, etc.). Move cards one at a time, never in groups or sets. When you have no moves left, turn up the topmost stock card and play it to either the tableau/foundation or to the waste pile. The topmost waste card may be played at any time.

There is no redeal in German Patience, which makes it a very difficult game to win.

GOLF

DIFFICULTY *high*	TIME LENGTH *medium*	DECKS 1

Solitaire golf is not exactly a gimme: The odds of winning are less than 1 in 20 games. Luck plays a role, but skill does, too. And like the real game of golf, Solitaire Golf may be moving along very smoothly, then all of a sudden— shank, triple bogey, game over.

∾ **HOW TO DEAL** Start with a fifty-two-card deck, and deal seven tableau piles (five cards per pile) all face up, with all cards visible. The remaining seventeen cards are your stock.

∾ **WINNING** The goal is to clear away the entire tableau, moving all cards to a single waste pile. At the end of the game, count how many cards are left in the tableau; this is your score. As in golf, the lower the score, the better.

∾ **HOW TO PLAY** Tee off by taking the topmost stock card and placing it, face up, on the waste pile. You may now move the topmost tableau cards to the waste pile, one at a time, as long as they are one up or one down in rank (suits and colors do not matter). So, if your top waste card is 7♦, for example, you may remove any 6s or 8s from the tableau.

In Golf, aces are always low, and you may build A-2-A but not 2-A-K. In fact, you may not build up or down on a king at all. Simply deal another card from the stock and move along to the next tee. You may play through the stock pile only once. No mulligans allowed.

- -

VARIATION: DOUBLE GOLF

The two-player version of Golf is a good-spirited head-to-head competition. Each player plays his or her own game, following the rules of Golf exactly as above. Scores are compared at the end of a round to determine a winner. In Double Golf, it's traditional to play nine hands, the solitaire equivalent of a nine-hole golf round. Or go for master's status with an eighteen- or thirty-six-round tournament.

GRAND DUCHESS

DIFFICULTY *high*	TIME LENGTH *medium*	DECKS 2

The name Grand Duchess probably alludes to a French family of card games in which a portion of the deck is set aside and remains unused until the end of the hand. Grand Duchess has such a feature, in the form of a reserve that is continuously built upon but not played until the entire stock is exhausted. This unique feature is what makes this game more about skill than chance, with low odds of winning (about 1 in every 30 games).

∽ **HOW TO DEAL** Start with two fifty-two-card decks (104 cards total), and deal four cards, face up. This is your tableau. Next, deal two cards face down; these are your two reserve piles. All other cards form the stock.

∽ **WINNING** Build eight total foundation piles, four by suit in ascending rank from ace to king, four by suit in descending rank from king to ace.

∽ **HOW TO PLAY** Move aces and kings to the foundations as they become available.

You may not build on your tableau piles—the topmost tableau cards may be played only to the foundations. Because building is so heavily restricted, the process of dealing four face-up cards to the tableau and two face-down cards to the reserve is continued until the entire stock is exhausted.

At this point, turn up all cards in the reserve and play them in any order you like to the foundations. You still may play the topmost tableau cards to your foundations.

Once all moves are exhausted, pick up the tableau (stack the piles from left to right, one atop the other) and turn them over to form a new stock (do not shuffle!). Add the unplayed reserve cards to the bottom of the new stock. You are allowed to redeal this way three times. Do not deal any cards to the reserve on the third round. The game is over when you run out of cards on the third round, or when all cards have been appropriately moved to the foundations.

- -

VARIATION: LA PARISIENNE

This variation is slightly easier than Grand Duchess—the odds of winning are 1 in every 20 games. The rules are exactly as above, with one exception: Before the game begins, the foundations are "seeded" with one ace and one king from each suit.

GRANDFATHER

DIFFICULTY *low*	TIME LENGTH *medium*	DECKS 2

The odds of winning Grandfather are a morale-boosting 1 in every 3 games.

∾ **HOW TO DEAL** Start with two fifty-two-card decks (104 cards total), and deal twenty, face up, in five rows of four cards each, leaving space between rows. These are your twenty tableau piles.

∾ **WINNING** Build eight foundation piles, four by suit in ascending rank from ace to king, four by suit in descending rank from king to ace.

∾ **HOW TO PLAY** Play the topmost tableau cards to the foundations; move up aces and kings as they become available.

Though you may not build or move cards among tableau piles, you may play stock cards on *any* tableau pile regardless of rank, color, or suit. That's correct—it is legitimate to play, for example, 6♥ from the stock to a tableau starting with Q♠, A♣, or 5♣. The only restriction is that each tableau pile may never contain more than two cards total.

Your other option with the stock is to play cards directly to the waste pile (and you may always play the topmost waste card to the foundations or the tableau). Fill vacancies in the tableau either with a card from the stock or the topmost waste card (your choice).

Once you exhaust the stock, pick up all cards *not* in a foundation pile (e.g., all tableau and waste cards) and shuffle to form a new stock. You are allowed one redeal in Grandfather.

GRANDFATHER'S CLOCK

DIFFICULTY *low*	TIME LENGTH *short*	DECKS 1

This game has many of the same features as Clock; it's just a lot easier to play and to win. You should win 75 percent of the time (about 3 in every 4 games).

∾ **HOW TO DEAL** Start with a fifty-two-card deck, and remove the following: 2♥, 3♠, 4♦, 5♣, 6♥, 7♠, 8♦, 9♣, 10♦, J♠, Q♦, K♣. Arrange these twelve cards into a circle (mimicking a clock face) in sequence, starting with 9♣ at the 12:00 position, 10♦ at 1:00, J♠ at 2:00, etc., ending with 8♦ at the 11:00 position. These are your foundation cards.

Next, deal eight piles (five cards per pile) so that all cards are face up and visible. These are your tableau piles.

∾ **WINNING** The goal is to build each foundation pile, by suit and in ascending rank, to its corresponding position on the clock face. For example, the pile at the 2:00 position builds from J♠ to 2♠, the pile at 6:00 builds from 3♠ to 6♠, the pile at 12:00 builds from 9♣ to Q♣ (in this game jacks count as 11, queens as 12, aces as 1). This game allows *continuous ranking*, and all foundation piles require three cards, *except* the piles starting with 10♦, J♠, Q♦, and K♣, which require four cards.

∾ **HOW TO PLAY** The topmost tableau cards may be played to a valid foundation card, or you may use them to build by suit in descending rank on another tableau pile. You may move only one card at a time. Fill empty spaces with any available card. There is no redeal in Grandfather's Clock; the game is over once all moves are exhausted.

HAND

DIFFICULTY *medium*	TIME LENGTH *short*	DECKS 1

This simple and addictive game is played using just one hand, so it's perfect if you commute each day on crowded subways, buses, or trains. It's similar to Decade, another "Solitaire-to-go" game, except it is a little easier to win (the odds of winning are 1 in every 15 hands).

∽ **HOW TO DEAL**   Start with a fifty-two-card deck face down, and flip four cards from the bottom to the top of the deck, one at a time and face up.

∽ **WINNING**   The goal is to discard all but five of the fifty-two cards in the deck.

∽ **HOW TO PLAY**   Whenever the first and last cards on top of the deck are of the same suit, discard all cards between them. If they are of the same rank (two 7s, two Js, etc.), remove *all* cards, including the first and last card. Place all discards face up at the bottom of the deck. (With just a little practice, you can easily manage dealing with one hand.) Alternatively, if the first and last cards do not match in suit or rank, deal a fifth card, then a sixth, etc., until the first and last cards match in suit or rank.

INTELLIGENCE

DIFFICULTY *low*	TIME LENGTH *short*	DECKS 2

Befitting its name, skill and strategy are more important than raw luck in this game. The odds of winning are 1 in every 5 games.

∾ **HOW TO DEAL** Start with two fifty-two-card decks (104 cards total), and deal eighteen tableau piles (three cards per pile), all cards face up and visible.

∾ **WINNING** Build eight foundation piles by suit, each in ascending rank from ace to king.

∾ **HOW TO PLAY** Play the topmost tableau cards either to the foundations (move aces up as they become available) or another tableau pile, building in ascending or descending order by suit. You may move only one card at a time. The stock serves only one purpose: to fill empty spaces in the tableau (with three replacement cards). Otherwise, you may not play cards from the stock.

Once you no longer can move or build, it's time for a redeal. Pick up all cards *not* in a foundation, shuffle, and deal as many three-card tableau piles as possible. You are allowed two redeals.

INTERREGNUM

DIFFICULTY *medium*	TIME LENGTH *short*	DECKS 2

An interregnum is the period between the reigns of successive kings, popes, or governments. The name is a nod to the game's unique layout, featuring a row of cards that dictate how the hand must evolve. The odds of winning are 1 in every 7 hands.

∾ **HOW TO DEAL** Start with two fifty-two-card decks (104 cards total), and deal eight cards, face up, in a row. These are your "topper" cards. Leave an empty row below the toppers for your foundations, and below that deal another row of eight cards, face up. These are your tableau piles.

∾ **WINNING** The goal is to build eight foundation piles, each with thirteen cards organized by ascending rank (suits and colors do not matter). This game allows **continuous ranking**.

The complication is that each foundation must start with a card one rank higher than the topper card above it. So a 7♥ topper, for example, requires the foundation below it to start with any eight and build from there in ascending rank. When the foundation reaches twelve cards, the topper card is added to the pile, making thirteen cards total, and the entire pile is set aside. The game ends when all eight foundations are set aside.

∾ **HOW TO PLAY** Move foundation cards as they become available. You may not build or move cards among tableau piles; cards may be moved only from the tableau to the foundations. Once all moves are exhausted, deal eight new tableau cards from the stock. You are allowed one redeal.

INTRIGUE

DIFFICULTY *low*	TIME LENGTH *medium*	DECKS 2

Intrigue has plenty to recommend it. The odds of winning are good (1 in every 3 games), and yet it's not a blind-luck game. You need to concentrate in order not to miss the obvious plays.

∾ **HOW TO DEAL** Shuffle two fifty-two-card decks (104 cards total), and remove a random queen. This is your first tableau card. Next, continue dealing cards, face up, on the queen until one of three things happens: you turn up a 6 (which you then should move to the foundation row above); you turn up a 5 (which you then should move to the foundation row below); or you turn up another queen (with which you should start a new tableau pile). Continue until the last queen is dealt.

∾ **WINNING** Build sixteen total foundation piles: eight piles above, built in ascending rank from 6 to jack regardless of suit; and eight piles below, built in descending rank from 5 to king. This game allows ***continuous ranking,*** and suits do not matter.

HOW TO PLAY There is no redeal, so take a minute to review the board after you deal that final queen. The topmost tableau cards may be played to the foundations or—this is the *only* tableau building allowed in Intrigue—on an uncovered queen. An uncovered queen is considered a "vacant" space, and any available card may be played to it.

The topmost stock card may be played to the foundations or any tableau pile. When the stock runs out, the game is over.

- -

VARIATION: LAGGARD LADY

The rules are exactly as above, with one critical difference. You may not move 5s or 6s to the foundations faster than you deal queens to the tableau. For example, with four queens on the tableau and four 6s in the foundations, the next 6 turned up may not be played to the foundations. Instead, it must be played to the tableau, which makes it harder to retrieve later in the game once all queens are dealt.

JUBILEE

DIFFICULTY *low*	TIME LENGTH *short*	DECKS 2

It's likely this game was invented by a patriotic Brit in honor of Queen Victoria's Golden Jubilee in 1887, celebrating her fifty years as monarch. Jubilee is an easy game to win. The hardest decision is how to organize your tableau.

Hint: Put all your queens into a single pile.

HOW TO DEAL Start with two fifty-two-card decks (104 cards total), remove all kings, and arrange them in a single row. These are your eight foundation cards. There is no starting tableau in Jubilee; the remaining cards are your stock.

WINNING Build each foundation pile *by suit* in the following order: K, A, J, 2, 10, 3, 9, 4, 8, 5, 7, 6, Q.

∾ **HOW TO PLAY**   The stock starts with ninety-six cards. Turn these up one at a time and play them either to the foundations or to one of four tableau piles (the game starts with four empty tableau piles). The topmost tableau cards may always be played. There is no other building in Jubilee.

You are allowed one redeal once the original stock is exhausted. Gather the tableau piles (starting with the rightmost) and place one atop the other. Turn them over (do not shuffle) and continue dealing as before.

KING ALBERT

DIFFICULTY *high*	TIME LENGTH *medium*	DECKS 1

King Albert was the king of Belgium until 1934. Though we don't know why the game was named in his honor, we do know that King Albert is a difficult game to win (you should win 1 in every 26 games), which is why it's widely known as "Idiot's Delight." That's no insult intended to King Albert or his noble descendants.

∾ **HOW TO DEAL**   Start with a fifty-two-card deck, and deal nine cards (all face up and visible) in the first tableau pile, eight cards in the second, seven in the third, etc. Your ninth and final tableau pile will have just a single card. Next, deal the remaining seven cards (all face up and visible) to your reserve.

∾ **WINNING**   Build four foundation piles by suit in ascending rank from ace to king.

∾ **HOW TO PLAY**   Move aces to the foundations as they become available. Play the topmost tableau cards to the foundations, or use them to build on other tableau piles in descending rank by alternating color (e.g., on 8♥, build 7♣ or 7♠). You may move cards only one at a time, not in groups or sets. Fill vacant tableau slots with any available card. Each of the seven reserve cards may be played at any time. And no, you may not move cards from the tableau to the reserve. Nice try. There is no redeal.

------- *Klondike* -------

(Basic Solitaire)

DIFFICULTY *medium*	TIME LENGTH *short*	DECKS 1

At the risk of inciting a heated debate, we are using the most common American version of Solitaire—generally known as Klondike—as the "basic" or standard version of the game. This is likely to upset more than one group of passionate players who claim their version of Solitaire is the true, original, and authentic version of the game. However, once you master Klondike, you are ready to play nearly every other version of Solitaire. The odds of winning Klondike are about 1 in every 30 hands.

∾ **HOW TO DEAL** Shuffle a fifty-two-card deck, and deal twenty-eight cards into seven piles like this: one card to the first pile, two cards to the second pile, three cards to the third pile, etc., until you have seven piles. All cards are dealt face down, except for the last or topmost card in each pile, which is turned up. So the first pile consists of just one card turned face up.

Traditionalists argue you should deal one card at a time to each pile; modernists prefer to deal out each pile completely before moving on to the next. Either way, the opening layout should look something like this:

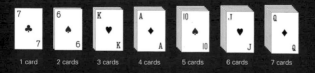

| 1 card | 2 cards | 3 cards | 4 cards | 5 cards | 6 cards | 7 cards |

After dealing, set aside all remaining cards, face down, in a single pile. This is your **stock pile**.

∾ **WINNING** Klondike is difficult to win—the odds are less than 4 percent (about 1 in 30 hands). The goal is to rearrange your seven piles of random cards into four new piles, called foundations, organized by suit (spades, hearts, diamonds, clubs), and within each suit by rank from low to high (A-2-3-4-5-6-7-8-9-10-J-Q-K).

Each pile must contain all thirteen cards of its appropriate suit. More often than not, you end up swallowing the bitter pill of defeat, having exhausted all moving and building options and turning up your final stock cards.

∾ **HOW TO PLAY** Klondike, like most Solitaire games, has five distinct "plays" or moves: building cards within the tableau (your original seven piles); promoting an exposed ace above the board to start a new foundation pile; removing cards from the main board to an appropriate (suited) ace foundation above the board; moving kings to occupy any vacant slots in your original seven piles; and, when all else fails, drawing a card from your stock pile. Each play is described below.

∾ **BUILDING** Once all cards are dealt, start by moving one card onto another that is higher in rank and of the opposite color. This is called *building*. In the tableau below, for example, you may build 10♠ on J♥. You may not build Q♦ on K♥ (they're both red) or 6♠ on 7♣ (they're both black).

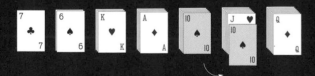

Any time you expose a face-down card, turn it up. In the example on the next page, after building 10♠ on J♥, there was a face-down card below 10♠, the Q♣. You may build that Q♣ on K♥, and then build the existing J♥-10♠ set on top of that! All face-up cards on a pile may be moved as a single unit, as long as the suit-matching and ranking rules are followed.

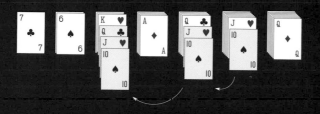

∾ **FOUNDATIONS** In Klondike and most other Solitaire games, when you encounter an exposed ace, you move it to a new row above the original tableau (see illustration below). This allows you to begin building the four piles, or foundations, that you need to win the game. Keep in mind there is no requirement to immediately promote an exposed ace—sometimes it makes sense to wait a turn a two before promoting an ace.

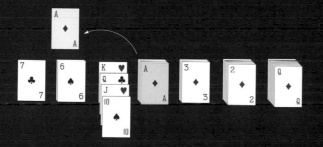

∾ **BUILDING ON THE FOUNDATIONS** Once you create an ace foundation, start building cards of the same suit in *ascending* order. This is how you win (or more often lose!) a game of Klondike. So in the example above, you may build 2♦ and then 3♦ onto A♦. Just remember that once you move an ace up or start building on an ace foundation, you may not reuse or replay these cards. Once played to the foundations, a card stays on the foundations.

∾ **FILLING VACANT TABLEAU SLOTS** When one of your original tableau piles is vacant (typically because you have built its cards onto other tableau piles or to the foundations), you are allowed to move any king into the vacant slot. As with promoting aces, there is no requirement to immediately move a king into an empty slot. Do so at your leisure. However, if a king has cards already built on it, you must move the entire pile of cards as a single unit to the new slot.

∾ USING YOUR STOCK PILE Any time you cannot move or build cards on the tableau, expose the top card of your stock pile. If the card can be played anywhere on the tableau, do so immediately, like so:

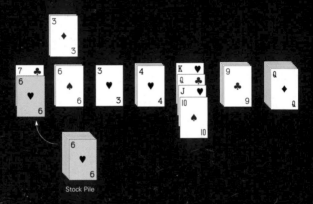

Stock Pile

If the card cannot be played, you must toss it into a separate garbage pile. In Klondike and most other Solitaire games, you are allowed to play the topmost "garbage" card at any time.

Continue turning up cards from your stock pile, one at a time, as needed. But remember: You may shuffle through the stock pile only once. That's the official rule, despite protestations from loosey-goosey Solitaire players who claim it's OK to shuffle the garbage pile when your stock pile is exhausted.

The game ends when you build all cards from the tableau to the appropriate ace foundations, or, more likely, you exhaust the stock pile and run out of moves.

VARIATION 1: DOUBLE KLONDIKE

This is a superb two-deck variant (hence the "double" in the title) of the standard Solitaire game, with plenty of scope for skill. Like the standard game, Double Klondike is not easy to win. You're doing well to win 1 in every 50 games.

Start with two fifty-two-card decks (104 cards total), and deal nine tableau piles from left to right: one card in the first pile, two cards in the second pile, etc. The top card in each pile should be face up. The remaining cards are your stock.

Double Klondike does have one nasty little twist: even with two decks of cards in play, there are only four foundation piles—one ace from each suit. As the first four aces become available, move them to a foundation pile and continue building by suit in ascending rank (A-2-3 etc.). You may play the second ace of that suit only when each foundation pile has its first king (A-2-3 . . . Q-K-A), then you may continue building up to the second and final king. The game is won when all four foundation piles have been built from ace to king twice.

The topmost tableau cards (as well as the topmost card in the waste pile) may be played either to a foundation or to another tableau pile. As in standard Klondike, build tableau piles in *descending* rank in alternating colors (suits do not matter). Fill empty tableau piles with the topmost card from any tableau or waste piles. It is OK to fill empty tableau piles with cards other than kings.

Whenever you run out of moves, deal three cards from the stock and flip them over as a set, playing the topmost card if possible. When the stock is empty, recycle the waste pile by turning it over (do not shuffle). Redeal as many times as you like.

VARIATION 2: BLOCKADE

If Klondike is too simple for you, try Blockade. It's essentially the same game but with two decks of cards. This makes the game play longer and—if you're into that sort of thing—much, much harder to win.

Start with two fifty-two-card decks (104 cards total), and deal twelve cards, face up. These are your tableau piles. All other cards are set aside as the reserve. The goal is to build up eight foundation piles by suit, from ace to king.

The top card from each tableau pile may be used to build on foundation piles by suit in *ascending* rank (A♥-2♥-3♥ . . . Q♥-K♥) or on other tableau piles by suit in *descending* rank (8♣-7♣-6♣ . . .). If one of your tableau piles becomes empty, fill it immediately with a card from your reserve. You are allowed to fill vacancies with the top card from a tableau pile only once your reserve is exhausted.

Once you move or build all available cards, you must deal one card to each of your twelve tableau piles. There are no exceptions to this rule. When this happens, you may not move the underlying sequence among your tableau piles until the off-suit or off-rank card on top is moved or played. In other words, if your Q♥-J♥-10♥-9♥ sequence becomes buried beneath 4♣ dealt from the reserve, you may not move the Q♥-J♥-10♥-9♥ sequence as a unit until the 4♣ is played or moved. The game is over once the reserve is exhausted. There is no redeal.

- -

VARIATION 3: WESTCLIFF

This is another common Klondike variation. Start with a fifty-two-card deck, and deal ten tableau piles with three cards each, with the topmost card of each pile face up. All other rules are the same. There is no redeal in Westcliff. The game ends when the stock is exhausted.

LA BELLE LUCIE

DIFFICULTY *medium*	TIME LENGTH *short*	DECKS 1

There's not much scope for strategy in La Belle Lucie, but even so, it's not an easy game to win (the odds of doing so are 1 in every 8 hands).

∾ **HOW TO DEAL** Start with a fifty-two-card deck, remove one ace as a foundation, and deal seventeen *fans* of three cards each. This is your tableau.

∾ **WINNING** Build four foundation piles by suit in ascending rank from ace to king.

∾ **HOW TO PLAY** Move aces to the foundations as they become available. Play the top tableau cards to the foundations, or use them to build other tableau piles by suit in descending rank. You may move only one card at a time. Fill a vacant tableau slot with any available card.

You are allowed two redeals, so when all moves are exhausted, pick up all tableau cards, shuffle, and redeal as many tableau piles as possible (in fans of three cards each).

LA CROIX D'HONNEUR

DIFFICULTY *high*	TIME LENGTH *long*	DECKS 1

You'll love this game if you're a connoisseur of unique Solitaire layouts. La Croix d'Honneur (French for "cross of honor") replaces foundations with inner and outer circles of cards that are extremely difficult to clear (the odds of winning are 1 in 40 games).

∾ **HOW TO DEAL** Start with a fifty-two-card deck, and deal an inner circle of eight cards (face up) and an outer circle of eight cards (also face up). These are your tableau cards. The remaining cards are your stock.

∾ **WINNING**   The goal is to remove all cards from the tableau in pairs (two 5s, two 10s, etc.).

∾ **HOW TO PLAY**   Turn stock cards over one at a time. Pair them with cards in the *inner* circle (and then discard both), or place them in a single waste pile. Whenever you make a successful pair, replace the inner circle card with its corresponding outer circle card.

After the initial stock runs out, pick up the waste pile and turn it over (do not shuffle). This time around, in addition to using the stock to pair with inner circle cards, use the stock to fill inner circle vacancies. When the stock is exhausted a second time, you may finally pair inner circle cards with one another. There is no further redeal.

LABYRINTH

DIFFICULTY *high*	TIME LENGTH *medium*	DECKS 1

The game is well named, because it's not easy to find your way out of this maze. Luck is a prominent feature, but this does not detract from the thrill of actually winning a game of Labyrinth, where the odds of winning are 1 in every 30 hands.

∾ **HOW TO DEAL**   Start with a fifty-two-card deck, and remove all aces. Place these face up in a row (these are your foundations) and deal a row of eight cards, face up, below the foundations. This is your first tableau row.

∾ **WINNING**   Build four foundations by suit in ascending rank from ace to king.

∾ **HOW TO PLAY**   Play cards from the top tableau row directly to the foundations. Throughout the game, whenever a card from the *top* tableau row is played, replace it with a card from the stock.

When your moves are exhausted, deal a second tableau row of eight cards. If you play cards from this row to the foundations, do not replace them with a stock card; the vacancies must remain.

When your moves once again are exhausted, deal a third tableau row of eight cards. From this point on, only cards in the top and bottom tableau rows may be moved to the foundations. In the example below, after dealing a fourth tableau row, you may play any card from Row 1 or Row 4 to the foundations, as well as 10♣ or A♦, since they are at the bottom of their respective columns. Gaps in all rows (except the first) must remain vacant throughout the game.

Tableau Row 1:	A♥	5♣	7♦	10♠	10♦	6♣	Q♥	2♠
Tableau Row 2:	K♦	—	9♠	Q♣	A♦	7♠	4♦	8♣
Tableau Row 3:	—	J♥	10♣	8♦	—	2♦	6♠	4♣
Tableau Row 4:	9♦	K♥	—	9♦	—	3♠	10♥	2♣

There is no redeal; the game ends once the stock is exhausted.

LEONI'S OWN

| DIFFICULTY *high* | TIME LENGTH *short* | DECKS 2 |

Leoni's Own seems simple enough. Yet the odds of winning are a disheartening 1 in every 80 hands.

∾ **HOW TO DEAL** Start with two fifty-two-card decks (104 cards total), and remove all kings and aces. These are your eight foundations. Deal the remaining cards, face up and one at a time, into thirteen piles. Any time a card is dealt to a pile corresponding to its rank (5 to the fifth pile, jack to the eleventh pile, king to the thirteenth pile, etc.), place the card face down in a fourteenth pile of "exiles." Deal a replacement card to the original pile in place of the exiled card.

∾ **WINNING** Build eight total foundations: four by suit in ascending rank from ace to king, and four by suit in descending rank from king to ace.

∾ **HOW TO PLAY** Build the top card from the first twelve piles, plus *any* card from the thirteenth pile, on the foundations.

When your moves are exhausted, turn up a card from the exiles pile and play it to a foundation if possible. If it cannot be played, you must '"weave" it into the game as follows: Put the exiled card at the bottom of the pile corresponding to its rank, then put the top card of that pile at the bottom of the pile corresponding to its rank. Repeat until you uncover a card that may be played to the foundations. If any of your exile cards happen to be kings, immediately place them in the thirteenth pile (along with the other kings) and draw another exile card.

When your moves are once again exhausted, weave another exile card into the game. The deal is over when you run out of exile cards. Fortunately, you are allowed two redeals: Place pile one on top of pile two, place these on top of pile three, etc., until all thirteen piles are gathered. Turn the cards over (do not shuffle) and redeal into thirteen piles, removing new exiles along the way.

MARTHA

DIFFICULTY *low*	TIME LENGTH *short*	DECKS 1

Martha is a founding member of the "easy to learn, easy to play, easy to win" group of Solitaire games. There's nothing here to cause you much trouble, which is half the fun of playing. The odds of winning are 1 in every 2 hands.

ↅ **HOW TO DEAL** Start with a fifty-two-card deck, and remove all aces. These are your foundations. Next, deal twelve tableau piles of four cards each, alternating face down and face up within each pile.

ↅ **WINNING** Build four foundations by suit in ascending rank from ace to king.

ↅ **HOW TO PLAY** Play the topmost tableau cards to the foundations at any time. As face-down cards become exposed, flip them over and play them to the foundations. You also may build the topmost tableau cards on other tableau piles in descending rank and alternating color (e.g., 7♠ or 7♣ on 8♥). Cards may be moved as a group as long as rank and color-matching rules are followed. Fill vacancies in the tableau with any single card (not a group of cards).

MAZE

DIFFICULTY *low*	TIME LENGTH *medium*	DECKS 1

Here's another novel tableau for players who appreciate them. Once you get the hang of its unique layout, Maze is a relatively simple game to play and win. You should win 1 in every 4 hands.

∾ **HOW TO DEAL** Deal an entire fifty-two-card deck as follows: two rows of eight cards each, followed by four rows of nine cards each. Remove all four aces from the tableau—these are discarded from the game, thereby creating the initial "gaps" in the tableau.

∾ **WINNING** The goal is to reorganize the tableau into four twelve-card sequences arranged by suit, in ascending rank, from 2 to king. Despite the six-row tableau at the start of the game, the tableau is actually continuous—think of the layout as a single line of cards reading from top left to bottom right. As you properly sequence the cards, the king of each suit will by followed by the 2 of a different suit, and that's OK. It does not matter in what order the suits are played. Nor does it matter where the gaps ultimately fall.

∾ **HOW TO PLAY** Maze is all about filling gaps. Look at the cards to the left and right of each gap, and fill any gap with either a suited card one rank higher than the card to the left of the gap, or with a suited card one rank lower than the card to the right of the gap. For example, in the sequence 5♥—8♦—10♠—**gap**—4♦—9♣—Q♠—**gap**—2♦, the left gap may be filled with J♠ (one rank higher than 10♠) or 3♦ (one rank lower than 4♦).

Note that you may not play a king to the left of a 2, though you may play a 2 (of a different suit) to the right of a king. Also note that rows are continuous, so the last card of each row is followed by the first card of the next row.

MISS MILLIGAN

DIFFICULTY *medium*	TIME LENGTH *short*	DECKS 2

This game starts with the most basic Solitaire model and adds just a single innovation: a temporary reserve. This novel twist is enough to recommend Miss Milligan. The odds of winning are 1 in every 6 hands.

∾ **HOW TO DEAL** Start with two fifty-two-card decks (104 cards total), and deal eight tableau cards, face up, in a row.

∾ **WINNING** Build eight foundations by suit in ascending rank from ace to king.

∾ **HOW TO PLAY** As they become available, move aces to the foundations, and play the topmost tableau cards to the foundations whenever possible. When you're out of moves, deal a new row of eight tableau cards.

You also may build within the tableau in descending rank and alternating color. As you build on the tableau, you may move any group of cards, as long as rank and color-matching rules are followed. Fill empty spaces only with a king or a king-led sequence of cards.

Miss Milligan's unique feature is that once the stock is exhausted, you may create a temporary reserve pile. Any single card (or properly built sequence of cards) may be transferred to the reserve in order to clear space in the tableau. You may play cards from the reserve at any point; however, the reserve must be empty before you move any additional cards into it.

MONTE CARLO

DIFFICULTY *high*	TIME LENGTH *short*	DECKS 1

This is a game of chance with unfriendly odds—just what you'd expect from something named after a European principality famous for its casinos. Don't expect to win more than 1 in every 25 hands.

꙰ **HOW TO DEAL**   Start with a fifty-two-card deck, and deal twenty-five cards, face up, in five rows of five. This is your tableau.

꙰ **WINNING**   The goal is to remove all cards from the tableau by pairing them. The game is won when the entire deck is discarded.

꙰ **HOW TO PLAY**   Remove cards from the tableau by pairing off any two cards that match in rank (e.g., 10♣ and 10♦) *and* that adjoin either vertically, horizontally, or diagonally. When all moves are exhausted, move all remaining tableau cards one position to the left and one position up in the tableau, and fill gaps with cards dealt from the stock. There is no redeal.

MOUNT OLYMPUS

DIFFICULTY *medium*	TIME LENGTH *short*	DECKS 2

We can't prove it, but the reason behind the name of this game has got to be the phrase "scaling the heights of Mount Olympus." With sixteen foundation piles, there is plenty of scaling to be done here. You're unlikely to win more than 1 in every 17 games.

꙰ **HOW TO DEAL**   Start with two fifty-two-card decks (104 cards total), and remove all aces and 2s. These sixteen cards are your foundations. Next, deal a row of nine cards face up; this is your tableau.

꙰ **WINNING**   Build sixteen foundations in total. Eight foundations ascend from ace to king by suit, skipping every second card (A, 3, 5, 7, 9, J, K), while eight foundations ascend from 2 to queen by suit, also skipping every second card (2, 4, 6, 8, 10, Q).

꙰ **HOW TO PLAY**   The topmost cards in the tableau may be played on any foundation. They also may be built on other tableau piles by suit in descending rank, as long as you also skip every second card (e.g., build 9♥ on J♥, 8♠ on 10♠). Groups of cards may be moved within the tableau as long as the rules for building are followed. Once you're out of moves, deal a new row of nine tableau cards from the stock.

Empty spaces must be filled with cards from the stock; if the stock is empty, use any card or group of cards from the tableau. There is no redeal in Mount Olympus.

MRS. MOP

DIFFICULTY *low*	TIME LENGTH *short*	DECKS 2

Here's another well-known Solitaire game with a unique tableau layout. The odds of winning are 1 in every 5 hands.

∾ **HOW TO DEAL** Start with two fifty-two-card decks (104 cards total), and deal thirteen piles in a single row (eight face-up cards per pile); this is your tableau.

∾ **WINNING** The goal is to create, within your *tableau* (foundations are not used in Mrs. Mop, nor is a stock), eight sequences of thirteen cards each, organized by suit in descending rank from king to ace. Each time you successfully build a thirteen-card "suited sequence," you may (and must) remove it from the tableau. The game is won when no cards are left on the tableau.

∾ **HOW TO PLAY** Use the topmost tableau cards to build down in rank on other tableau piles—suits do not matter, just descending rank. Of course, in order to win the game, you eventually must build sequences both by suit and in descending rank. Move cards one at a time. You may move sets of cards as long as the set is ordered by both suit and rank. The game ends when all cards are removed from play or until you can no longer move.

NAPOLEON'S SQUARE

DIFFICULTY low	TIME LENGTH short	DECKS 2

There are no twists, turns, or surprises here. Napoleon's Square is your no-frills textbook example of two-deck Solitaire. The odds of winning are 1 in every 3 hands.

∾ **HOW TO DEAL**   Start with two fifty-two-card decks (104 cards total), and deal twelve piles (four cards face up per pile) in a single row. This is your tableau. The remaining cards are your stock.

∾ **WINNING**   Build eight foundations by suit in ascending rank from ace to king.

∾ **HOW TO PLAY**   Move aces to the foundations as they become available. The topmost tableau and waste cards always may be played. Build tableau piles by suit in descending rank. You may move cards in sets as long as the set is ordered by both suit and rank.

When all moves are exhausted, deal cards one at a time from the stock. The game ends when all cards are played to the foundations, or until you can no longer move. There is no redeal.

NESTOR

DIFFICULTY low	TIME LENGTH short	DECKS 1

Nestor is similar to La Croix d'Honneur in that the goal is to remove cards by pairing them. The rules of Nestor are pure and simple, the odds of winning are 1 in every 3 hands.

∾ **HOW TO DEAL**   Start with a fifty-two-card deck, and deal seven tableau piles in a row, six cards per pile and all face up. Deal the remaining ten cards face up, in a single row below the tableau. This is your reserve.

∾ **WINNING**   Remove all cards in pairs, two at a time.

∾ **HOW TO PLAY**   Pair the topmost tableau cards with one another, or with any card from the reserve. Once cards are paired, you may remove them from the game. You may not move cards among tableau piles, nor may you move cards to or from the reserve. There is no redeal.

NINETY-ONE

DIFFICULTY *medium*	TIME LENGTH *medium*	DECKS 1

If you can handle the mathematics—Ninety-one requires quick-footed addition and multiplication of numbers—then you will love this game. You should win 1 in every 7 hands.

∾ **HOW TO DEAL**   Start with a fifty-two-card deck, and deal four piles of thirteen cards each, all face up.

∾ **WINNING**   Build each of the four piles to a total of 91 points. Numbered cards are worth their face value, aces are worth 1, jacks 11, queens 12, and kings 13.

∾ **HOW TO PLAY**   Move the topmost cards to any pile, regardless of suits or rank. That's right! Suit and rank do not matter in this game; your only concern is the total value of cards in each pile. You can make 91 points in many ways. For example, a pile with four kings (13 x 4 = 52), three 10s (30), one 8, and one ace. A complete run from ace to king is also worth 91 points.

It does not matter how you get there, you simply must end the game with four piles that each add up to 91 points. You may fill empty spaces with any available card, but at the end of the game, each pile must have at least one card.

OCTAVE

| DIFFICULTY *low* | TIME LENGTH *medium* | DECKS 2 |

Octave offers excitement and novelty, and is an all-around fantastic Solitaire game. The odds of winning are 1 in every 5 hands.

∾ **HOW TO DEAL** Start with two fifty-two-card decks (104 cards total), and deal all eight aces to the foundations. Next, shuffle and deal eight tableau piles; each pile has three cards, the bottom card face down, the others face up. The remaining cards are your stock.

∾ **WINNING** You have two objectives in Octave. The first is to build eight foundations from ace to 10 by suit in ascending rank. The second is to build each of the eight tableau piles in descending rank and alternating color from king to jack (K♥-Q♠-J♦, K♠-Q♦-J♠, etc.). Accomplishing one or the other is not good enough; to win you must properly build both the foundations and the tableau!

∾ **HOW TO PLAY** Move the topmost tableau cards to the foundations or another tableau pile. Fill tableau vacancies with any available card. Once you're out of moves, turn over the topmost stock card and play it either to the foundations or the tableau. Otherwise, place it face up in a waste pile. The topmost waste card may always be played.

Things get interesting once the stock is exhausted. Turn over the waste pile (do not shuffle), and deal eight cards face up. This is your new reserve. Play any reserve card to the foundations or the tableau, but do not build on other reserve cards. When you play a reserve card, replace it with another card from the stock. Once you can no longer play cards from the reserve, turn over the topmost stock card. In an unexpected twist, if you cannot play this card immediately to a foundation or tableau pile, the game is lost. Otherwise, keep on playing.

There is no second redeal in Octave. The game is lost once the stock is exhausted a second time.

OSMOSIS

DIFFICULTY *medium*	TIME LENGTH *short*	DECKS 1

Osmosis is unique in two ways. First, it is one of the few Solitaire games where foundations are built exclusively by suit rather than by suit and rank. Second, you may not play cards to the foundations until a card of the same rank has already been played on the foundation directly above. These two twists make Osmosis a worthy challenge. The odds of winning are 1 in every 15 hands.

∾ **HOW TO DEAL**   Start with a fifty-two-card deck. In a single column, deal four tableau piles, each with three cards face down and a fourth card face up. Next, in a column immediately to the right, deal one card face up. This is your first (of four) foundations. The remaining cards are your stock.

∾ **WINNING**   Build four foundation piles, each with thirteen cards of the same suit.

∾ **HOW TO PLAY**   You start the game knowing the suit of your first foundation pile. If you dealt 7♠, for example, move any visible spade from the tableau to the spade foundation. The rank of the first foundation also determines the starting rank for the three other foundations. In this example, the three remaining foundations must each start with 7 (7♦, 7♣, 7♥). So move up the remaining 7s as they become available.

There's one additional complication: You may not play a card to the foundations until a card of the same rank is played to the foundation pile directly above it. Here's an example: Your first foundation pile starts with 7♠ and one of your tableau piles has J♠ showing. You move J♠ to the spade foundation. Let's also assume that 7♦ is showing in your tableau, so you move that over to start a second foundation pile. At this point, you may only build

J♦ to the diamond foundation, because only J♠ has been built on the pile directly above. You must build another card to your spade pile before you may play a card of the same rank to your diamond pile. This rule holds true for all four foundation piles.

When you run out of moves, turn up the topmost stock card and play it to the foundations, if possible. Otherwise, play it face up onto a waste pile (the top waste card may always be played). You may turn over and redeal the stock as many times as you like.

PARALLELS

DIFFICULTY *high*	TIME LENGTH *medium*	DECKS 2

Some Solitaire games appear easy to win, and are easy to win. Other games appear easy yet have some twist that makes them difficult to win. Parallels belongs to the latter group. The odds of winning here are 1 in every 25 hands.

∾ **HOW TO DEAL** Start with two fifty-two-card decks (104 cards total), and deal four aces and four kings (one per suit) to your foundations. Next, shuffle and deal ten cards face up, in a row. This is the first row in your tableau.

∾ **WINNING** Build eight total foundations: four by suit in ascending rank from ace to king, four by suit in descending rank from king to ace.

∾ **HOW TO PLAY** Build cards from your tableau to the foundations, and fill any gaps in the tableau with cards from the stock.

If all gaps are filled and you still cannot move, deal ten new face-up cards in a row directly below the original row of ten tableau cards. Continue building your foundations, filling any gaps in the tableau from the stock. Deal another row of ten cards to the tableau each time you run out of moves.

As your tableau grows, note that you may play any tableau card to the foundations as long as there is at least one empty space either above or below the card. Because of this rule, don't be in a rush to full gaps in the tableau. The gaps definitely come in handy!

There is no redeal in Parallels; the game is over when the stock is exhausted.

PATRIARCHS

DIFFICULTY *high*	TIME LENGTH *medium*	DECKS 2

This game enjoyed its fifteen minutes of fame back in the 1920s, when it was featured in a silent Mary Pickford film titled Sparrows. *The game has since fallen out of favor, placing it near the top of any "Endangered Solitaire Games" list. Even though luck plays only a minor role in Patriarchs, the odds of winning are a daunting 1 in every 80 hands.*

∾ **HOW TO DEAL** Start with two fifty-two-card decks (104 cards total), and deal four aces and four kings (one per suit) to your foundations. Next, shuffle and deal three rows of three cards, all face up. This is your tableau. The remaining cards are your stock.

∾ **WINNING** Build eight foundations in total: four by suit in ascending rank from ace to king, four by suit in descending rank from king to ace.

∾ **HOW TO PLAY** Tableau cards may be built only on the foundations; they may not be built upon or moved to other tableau piles. When two foundations of the same suit meet (e.g., when one is built up to an 8 and the other is built down to a 9), you may transfer cards between them. However, you may not transfer the bottom card of a foundation.

When you cannot move, turn up a stock card and build it on a foundation. Or, discard it face up on the waste pile (the topmost waste card may always be played). Fill any tableau vacancies with the topmost waste card, or if the waste pile is empty, with a stock card.

There is just one redeal in Patriarchs. When the stock is empty, pick up the waste pile and turn it over (do not shuffle) to create a new stock.

PERSIAN PATIENCE

DIFFICULTY *medium*	TIME LENGTH *short*	DECKS 2

This version of Solitaire is popular in Iran, hence the name. The game uses a "short" or stripped deck, a legacy of the thirty-two-card decks common through-out ancient Persia and modern Iran. The odds of winning are 1 in every 6 hands.

∾ **HOW TO DEAL** Start with two fifty-two-card decks, and remove all 2s, 3s, 4s, 5s, and 6s, leaving sixty-four cards total. Deal eight tableau piles in a row, with eight face-up cards per pile.

∾ **WINNING** Build eight foundations, each by suit in ascending rank from ace to king (A-7-8-9-10-J-Q-K).

∾ **HOW TO PLAY** The topmost tableau cards may be built on your founda-tions, or on other tableau piles in descending rank and by alternating color (e.g., J♥-10♠-9♦ . . .). You may move only one tableau card at a time.

When all moves are exhausted, pick up all cards *not* in a foundation pile (gather one pile at a time, top to bottom and left to right, and do not shuffle). Redeal eight tableau piles, one card at a time, moving left to right until you run out of cards. You may redeal twice in Persian Patience.

POKER SOLITAIRE

DIFFICULTY *medium*	TIME LENGTH *short*	DECKS 1

Here's a game that blends Poker hands with Solitaire sensibilities. With two play-ers, you can even play head to head for a small wager. This is Poker, after all.

∾ **HOW TO DEAL** Start with a fifty-two-card deck, and deal one face-up ***starter card*** in the center of an otherwise empty five-by-five grid of cards. The remaining fifty-one cards are your stock.

∾ **WINNING** The goal is to score as many points as possible by creating ten poker hands in a five-by-five grid of cards. Hands are judged according to traditional poker rankings (see page 313), with the following points awarded:

Royal straight flush = 100 points

Straight flush = 75 points

Four of a kind = 50 points

Full house = 25 points

Flush = 20 points

Straight = 15 points

Three of a kind = 10 points

Two pair = 5 points

Pair = 2 points

∾ **HOW TO PLAY** Turn up a stock card and place it immediately above, below, or next to (but not diagonal from) the starter card. The goal is to build five-card poker hands in both rows and columns; continue building out the five-by-five grid until each row and column has five cards total. A card may not be moved once you place it on the grid.

PUSS IN THE CORNER

DIFFICULTY *low*	TIME LENGTH *short*	DECKS 1

This game has been around since the 1860s. The "puss" in the title refers to a cat, presumably waiting to pounce on prey in the center of the tableau. Luck is more important than skill in this game, and the odds of winning are 1 in every 4 hands.

∾ **HOW TO DEAL**   Start with a fifty-two-card deck, remove the aces, and place them face up in a two-by-two square. These are your foundations. You begin the game with four empty reserve piles (traditionally the placeholders for these reserve piles are on the diagonal from each ace, but this is not required). The remaining cards are your stock.

∾ **WINNING**   Build four foundations, each by color in ascending rank from ace to king. Suits don't matter, just the colors.

∾ **HOW TO PLAY**   Turn up four stock cards, one at a time, and play them to any reserve pile. Suits and ranks don't matter, and it's absolutely OK to play all four cards to a single pile, or to distribute them however you see fit for easy access later in the game.

The trick, of course, is that you may play cards only from the stock to the reserve, and then from the reserve to the foundations. You may not play cards directly from the stock to the foundations. Herein lies the challenge of Puss in the Corner.

When you cannot move, deal four cards from the stock to the reserves, and repeat until the stock is exhausted. You are allowed one redeal when the stock is empty. Simply pick up the reserve piles and turn them over (do not shuffle).

PYRAMID

DIFFICULTY *medium*	TIME LENGTH *medium*	DECKS 1

Pyramid is a well-rounded game. It has an innovative layout, moves quickly, and requires skillful play plus a little bit of luck. The odds of winning are 1 in every 15 hands.

∾ **HOW TO DEAL**   Start with a fifty-two-card deck, and deal a seven-row pyramid, all cards face up, with one card in the top row, two in the second, three in the third, etc. Deal each row so that it slightly overlaps the row above it:

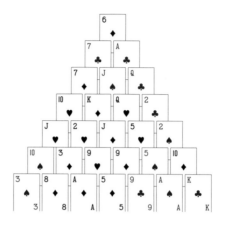

The remaining cards are your stock.

∾ **WINNING** The goal is to make pairs of all cards and remove them from the game. In Pyramid, you may pair any two cards that add up to thirteen.

∾ **HOW TO PLAY** Pair any uncovered cards (not blocked by cards on top) that add to thirteen. Only cards in the seventh row are considered "uncovered" at the start of the hand.

Numbered cards are worth face value, aces are worth 1 point, jacks 11, and queens 12. Kings (13 points) may be removed immediately from the game, even if they are "covered."

When you've exhausted all moves, turn up the topmost stock card, and remove a pair, if possible. Otherwise, place the card face up in a waste pile (the topmost waste card may always be played). Once you exhaust the stock, pick up the waste pile and turn it over (do not shuffle) to form a new stock. You may redeal in this manner a total of two times.

QUEEN OF ITALY

DIFFICULTY *medium*	TIME LENGTH *short*	DECKS 2

Queen of Italy is a member of Solitaire's "variable foundations" family of games, in which the starting rank of the foundations varies from hand to hand. This makes it difficult to win. If you succeed more than once in every ten games you are doing very well.

∾ **HOW TO DEAL** Start with two fifty-two-card decks (104 cards total), and deal eleven cards face up, each card slightly overlapping the previous one. This is your reserve.

Next, deal four cards face up, and select one as your first foundation. The card you choose determines the rank for the other seven foundation cards in the game (the idea is to nominate a foundation card that works well with the eleven cards already in your reserve). Now deal six additional cards face up, for a total of nine tableau cards and one foundation. The remaining cards are your stock.

∾ **WINNING** Build eight foundations by alternating color in ascending rank so that each pile ends with thirteen cards total. This game allows *continuous ranking*.

∾ **HOW TO PLAY** The starting rank of your foundations will vary from game to game, based on the card you select at the start of the hand. Move the other seven cards of matching rank to the foundations as they become available.

Play the topmost tableau cards to the foundations, or use them to build on other tableau piles by alternating color in descending rank. Fill vacancies immediately with a card from the stock. You may move cards within the tableau one at a time only, not in groups. Use the topmost reserve card to build directly on a foundation pile (you may not use reserve cards to build on the tableau).

When all moves are exhausted, turn up a stock card and play it to a foundation or tableau pile, or leave it face up in a waste pile (the topmost waste card may always be played). There is no redeal—the game ends when the stock is exhausted.

RED & BLACK

DIFFICULTY *low*	TIME LENGTH *short*	DECKS 2

There's not much to this game—it's a straightforward red-on-black building game, with decent odds of winning (roughly 1 in every 5 hands). It's included here mainly because it was purportedly the favorite Solitaire game of Frank Sinatra.

∾ **HOW TO DEAL** Start with two fifty-two-card decks (104 cards total), place the eight aces face up as your foundations, then shuffle and deal eight cards face up in a row. This is your tableau.

∾ **WINNING** Build eight foundations in alternating color and ascending rank from ace to king.

∾ **HOW TO PLAY** Play only the topmost tableau cards to the foundations, or use them to build on another tableau pile in alternating color and descending rank. (To clarify, you build ascending to foundations, and descending to the tableau.) Immediately fill tableau vacancies with the topmost waste card or, if the waste pile is empty, the topmost stock card.

You may move cards as groups within the tableau as long as they're grouped in proper sequence and color. When all moves are exhausted, turn up a stock card and play it to the foundations or tableau, or leave it face up in a waste pile (the topmost waste card may always be played). There is no redeal—the game ends when the stock is exhausted.

ROYAL COTILLION

DIFFICULTY *medium*	TIME LENGTH *short*	DECKS 2

If you've played Mount Olympus or Calculation, you will instantly recognize Royal Cotillion. The games share an "every second card" foundation-building scheme. This feature, plus the fact that you may not build on the Royal Cotillion tableau, gives the game an added layer of difficulty. The odds of winning are 1 in every 9 hands.

∾ **HOW TO DEAL** Start with two fifty-two-card decks (104 cards total), and deal four rows of four cards each, all face up, for a total of sixteen cards. This is your tableau. Next, deal four piles of three cards each, all face up and with the cards **fanned**. This is your reserve.

∾ **WINNING** Build eight foundations in total, four ascending by suit from ace to queen, skipping every second card (A, 3, 5, 7, 9, J, K, 2, 4, 6, 8, 10, Q), four ascending by suit from 2 to king, also skipping every second card (2, 4, 6, 8, 10, Q, A, 3, 5, 7, 9, J, K).

∾ **HOW TO PLAY** Move aces and 2s to the foundations as they become available. Use tableau cards only to build directly on the foundations. In Royal Cotillion, you may not build on the tableau, ever. Fill any tableau vacancies immediately with the topmost waste card or, if the waste pile is empty, with the topmost stock card.

Use the topmost reserve cards to build on the foundations (you may not move them to the tableau). Once a reserve pile is empty, it stays empty for the remainder of the game. When your moves are exhausted, turn up a stock card and play it on a foundation, or leave it face up in a waste pile (the topmost waste card may always be played). There is no redeal—the game ends when the stock is exhausted.

ROYAL MARRIAGE

DIFFICULTY *high*	TIME LENGTH *short*	DECKS 1

Here's another excellent choice for connoisseurs of nontraditional Solitaire vari-
ants. Royal Marriage is further distinguished by the fact that almost no skill is
required (what you really need is luck), and yet the odds of winning are still very
poor—about 1 in every 35 hands.

∾ **HOW TO DEAL** Start with a fifty-two-card deck, remove Q♥ and K♥, and
shuffle. Place K♥ on the bottom of the deck (this will be your last card) and
place Q♥ face up on the table.

∾ **WINNING** The goal is to remove all cards from the table except Q♥ and K♥.

∾ **HOW TO PLAY** The game starts with just one card—Q♥—on the table.
Next, deal a row of ten cards face up, stopping to remove up to two cards that
fall between cards of matching suit, or up to two cards that fall between cards
of matching rank.

For example, with Q♥-7♦-9♠-10♣-J♦ on the table, you may remove 9♠
and 10♣ because they fall between two diamonds. Close up empty spaces
and continue dealing. Assume the table now shows Q♥-7♦-J♦-A♠-7♠, and
remove J♦ and A♠, since they fall between two 7s.

Continue dealing cards in rows of ten, all face up, stopping to remove cards
as appropriate. When your first row reaches ten, start a new row (this is not
a requirement; it simply makes dealing more manageable). The final twist is
that you are allowed to remove more than two cards at a time from the table
at any point, but *only if* they fall between cards of matching suit or rank and
are themselves of matching suit. For example, with Q♥-7♦-8♠-J♦-A♠-K♣-7♠,
your only option is to remove J♦ (since it falls between two spades). However, with Q♥-7♦-8♠-J♠-A♠-K♠-7♣, you may remove all four spades.

There is no redeal in Royal Marriage.

SALIC RULE

DIFFICULTY *low*	TIME LENGTH *long*	DECKS 2

In medieval Europe, a collection of ancient Frankish customs called The Salic Law prevented women from inheriting property. This game plays on this theme by removing all queens to a lonely, powerless row in the foundations. Luck is the driving force here; your only decision is when to play cards to the foundations or to leave them in the tableau. The odds of winning are 1 in every 5 hands.

∾ **HOW TO DEAL** Start with two fifty-two-card decks (104 cards total), remove one king, and place it face up on the table. This is your first (of eight) tableau piles. The remaining cards are your stock.

∾ **WINNING** The goal is to build two completely different foundation sets. The first set comprises eight piles built in ascending rank from ace to jack (suits and colors do not matter). The second set is a single row of eight queens.

∾ **HOW TO PLAY** Move aces and queens to the foundations as they become available. Turn over a stock card and play it to the foundations if possible; otherwise you *must* move it to the existing tableau pile (on top of the king), regardless of suit or rank. Continue turning up stock cards until you uncover a second king, with which you start a new tableau pile. Each time you uncover a fresh king, start a new tableau pile.

The top card of each tableau pile may be played directly to the foundations. You may not move cards between tableau piles.

When the stock is empty, any lone king is considered an "empty" space, which means you may play any single card on top of it. There is no redeal; the game ends when the stock is empty and you've exhausted all moves.

SCORPION

DIFFICULTY *medium*	TIME LENGTH *short*	DECKS 1

This is a popular variant, mainly due to its unique open-ended style of building cards within the tableau. The game moves quickly and has decent odds of winning (1 in every 6 hands).

∾ **HOW TO DEAL** Start with a fifty-two-card deck, and deal a tableau in the following seven-by-seven pattern:

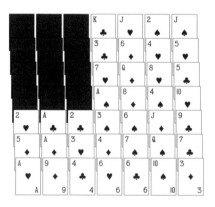

The remaining three cards are your stock.

∾ **WINNING** Build four foundations by suit in descending rank from king to ace.

∾ **HOW TO PLAY** The majority of cards are visible at the start of the game, so take a moment to plan your moves. Scorpion takes a liberal approach to moving cards among tableau piles. All moves are legal as long as the top card in the set being moved matches the suit and is one rank lower than the card it moves onto. In the example on the previous page, the sequence 8♦-6♠-7♠-6♣ may be moved onto the 9♦ because 8♦ is one rank lower and of the same suit as 9♦.

The cards in the bottom tableau row—in this example, the row starting with A♥—may always be played to the foundations. Move kings to the foundations as they become available. Alternatively, fill an empty tableau column with an uncovered king from the tableau.

Whenever a face-down tableau card is exposed, turn it face up. And do everything possible to uncover these face-down tableau cards. They're the key to winning.

When all moves are exhausted, deal the three stock cards face up, one at the bottom of the first column, one at the bottom of the second, and one at the bottom of the third. There is no further redeal in Scorpion.

SEVEN DEVILS

DIFFICULTY *high*	TIME LENGTH *medium*	DECKS 2

Devilishly hard and fiendishly difficult: That's this game's motto, because wins are so very rare (1 in every 40 hands).

∾ **HOW TO DEAL** Start with two fifty-two-card decks (104 cards total), and deal seven tableau columns in the following pattern:

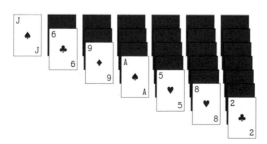

Next, deal seven cards to a reserve pile, with the top card face up. The remaining cards are your stock.

∾ **WINNING** Build eight foundations by suit in ascending rank from ace to king.

∾ **HOW TO PLAY** Move aces to the foundations as they become available. The topmost tableau cards may be played directly to the foundations, or use them to build on another tableau pile, in descending rank and alternating color. Whenever a face-down tableau card is the leading card in its column, turn it face up.

Play the topmost reserve cards to the foundations only; reserve cards may not be played to the tableau.

When you're out of moves, turn over a stock card and play it either to the foundations or tableau, or leave it face up on a waste pile (the top waste card may always, and only, be played to the foundations). There is no redeal in Seven Devils.

SEVEN UP

DIFFICULTY *low*	TIME LENGTH *short*	DECKS 1

Please stop reading and skip immediately to the next game if you hate math. This game is easy to master, it's just the constant adding and multiplying that can injure some brains. The odds of winning are 1 in every 2 hands.

∾ **HOW TO DEAL** Start with a fifty-two-card deck, and deal a single card, face up.

∾ **WINNING** The goal is to remove all cards from the table.

∾ **HOW TO PLAY** Deal cards one at a time in a row, and remove any adjacent card or combination of cards that totals seven or a multiple of seven (14, 21,

28, etc.). For example, you may not remove any cards in the sequence 8-9-J-6, but in the sequence 8-9-J-6-A, you may remove both the 6 and the ace because $6 + 1 = 7$. In this game, aces are worth 1, jacks 11, queens 12, kings 13. Once a pair has been removed, close the gap and continue dealing.

There is no redeal in Seven Up; the game ends when all cards are dealt.

SHAMROCKS

DIFFICULTY *medium*	TIME LENGTH *short*	DECKS 1

The legendary luck of the Irish comes in handy here. Shamrocks is not a difficult game (the odds of winning are 1 in every 10 hands), but it always seems that one measly card stands between you and victory.

∽ **HOW TO DEAL** Start with a fifty-two-card deck, remove one ace, and place it face up on the table. This is your first (of four) foundations. Next, shuffle and deal sixteen *fanned* tableau piles of three cards each, all face up. Move aces to the foundations as they become available.

∽ **WINNING** Build four foundations by suit in ascending rank from ace to king.

∽ **HOW TO PLAY** The topmost tableau cards may be played directly to the foundations, or use them to build on another tableau pile in descending *or* ascending rank (regardless of suit or color). The twist is that no tableau piles may ever contain more than three cards total. Move cards one at a time only, never in groups or sets. Once a tableau slot is empty, it remains empty for the entire game.

SIMPLE SIMON

DIFFICULTY *low*	TIME LENGTH *short*	DECKS 1

This is a simplified version of the much tougher game Spider. Whereas wins in Spider are rare, in Simple Simon you should experience the thrill of victory every 1 in 3 hands.

∾ **HOW TO DEAL** Start with a fifty-two-card deck, and deal ten tableau piles in the following pattern: three columns with eight cards each, all face up; a fourth column with seven face-up cards; a fifth column with six face-up cards; a sixth column with five face-up cards; a seventh column with four face-up cards, etc.

∾ **WINNING** Build four foundations by suit in descending rank from king to ace.

∾ **HOW TO PLAY** Move kings to the foundations as they become available. The topmost tableau cards may be played directly to the foundations, or use them to build on another tableau pile in descending rank (suits and colors do not matter). The one caveat is that you may not build kings on aces—in other words, ranking is not continuous.

Move cards one at a time or, if they are grouped in descending rank, in sets. Whenever a tableau slot is empty, fill it with any card or properly grouped set of cards. There is no redeal.

SPIDER

DIFFICULTY *low*	TIME LENGTH *short*	DECKS 2

Like Yukon, Spider is one of the quintessential Solitaire games. It's a true classic, balancing luck and skill, and requiring a decent amount of stamina. The odds of winning are 1 in every 5 hands.

HOW TO DEAL   Start with two fifty-two-card decks (104 cards total), and deal ten tableau columns in the following pattern: four columns of six cards each, with the top card in each column face up; and six columns of five cards each, also with the top card in each column face up. The remaining cards are your stock.

WINNING   The goal is to remove all cards from the tableau by building eight sequences of thirteen cards, each by suit and in descending rank from king to ace. Every time you successfully build a sequence of thirteen cards, remove it from the tableau.

HOW TO PLAY   Use the topmost tableau cards to build on another tableau column in descending rank (suits and colors do not matter). You are allowed to move cards in groups, as long as the cards being moved are properly sequenced in descending rank. ***Continuous ranking*** is not permitted, so you may never build kings on aces. The ultimate goal, of course, is to build descending sequences of *matching* suits, and this always should be your default choice when choosing which cards to build.

Whenever a face down tableau card is the leading card in its column, turn it face up. Fill vacant tableau slots with any available card (or group of properly sequenced cards).

When you've exhausted all moves, deal one card face up from the stock to each of the ten tableau piles. The only limitation here is that you may not deal a stock card to an empty tableau slot. Instead, you must first fill the empty slot with a card (or cards) from an existing tableau pile. There is no redeal in Spider. The game ends once the stock is exhausted and you're out of moves.

- -
VARIATION: SPIDERETTE

If Spider is too intimidating, try its simplified cousin, Spiderette, where the odds of winning are a gentler 1 in every 3 hands. The rules are identical, except that you play Spiderette with one deck of cards instead of two. Start by dealing seven tableau piles, with the number of cards per pile increasing left to right from one to seven cards. The top card in each pile is dealt face up. As in Spider, the goal here is to remove all cards from the tableau by building sequences (four total) of thirteen cards by suit and in descending rank from king to ace.

ST. HELENA

DIFFICULTY *medium*	TIME LENGTH *long*	DECKS 2

St. Helena throws a wrench in the standard foundation-building process, which makes the game both memorable and hard to win. The odds of winning are 1 in every 12 hands.

∾ **HOW TO DEAL** Start with two fifty-two-card decks (104 cards total), and remove all kings and aces; place these with aces in the top row, kings in the bottom row. These are your foundations. Shuffle and deal twelve tableau piles (eight cards per pile) in a box surrounding the foundations, like so (T = tableau, F = foundations):

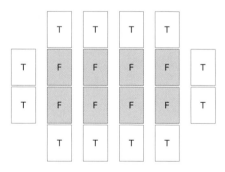

∾ **WINNING** Build eight total foundations: four by suit in ascending rank from ace to king, four by suit in descending rank from king to ace.

HOW TO PLAY The topmost tableau cards may be played to the foundations or another tableau pile. Within the tableau, you may build up or down by rank, regardless of suit or color. Only one card may be moved at a time. Ranking is not continuous. Fill tableau spaces with any available card.

St. Helena has one truly unique feature. On the first deal only, cards from the top tableau row may be played only to king foundations; cards from the bottom row may be played only to ace foundations; and cards from the sides may be played to both. These restrictions don't apply on the second and third deals.

When you're out of moves, pick up the twelve tableau piles in reverse dealing order, turn them over (do not shuffle), and redeal cards one at a time to the twelve tableau piles until you run out of cards. You are allowed two redeals in St. Helena.

STALACTITES

DIFFICULTY *medium*	TIME LENGTH *short*	DECKS 1

If you paid attention in school, you'll remember that stalactites are mineral deposits that "grow" down from the ceilings of caves. This game "seeds" its stalactites with four cards and forces you to build foundations down from there. The game is easy to master but hard to win (odds of winning are 1 in every 7 hands).

HOW TO DEAL Start with a fifty-two card deck, and deal four cards face up. These are your "starter" cards. Leave space below for a row of four foundation piles, and below that deal eight tableau piles with six cards each, all face up. Leave room for a reserve pile, which you may use later in the game.

WINNING Build four foundations in ascending rank (suits and colors do not matter), each starting with the card one rank higher than its corresponding starter card. For example, if the starter cards are 4, J, A, 7, your foundations must start with 5, Q, 2, 8, respectively. You play foundation cards as they become available. ***Continuous ranking*** is permitted. The game is won when all four starter cards are played onto their corresponding foundation piles.

∽ **HOW TO PLAY** Only the top tableau cards may be played, either to the foundations or the reserve. There is no building within the tableau. The reserve may never contain more than two cards, and both of these may always be played directly to the foundations. There is no redeal. The game ends when you're out of moves.

STONEWALL

DIFFICULTY *medium*	TIME LENGTH *medium*	DECKS 1

Stonewall is a game that seems easier to win than it really is. It's not too complex, and the building rules are very generous. Even so, you're doing well to win more than 1 in every 14 hands.

∽ **HOW TO DEAL** Start with a single fifty-two-card deck, and deal six tableau piles, each with six cards alternating between face up and face down. Next deal the remaining sixteen cards, all face up, into the reserve.

∽ **WINNING** Build four foundations by suit in ascending rank from ace to king.

∽ **HOW TO PLAY** Move aces to the foundations as they become available. Play the topmost tableau cards to the foundations, or build on other tableau piles in descending rank and alternating color (e.g., on 8♥, either 7♣ or 7♠ may be played). Move cards one at a time or in groups of properly sequenced cards. Fill vacancies at your discretion with any available card (or group of properly sequenced cards).

The sixteen reserve cards may be played at all times, either to the tableau or directly to the foundations. Cards played from the reserve are not replaced, and you may not move cards into the reserve. There is no redeal; the game ends when you're out of moves.

SULTAN

DIFFICULTY *medium*	TIME LENGTH *short*	DECKS 2

The "sultan" in this game is the K♥, which ends the game surrounded by eight queens. It's another fine example of simple rules creating a game that is surprisingly difficult to win (the odds of doing so are 1 in every 11 hands).

☙ **HOW TO DEAL** Start with two fifty-two-card decks (104 cards total), remove all kings and the A♥, and lay them out as shown (one K♥ is always in the center, the A♥ is always above). These are your foundations.

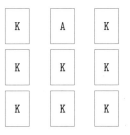

Next, deal six cards, face up, in two rows of three. This is your tableau. The remaining cards are your stock.

☙ **WINNING** The goal is to build eight foundations by suit and in ascending rank. Build the A♥ up to Q♥, and the seven outer kings up to the queens. At the end of the game, K♥ is surrounded by eight queens.

❧ **HOW TO PLAY** No tableau pile may ever have more than one card, and there is no building within the tableau. When you're out of moves, turn the topmost stock card over and play it to the foundations or to an empty tableau pile, or leave it face up in a waste pile. The topmost waste card may always be played to the foundations. You may redeal three times (do not shuffle).

TOURNEY

DIFFICULTY *medium*	TIME LENGTH *long*	DECKS 2

Tourney is neither the most innovative nor most challenging Solitaire variant. The twist is that with so few cards in play, your tourney may last a long, long time. The odds of winning are 1 in every 20 hands.

❧ **HOW TO DEAL** Start with two fifty-two-card decks (104 cards total), remove all kings and aces, and place these on the table as your foundations. Next, deal six tableau piles, each with four face-up cards. Finally, deal eight face-up cards to a reserve. The remaining cards are your stock.

❧ **WINNING** Build eight total foundations: four by suit in ascending rank from ace to king, four by suit in descending rank from king to ace.

❧ **HOW TO PLAY** Play the topmost tableau cards directly to the foundations. There is no building within the tableau. Fill vacant tableau slots with four cards from the stock.

You may play any reserve card at any time, but only to the foundations. Replace gaps in the reserve with any available tableau card.

When you're out of moves, turn up stock cards one at a time and play them directly to the foundations, if possible. Otherwise, place them face up in a waste pile (the topmost waste card may always be played directly to the foundations). When the stock is empty, turn over the waste (do not shuffle) to create a new stock. You are allowed to do this two times.

TOWER OF HANOI

DIFFICULTY *medium*	TIME LENGTH *medium*	DECKS 1

This is the card version of the famous "Tower of Hanoi" puzzle, which has three pegs and nine wooden disks of various sizes. The puzzle starts with the disks stacked together in a pyramid shape. The goal is to move the entire pyramid from one peg to any another. Fortunately, where the puzzle version takes hundreds of moves to complete successfully, the card version can be won in much less time.

∾ **HOW TO DEAL** Start with a fifty-two-card deck, and set aside all cards except the ace through 9 of any suit (suits are irrelevant in this game). Shuffle these nine cards and deal them, face up, into a random three-by-three grid:

∾ **WINNING** The goal is to build a single vertical column of nine cards, the 9 at the top and ace at the bottom, following the rules below.

∾ **HOW TO PLAY** Move cards however you like, as long as you follow these simple rules:

Only the exposed card in each column may be moved.

Only one card at a time may be moved.

A card may never be played on lower-ranked cards, only on higher-ranked cards.

In the example above, you may move the 2 onto the 4 or 9, since both cards rank higher than the 2, or move the 4 onto the 9. But you may not move the 9 onto the 4, or the 4 onto the 2. It's up to you if and when to fill an empty column with any non-buried card from another column.

TRI PEAKS

DIFFICULTY *medium*	TIME LENGTH *medium*	DECKS 1

Tri Peaks combines the frenzy of Golf with the strategy of Pyramid. The resulting mashup is completely addictive. The odds of winning are 1 in every 6 hands.

∾ **HOW TO DEAL**   Start with a fifty-two-card deck, and deal twenty-eight cards to the tableau in the pattern below, with each row slightly overlapping the row above it. The remaining cards are your stock.

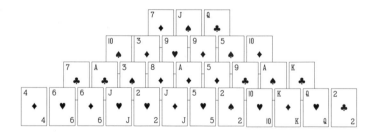

∾ **WINNING**   Remove every card from the tableau, according to the rules below.

∾ **HOW TO PLAY**   At the start of the game, cards at the bottom of each pyramid are considered "uncovered." As you discard them, cards higher up the pyramid become available to be played. Start by placing the topmost stock card onto a waste pile, face up. You now may discard any "uncovered" card in the tableau to the waste pile, as long as it is one rank higher or lower. If the waste card is 5, for example, you may remove any uncovered 6 or 4 from the tableau.

Turn over another stock card when you run out of moves. The game ends once the stock is exhausted.

WINDMILL

DIFFICULTY *medium*	TIME LENGTH *short*	DECKS 2

This game earns high marks in both the "creative layout" and "highly entertaining" categories. Building a windmill is not easy, but the pace of the game is quick, and there's just enough skill required to keep things interesting. The odds of winning are 1 in every 12 hands.

∾ **HOW TO DEAL** Start with two fifty-two-card decks (104 cards total), remove one ace and four kings, and place these foundation cards on the table with the ace in the center and the kings on the diagonal. Next, deal eight tableau piles (one card per pile, face up) in the form of a cross like so (T = tableau):

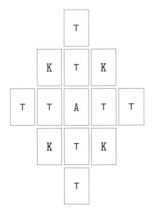

The remaining cards are your stock.

∽ **WINNING** Build the king foundations in descending rank (suits and colors do not matter) from king down to ace. The tricky part is building the lone ace foundation with all remaining cards (fifty-two total) in ascending rank. Once again, suits and colors do not matter. ***Continuous ranking*** is permitted.

∽ **HOW TO PLAY** Tableau piles may never contain more than one card, which means no building on the tableau. Fill tableau vacancies with cards from the stock or waste. The topmost cards on the king foundations may be played to the ace foundation. When you run out of moves, turn up a stock card and play it to the foundations, or leave it face up on a waste pile. The topmost waste card may always be played. There is no redeal.

- -

VARIATION: SINGLE-DECK WINDMILL

This Windmill variant uses only one deck of cards. Start by removing all 2s and placing them on the table as your tableau piles, leaving spaces for the foundations and reserve in a windmill pattern like so (F = foundations):

The goal is to build the foundations from **3** to ace by suit in ascending rank. You may build down on the tableau by suit in descending rank (ranking is continuous). Only the topmost tableau cards may be moved. The reserve card may be played either to the foundations or the tableau. When the reserve is empty, fill it with any available card. All other rules are the same as the basic game, except in the single-deck game, you are allowed one redeal (pick up the waste pile, turn it over, and continue dealing).

YUKON

DIFFICULTY *medium*	TIME LENGTH *short*	DECKS 1

Yukon is a close relative of Klondike, and a logical game to graduate to. Nobody is sure of the Alaskan connection with these two games—it's a mystery lost in the mists of time. The odds of winning Yukon are 1 in every 13 hands.

∾ **HOW TO DEAL** Start with a fifty-two-card deck, and deal seven tableau columns in the pattern below (D = face down):

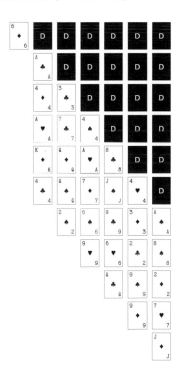

∾ **WINNING**   Build four foundations by suit and in ascending rank from ace to king.

∾ **HOW TO PLAY**   Move aces to the foundations as they become available. Play the topmost tableau cards to the foundations, or use them to build on other tableau piles in descending rank and in alternating color (e.g., on 8♥ you may play 7♠ or 7♣).

Move cards one at a time or in groups; unlike many other solitaire games, it is OK to move groups of cards even if they are not properly sequenced; the only requirement is that the two cards *being joined* follow the building rules above.

Fill tableau vacancies with any king or group cards starting with a king. Whenever a face-down tableau card is the leading card in its column, turn it face up. There is no stock. The game ends when you're out of moves.

ZODIAC

DIFFICULTY *high*	TIME LENGTH *medium*	DECKS 2

Zodiac has a solid pedigree. Its rules were standardized in 1914, and ever since, the game has remained popular in Solitaire circles. The odds of winning are 1 in every 25 hands.

∾ **HOW TO DEAL**   Start with two fifty-two-card decks (104 cards total), and, in a single row, deal eight reserve piles with one card per pile, face up. In Zodiac, the reserve is also called the "equator." Next, deal twenty-four tableau piles (also one card per pile, face up) in a circle surrounding the equator. The tableau is also called the "zodiac."

∾ **WINNING**   The ultimate goal (phase two) is to build eight total foundations by suit in ascending rank from ace to king. The interim goal (phase one) is to empty the stock and waste piles according to the rules below.

HOW TO PLAY Zodiac has two phases. In phase one, your goal is to build the zodiac (the tableau) with cards from the equator (the reserve), the stock, and the waste piles. You may not proceed to phase two until *all* stock and waste cards are played either to the equator or to the zodiac.

Build on zodiac piles by suit in descending *or* ascending rank. As often as you like, switch the direction of ranking within the same zodiac pile. However, once you play a card to the zodiac in phase one, you may not move it again until phase two. Another restriction in phase one: you may not move cards among zodiac piles.

Play cards from the equator directly to the zodiac, and fill empty equator cards at your discretion with cards from the stock or the topmost waste card. You may not build on the equator, and equator piles may never contain more than one card.

When you're out of moves, turn stock cards up one at a time and play them to the zodiac, the equator, or to a waste pile. The topmost waste card may always be played. Redeals are infinite in the zodiac! Redeal by picking up the waste pile and turning it over, as many times as you like.

If you successfully play every stock and waste card to the zodiac and equator, you may then start phase two of the game. Play the topmost zodiac cards, plus any equator card, directly to the foundations. In phase two, you may move cards among the zodiac piles, if it helps. The game is won if you successfully build all eight foundations.

.03 ~

Games Especially for Two Players

CHAPTER THREE

Games Especially for Two Players

TWO IS A MAGICAL NUMBER IN CARDS. Certainly one-player Solitaire games are a fun challenge. But with two players, card games take on a whole new life. Competition, strategy, head-to-head battles, the thrill of victory, the sting of defeat—these are what define two–player games. Most people have heard of Cribbage and Gin Rummy. These are quintessential two-player games. Yet few people have heard of—let alone played—Bezique, Casino, Piquet, or Klaberjass, all of which should be more popular than they are. The next time you and a friend have an afternoon to spare, spend time learning some of these underappreciated two-player gems. Your investment will be amply rewarded.

BEZIQUE (TWO-HAND)

DIFFICULTY *medium*	TIME LENGTH *medium*	DECKS 2

It's likely you've never played a game quite like Bezique—even though the game's original version (Two-Hand Bezique) is the predecessor of modern Pinochle. For the most part, Bezique is a game with no loyal following and few hardcore fans. We wish it were otherwise.

In the 1840s and '50s, Bezique was the most popular game in France, and for many years thereafter it was played by European royalty and high society. Its popularity peaked in the 1920s, thanks in no small part to Winston Churchill. He was an expert in the game, swept up in the Bezique mania that roared through London in the early twentieth century. There are many variations in Bezique. Two Hand Bezique, the easiest to learn and master, is outlined below. Other variations are covered later.

❧ **HOW TO DEAL** Start with two fifty-two-card decks, and discard all cards between 2 and 6, so that you're left with 7 to ace in each suit (for a total of sixty-four cards). Note that in Bezique the cards rank (high to low) A, 10, K, Q, J, 9, 8, 7.

Shuffle and deal each player eight cards, face down, in bundles of three, two, three. Turn the seventeenth card face up to determine **trump** for the round. Place the remaining cards (the stock) face down in the center of the table. The non-dealer then leads the first **trick**.

❧ **SCORING** The goal of Two-Hand Bezique is to score points. Games of Two-Hand Bezique are typically played to 1,000 points.

Points are awarded in two distinct phases. First is the *declaration phase*, in which each player tries to **meld** his or her cards according to the scoring chart below. What's unique about Bezique is that it's possible to use the same card to form multiple melds. In this phase, you're also trying to capture *brisques* (10s and aces), each worth 10 points.

MELDS	FORMATION	POINTS
7 of trumps	Exchanged for the exposed trump card	10
Marriage	Q and K of same suit (not trump)	20
Royal Marriage	Q and K of trump suit	40
Bezique	J♦, Q♠	40
Four Jacks	One from each suit	40
Four Queens	One from each suit	60
Four Kings	One from each suit	80
Four Aces	One from each suit	100
Sequence	J, Q, K, 10, A in same suit (not trump)	150
Royal Sequence	J, Q, K, 10, A of trump suit	250
Double Bezique	A second J♦ and Q♠ played on an existing J♦ and Q♠ meld	500

The declaration phase lasts until the entire stock of cards is exhausted. At this point, the game switches to the *play-off phase;* each player picks up all his or her eight remaining cards and plays them one at a time in standard tricks. The goal here is to capture more and to win the very last trick (worth 10 points).

᭺ HOW TO PLAY   After dealing, a game of Two-Hand Bezique begins with the declaration phase. The non-dealer opens by playing a single card face up. The dealer then plays any card he or she chooses—in the declaration phase you are not required to follow suit. Tricks are won by the highest card in the leading suit, or by the highest trump card played. If identical cards are played in the same trick, the one that led wins. Tricks are always opened by the winner of the previous trick.

The winner of each trick sets the trick aside (any brisques captured are scored at the end of the hand), and either declares a meld or takes one card from the top of the stock. If the winner cannot meld, he or she simply takes a card from the top of the stock. So, too, does the opposing player. This way each player always has eight cards in his or her hand, until the stock is exhausted.

∾ **DECLARING MELDS** Melds may be declared only during the declaration phase, only by the winner of a trick, and only before the winner takes a card from the stock. You may declare only one meld per trick. When declaring a meld, simply place the cards face up on the table and score yourself the appropriate number of points.

FOR EXAMPLE If player one leads 7♣, player two follows with any card in his hand. A higher club or any trump (assuming clubs are not trump) wins the trick. If player two follows with 8♣, then player two wins the trick. If identical cards are played in the same trick, the one that led wins.

Once cards have been melded, they are not dead or out of play. Instead, they remain a part of your active hand and may be played again as part of a different meld. In the declaration phase, each player always has eight cards in hand, and it doesn't matter if some of these cards are literally in your hand or are face up on the table as part of a scoring meld.

FOR EXAMPLE Here's the basic outline of a complete turn (assuming hearts are trump). Player one leads 7♦ and player two wins the trick with J♦. Player two melds a Royal Marriage by placing Q♥ and K♥ on the table, face up, and then takes one card from the stock. Player one takes a card from the stock. Player two then leads the next trick.

THINGS TO KNOW ABOUT MELDING Bezique has a few melding quirks. The first oddity is the 7 of trump. If the card indicating trumps happens to be a 7, score the dealer 10 points immediately. If you are holding the 7 of trump, you may exchange it for the face-up trump card next to the stock (and don't forget to score yourself 10 points). This counts as a declaration and, as a result, may happen only after you win a trick. The 7 of trump may be swapped this way only once.

In Bezique, it is also possible to use the same card more than once in a meld. For example, after winning a trick, you meld the queen and king of trump (Royal Marriage) for 40 points. Later in the game, you add 10, jack, and ace of trump to the existing queen and king on the table, thereby melding a Royal Sequence for 250 additional points.

Just remember that a card may be used only once to declare a different meld from the one already declared. In the example above, you may not use a card from your Royal Marriage to meld a second Royal Marriage unless you already have played a card from the Royal Marriage. In other words, with a marriage of Q♥-K♥ on the table, you may not meld a subsequent Q♥ for a second marriage. However, if you play the Q♥ on the table as part of a trick, you may create a marriage if you meld a subsequent Q♥ with the K♥ already on the table.

Because you may score only one meld per turn, it's also possible that the same card fits more than one of your existing melds. For example, assume that spades are trump and that you already have Q♠ and K♠ on the table (40 points for the Royal Marriage). Now you declare four jacks (40 points) and announce "Bezique to come." This entitles you to score the Bezique (J♦-Q♠) the next time you win a trick.

∾ **PLAY-OFF PHASE** Once the stock is exhausted, the winner of the last trick takes the final stock card, and the loser takes the exposed trump card. Both players pick up all their cards (eight each). The goal of the play-off phase is simple: capture brisques and win the final trick. No further declarations (melds) are allowed.

The player who wins the last trick in the declaration phase leads the first trick. And from this point forward, you must follow suit if possible. If you cannot, you must play a trump. Only as a last resort may you play from your other suits.

FOR EXAMPLE Assume spades are trump. Player one leads 8♣. Player two must follow with a club, if possible, or a trump spade. If player two has neither clubs nor spades, she may play a diamond or heart. Either way, the trick is won by the highest card in the suit that led, or the highest trump.

The player who wins the final trick scores all of his brisques first; if this puts you over 1,000 points, then you win the game immediately. Otherwise, the cards are shuffled and dealt, a new trump is exposed, and the game continues until either player achieves 1,000 points.

∾ **HOW TO WIN** If you must choose between melding a marriage or a Bezique, always choose the Bezique so you can possibly reuse Q♠ or J♦ in a future meld. And pay attention to sequences, because even a basic sequence is still worth 150 points.

If you are holding the 7 of trump, play a trick-winning card immediately if the exposed trump card is higher than 9. In the play-off phase, start by leading aces and 10s, if you are certain (based on what you saw of your opponent's face-up melded cards) that your opponent is holding lower cards in those suits. Then follow up with your trump (assuming you are long in trump), in order to draw out your opponent's trump cards and any brisques.

Finally, if your opponent is blessed with a handful of aces (especially the ace of trump), play your 10s to over-trump suits for which you hold no other cards. In Bezique, there is nothing worse than losing your 10 to an opponent's ace in the final trick, thereby losing 20 points (10 for the brisque, 10 for the last trick) and possibly the game!

- -
VARIATION 1: THREE-HAND BEZIQUE
This game is specifically for three players, and follows the basic rules of Two-Hand Bezique. However, instead of two decks, Three-Hand Bezique uses three decks (removing all cards ranking 2 through 6) for a total of ninety-six cards in play.

Games typically last to 3,000 points. Three-Hand Bezique uses the standard scoring system; however, with the addition of more cards, it is now possible to score a "Triple Bezique," which is a third J♦-Q♠ set played on an existing set of two J♦-Q♠ melds. This very rare meld is worth 1,500 points.

- -
VARIATION 2: RUBICON BEZIQUE
Two-Hand is the simplest version of Bezique. Yet despite that advantage, the more complex Rubicon variation is the most commonly played, even today. Rubicon Bezique is a superb two-player game, requiring equal measures of luck, skill, and concentration. If you and your partner are starting to be bored by Cribbage, invest a little time learning Rubicon Bezique.

Add spice to your game of Rubicon Bezique with a small wager. Assign points a value (one-tenth of a penny per point is common), and agree to settle all accounts at the end of a predetermined time, say, after one player reaches 10,000 points or after a 90-minute clock has run out.

DEALING Start with four packs of cards, removing all cards ranking 2 through 6, for a total of 128 cards in play. There is only one deal in Rubicon Bezique; simply deal each player nine cards, face down and one at a time. The first stock card is not exposed, and the 7 of trump has no additional value.

DECLARING TRUMP Unlike in Two-Hand Bezique, the trump suit is established only when a marriage or sequence is melded; the suit of the first meld establishes trump. Until then, the game is played without a trump suit.

SCORING The winner of a hand in Rubicon is the player with the highest score at the end of a single hand (there is no second deal). That player receives 500 points, plus the difference between the two players' scores. For example, if you end the game with 1,150 points and your opponent ends with 1,100 points, you win the game with a final score of 500 points plus 50 points (your score minus your opponent's score), for a total of 550 points.

One exception to this scoring is called *rubicon*. The losing player is said to be "rubiconed" when their final score is less than 1,000 points. In this case, the winning player receives 1,000 points (rather than 500 points) plus the *sum* (rather than the difference) of the two scores.

Tricks (plus any brisques) won during the declaration phase are set aside and have no scoring value whatsoever. The final scoring anomaly is that brisques are not counted and have no scoring value, unless there is a tie or in order to avoid a possible rubicon. In these cases, both players count the brisques only from the play-off phase.

MELDS	FORMATION	POINTS
Marriage	Q and K of same suit (not trump)	20
Royal Marriage	Q and K of trump suit	40
Bezique	Q♠, J♦	40
Four Jacks	One from each suit	40
Four Queens	One from each suit	60
Four Kings	One from each suit	80
Four Aces	One from each suit	100
Sequence	J, Q, K, 10, A in same suit (not trump)	150
Royal Sequence	J, Q, K, 10, A of trump suit	250
Double Bezique	Two sets of Q♠, J♦	500
Triple Bezique	Three sets of Q♠, J♦	1,500
Quadruple Bezique	Four sets of Q♠, J♦	4,500

DECLARATION PHASE Melds are valued as in Two-Hand Bezique, with the following exceptions. First is a meld called *Carte Blanche*. If you are dealt only number cards and no face cards, you may declare Carte Blanche immediately without winning a trick, by exposing all eight of your cards and scoring yourself 50 points. On the next round, score yourself another 50 points if you draw a non-face card, and keep scoring yourself 50 points until you finally draw a face card.

Also note that melded cards may be reused (as often as possible!) to form further melds. For example, if you have already declared a meld of four queens, on the next trick you win, it is OK to use a fifth queen to declare a second "Four Queens" meld. Two marriages of the same suit may also be reused to form two additional marriages.

PLAY-OFF PHASE Play is the same as for Two-Hand Bezique, except that winning the last trick counts as 50 points (rather than 10 points).

--- -

VARIATION 3: SIX-PACK BEZIQUE

Six-Pack Bezique is played according to the rules of Rubicon Bezique. What's the main difference? Each player is dealt twelve cards, which places an emphasis on aggressive melding and re-melding of your cards.

Six-Pack Bezique is also more strategic, in that points are awarded exclusively for melds (brisques are neither counted nor scored). With so many combinations of cards to meld, it's best to devise a plan early for how to extract the maximum point value from your hand.

Tip: Move as quickly as possible to declare the trump suit. Even if you sacrifice a future meld or establish trump in a slightly weaker suit, it's always better for you to take that initiative rather than letting your opponent establish trump.

> **Winston Churchill's preferred variation is Six-Pack Bezique, better known in traditional circles as Chinese Bezique.**

DEALING Start with six packs of cards, removing all cards ranking 2 through 6, for a total of 192 cards in play. As with Rubicon Bezique, there is only one deal; each player receives twelve cards, in batches of three.

DECLARING TRUMP The trump suit is determined as in Rubicon Bezique (the suit of the first marriage or sequence determines trump). However, unlike in Rubicon Bezique, the same suit may not be trump on two successive deals (assuming you're playing a multihand game). So if the first sequence or marriage in a subsequent deal would establish the same suit, simply score the standard points for the declaration, and wait for the next marriage or sequence to establish trump.

SCORING The winner of a hand receives 1,000 points. A Rubicon is worth 3,000 points. Carte Blanche is worth 250 points. The last trick is worth 250 points. Brisques are never counted.

The composition of Beziques vary according to which suit is trump: diamonds (Q♦, J♠), clubs (Q♣, J♥), hearts (Q♥, J♣), spades (Q♠, J♦).

MELDS	FORMATION	POINTS
Marriage	K, Q of same suit (not trump)	20
Royal Marriage	K, Q of trump suit	40
Bezique	Q♠, J♦	40
Four Jacks	One from each suit	40
Four Jacks of Trump	Four Jacks of trump	400
Four Queens	One from each suit	60
Four Queens of Trump	Four Queens of trump	600
Four Kings	One from each suit	80
Four Kings of Trump	Four Kings of trump	800
Four 10s of Trump	Four 10s of trump	900
Four Aces	One from each suit	100
Four Aces of Trump	Four Aces of trump	1,000
Sequence	A, 10, K, Q, J in same suit (not trump)	150
Royal Sequence	A, 10, K, Q, J of trump suit	250
Double Bezique	Two sets of Q, J	500
Triple Bezique	Three sets of Q, J	1,500
Quadruple Bezique	Four sets of Q, J	4,500

- -

VARIATION 4: EIGHT-DECK BEZIQUE

This is a good variation for Rubicon enthusiasts who crave even more melding opportunities. The game is played under the standard Six-Pack Bezique rules, except there are 256 cards total in play and each player holds fifteen cards. It is melding madness!

DEALING Start with eight packs of cards, removing all cards ranking 2 through 6, for a total of 256 cards in play. As with Six-Pack Bezique, there is only one deal, and each player receives fifteen cards, dealt three at a time.

SCORING Follow the scoring guidelines for Six-Pack Bezique, except in this eight-deck version, a Rubicon is achieved only if the losing hand has fewer than 5,000 points.

MELDS	FORMATION	POINTS
Marriage	K, Q of same suit (not trump)	20
Royal Marriage	K, Q of trump suit	40
Bezique	Q♠, J♦	50
Four Jacks	One from each suit	40
Four Jacks of Trump	Four Jacks of trump	400
Five Jacks of Trump	Five Jacks of trump	800
Four Queens	One from each suit	60
Four Queens of Trump	Four Queens of trump	600
Five Queens of Trump	Five Queens of trump	1,200
Four Kings	One from each suit	80
Four Kings of Trump	Four Kings of trump	800
Five Kings of Trump	Five Kings of trump	1,600
Four 10s of Trump	Four 10s of trump	900
Five 10s of Trump	Five 10s of trump	1,800
Four Aces	One from each suit	100
Four Aces of Trump	Four Aces of trump	1,000
Five Aces of Trump	Five Aces of trump	2,000
Sequence	A, 10, K, Q, J in same suit (not trump)	150
Royal Sequence	A, 10, K, Q, J of trump suit	250
Double Bezique	Two sets of Q♠, J♦	500
Triple Bezique	Three sets of Q♠, J♦	1,500
Quadruple Bezique	Four sets of Q♠, J♦	4,500
Quintuple Bezique	Five sets of Q♠, J♦	9,000

VARIATION 5: FOUR-HAND BEZIQUE

It seems that all great two- and three-player games have a four-player version suitable for partnerships. Bezique is no exception. The game is played according to standard Rubicon Bezique rules, except that you may use your partner's declared cards to form melds. This gives the game a subtle flavor of Contract Bridge, although without the complexity of bidding and playing a dummy hand.

DEALING   Start with six packs of cards, removing all cards ranking 2 through 6, for a total of 192 cards in play. Deal each player nine cards, three at a time. The player to the left of the dealer always leads the first trick.

SCORING   The game works exactly as Rubicon Bezique, with two exceptions. If you win a trick, you may nominate yourself or your partner to declare a meld. If you nominate your partner, you still must lead the next trick.

More significant, you can also create melds using any of your partner's already declared cards (keep the cards separate, and simply call out which of your partner's cards are being included in the meld). Finally, if both players in a partnership score a Carte Blanche, each receives 500 points.

MELDS	FORMATION	POINTS
Marriage	K, Q of same suit (not trump)	20
Royal Marriage	K, Q of trump suit	40
Bezique	Q♠, J♦	40
Four Jacks	One from each suit	400
Four Queens	One from each suit	600
Four Kings	One from each suit	800
Four 10s	One from each suit	900
Four Aces	One from each suit	1,000
Sequence	A, 10, K, Q, J in same suit (not trump)	150

Continued

Royal Sequence	A, 10, K, Q, J of trump suit	250
Double Bezique	Two sets of Q♠, J♦	500
Triple Bezique	Three sets of Q♠, J♦	1,500
Quadruple Bezique	Four sets of Q♠, J♦	4,500
Quintuple Bezique	Five sets of Q♠, J♦	13,500
Sextuple Bezique	Five sets of Q♠, J♦	40,500

BURA

DIFFICULTY *low*	TIME LENGTH *short*	DECKS 1

Few people have heard of Bura. While it bears some resemblance to the Italian game of Briscola, Bura likely developed in Ukraine in the 1870s. From there it was brought by Ukrainian immigrants into western Europe and the United States. By the 1930s, the game's reputation had fallen on hard times, as it was associated (unfairly, no doubt) with drinking and gambling, having been played for high stakes in Ukrainian beer halls.

Bura is a fast-moving trick-taking game for two players (though up to six can conceivably play). The goal is to earn as many points as possible in tricks. It's not a difficult game to master—about the only nonstandard element is that a player may lead with one or more cards at the same time, forcing the other player to follow with the same number of cards.

The version described here does not include wagering, but it's simple enough to substitute money or poker chips for points.

∾ **HOW TO DEAL** Start with a fifty-two-card deck, and remove all 2s through 5s. You will end up with thirty-six cards total. In Bura, cards are always ranked (high to low) A, 10, K, Q, J, 9, 8, 7, 6.

Deal each player three cards, face down and one at a time. The dealer then turns over the top card to determine the trump suit, and places that card at the bottom of the stock so it remains partly visible.

∾ SCORING Each card in Bura is worth the following point values when taken in tricks. Games of Bura are typically played to 10 points.

BURA CARD VALUES	POINTS
Ace	11
10	10
King	4
Queen	3
Jack	2
9	0
8	0
7	0
6	0

∾ HOW TO PLAY The non-dealer leads the first trick, and tricks are won by the highest card in the leading suit, or by the highest trump played. The trick winner always leads the next trick.

When leading, you may play one card from any suit or, as long as all cards are in the same suit, up to three cards. Your opponent must always follow by playing the same number of cards as you, but they may play any cards they want—there is no requirement for your opponent to follow suit. However, to win the trick, your opponent must beat *each* card you play.

For example, assume spades are trump. Player one leads 7♣ and player two follows with 8♣, winning the trick and the lead. On the next trick, player two leads Q♥ and 9♥, and player one throws K♥ (beating Q♥) and J♥ (beating 9♥) to win the trick.

Either way, the trick winner captures all cards in the trick and places them face down. Neither player is ever allowed to look at cards he has captured, so it is important keep a mental tally of your points (and of your opponent's, if your brain can handle the math).

After the trick is complete, the winner draws new cards from the stock until he is again holding three cards. The trick loser then draws as many cards as needed to replenish his own three-card hand. If there aren't enough cards for *both* players to replenish, then *neither* draws cards. They simply play out the game with the cards they have.

∽ **SPECIAL COMBINATIONS** There are three combinations of cards players may use to alter the normal course of the game.

If a player can legally play three trump cards in the same trick, it's called a *Bura*. The hand is automatically won by that player. She earns 1 game point, and a new hand is dealt. If both players miraculously throw a Bura in the same trick, the higher Bura wins the hand.

If a player legally can play three aces in the same trick, that player earns the right to lead the next trick, even if three aces did not actually win the trick.

If a player legally can play three cards of the same suit (not trump), it's called a *Pannochka*. That player earns the right to lead the next trick, even if his cards did not win the trick.

The game ends when one player claims to have scored 31 or more points from tricks. Turn over the player's cards and tally the points. If he correctly crowned himself winner, score him 1 game point (if you're wagering, the player wins the pot). If he messed up the count and has less than 31 points, score 1 game point to the opponent (if you're wagering, a miscount means the loser must match whatever money is in the pot). Either way, the hand is over and new cards are dealt.

On the rare occasion that neither player declares 31 before the stock is exhausted, neither player wins. No game points are awarded, and new cards are dealt (if you're wagering, all players re-ante).

❧ **HOW TO WIN** Your main objective—besides winning tricks that contain points—is to force your opponent to throw point cards against her will. Inexperienced players tend to hold their point cards until later in a hand, so keep one high-ranking trump card for the later tricks.

If you have two cards in the same suit, don't assume it's always best to play them as a set. It's OK to play them as a set if they are mid- or high-ranking non-trump cards—for example K♣ and J♣. This lead forces your opponent to either beat both your cards (likely using trump), which depletes your opponent of trump; or it allows you to earn a few easy points. This strategy does not work well if your cards are of mixed ranks—for example K♣ and 6♣.

Similarly, it's not always a good idea to play three aces. Separately these cards may earn you a few points, which may be more important than capturing the lead.

CASINO

DIFFICULTY *high*	TIME LENGTH *medium*	DECKS 1

Few two-player games are as interesting—or challenging—as Casino. The rules are simple enough. Yet Casino handsomely rewards long-term planning, strategic play, and careful observation. Luck plays little role in Casino.

*Like Gin Rummy and other games that use a **board,** Casino players try to pair, combine, and build cards in their hands with communal cards on the table. Casino moves quickly, and gives players little room for error. That's half the fun of it.*

> Many modern card games originated in France, Italy, and Spain in the sixteenth century. Casino is an exception to the rule; it is originally from China. It's part of the Chinese family of "fishing" games, with a pool of cards that players attempt to capture by pairing them with cards from their own hand.

◆ HOW TO DEAL Casino uses a standard fifty-two-card deck. Cards are played according to their ***index value;*** face cards have no value, aces are worth 1.

On the first round, deal each player two cards, face down, and two cards to the table, face up. Repeat so that each player holds four cards and there are four face-up cards on the table.

Each time players empty their hands of cards, deal them four additional cards, two at a time. No additional cards are dealt to the table.

A single hand of Casino lasts six rounds (twelve cards in the first round, eight in each of the five subsequent rounds). Before the sixth and final round, the dealer must declare "last round," as it affects how the final few cards are played.

◆ SCORING Casino is a trick-taking game. The primary objective is to earn points by winning the most cards, the most spades, and by capturing high-value point cards such as 10♦ (the "Big Casino") or 2♠ (the "Little Casino").

No points are scored until all cards are played after the sixth and final round. At this point, players review the cards they have captured during the rounds, and tally scores based on the following:

CARD	POINTS
Most cards (27 or more)	3
Most spades (7 or more)	1
Big Casino (10♦)	2
Little Casino (2♠)	1
Aces (1 point for each)	4

So there are always 11 points to be won in a hand of Casino. Games are typically played to 21 points.

There is one further way to earn points. It's called a *sweep,* and it happens whenever a player captures all the cards on the table in a single round. This is worth 1 point each time it occurs.

HOW TO PLAY The non-dealer always leads first. In each round, you must always play one card from your hand. What makes the game so interesting is that there are many ways to play a card. Here are your options:

TRAIL A CARD This is Casino lingo for playing a single card to the table, face up. This is the most basic play, and it usually signals that you have no other options.

PAIR A CARD The simplest way to capture cards is by pairing them. Use a card from your hand to take a card of matching rank from the table. For example, assume you're holding 7♦, and 7♣ is face up on the table. Use your 7♦ to capture 7♣, then take both cards and place them face down in a pile in front of you. There's no limit to the number of cards you may capture this way (your 7♦ could capture both 7♣ and 7♥ on the table, for example). This holds true for aces (it's possible to capture three aces with a single ace), but not for face cards.

PAIR A FACE CARD Face cards may be paired, but only one card at a time. In other words, you may capture a jack with a jack, a queen with a queen, or a king with a king. You may not capture two kings, for example, with a single king.

COMBINING CARDS One of Casino's best features is the ability to capture cards in combinations. For example, 3♦ and 4♣ on the table may be captured by your 7♣, as 3 + 4 = 7; 9♥ and A♠ on the table may be captured by your 10♦; or 3♣, 5♥, A♦, A♠ on the table may be captured by your 10♠, etc. You may even combine multiple sets of cards on the table: For example, your 9♥ may capture 5♥ and 4♦ as well as 6♣ and 3♠ on the same turn.

PAIRING & COMBINING CARDS Yes friends, it is also possible to capture a pair and a combination (or multiple combinations) in a single turn. Your 8♥, for example, may capture 8♠ and 5♦-3♣ in the same turn.

BUILDING COMBINATIONS Another brilliant feature of Casino is the ability to build combinations over multiple turns. For example, assume 3♣ is on the table and you hold 5♥, 8♠ in your hand. You play 5♥ on top of 3♣ and announce that you are "building eights." On the next turn, you may capture the 5♥-3♣ build with your 8♠. Keep in mind that when building combinations, you may not trail a card on the subsequent turn; instead, you must capture the build, increase the build, or capture a different card. In other words, in the previous example, you may not leave the 5♥-3♣ build on the table on your following turn and then simply trail another card. However, you may leave the 5♥-3♣ on the table if you instead pair a different card (say, 10♦ from your hand with 10♥ from the table) or increase the existing 5♥-3♣ build.

INCREASING BUILDS You are allowed to increase an existing build (or an opponent's build) by adding a card from your hand. You may not use a card from the table. So in the previous example, you may add A♥ to the existing build of 5♥-3♣ on the table, announce you're "building nines," and then capture the build on the following turn with any 9 from your hand. The risk, of course, is that your opponent may swoop in and change the value of your build and capture it for herself on the following turn.

CAPTURING BUILDS There's nothing worse than watching your opponent capture one of your builds. Yet it's all part of the game—there's nothing to stop either player from doing so.

BUILDING & PAIRING COMBINATIONS Perhaps the ultimate play in Casino is building *and* pairing a combination. Assume you're holding 9♥, 5♣, 2♦, while 9♠, 4♦ are on the table. You could simply pair the 9s, or you might try this: play your 5♥ on the 4♦ (announce "building nines"), and add the 9♠ from the table onto the build, thereby "pairing" both builds. On your next turn, you could capture the 5♥, 4♦, 9♠ from the table with your 9♥. Or even better, if your opponent trails 7♦, play your 2♦ on 7♦, move these cards onto the build of nines, and on the following turn capture the 5♥, 4♦, 9♠, 2♦, 7♦ all with your 9♥. Note that neither player may increase the build of nines once that build is paired. In other words, you may not add A♥ to the 5♥-4♦-9♠ build and announce "building to tens." Once a build has been paired, its value is fixed and cannot be altered. Similarly, you may not unbundle or divide an existing build (for example, you may not split the 5♥-4♦-9♠ build into its components).

Remember that any player who captures all the table cards in a single turn earns 1 point for the sweep.

If any cards are left on the table after the final card in the last round is played, the remaining table cards are awarded to the player who most recently captured a card. And no, very sorry, this does not count as a sweep.

Once the hand is complete, each player counts the cards he has won and tallies his score based on the scoring table. In close games you are allowed to *count out* early if you think your score is greater, or equal to 21 points (or to whatever point total you're playing). When a player announces "count out," the game ends immediately and all cards taken to that point are tallied. If the player correctly claimed victory, well done; congratulations are in order. Otherwise the player scores -11 points and forfeits his next deal.

ᔦ **HOW TO WIN** Casino is considered a top-tier strategy game by professional card players. The challenge for newbies is to plan two or three moves ahead, because often the obvious play is not the most rewarding. Good Casino players know all about the "mind game" and are usually skilled bluffers.

Since one point is awarded to the player who captures the majority of spades, take every opportunity to capture (or to build and capture) spades, at least until a majority are won. Unless you are supremely confident, do not build with high-value cards such as aces or the Big and Little Casinos. Capture these cards straight away, or risk your opponent swooping in and robbing you of your build.

Similarly, avoid complex build-and-pairing combinations early in the game, unless you are certain your opponent does not possess the cards necessary to capture them. Since face cards may be played and captured only in sets of two, it's a good defensive maneuver to hold a face card late in the game. Use it either to capture the last trick (thereby winning any unclaimed table cards) or to throw yourself an easy win and the right to lead the subsequent trick (owning the lead late in the game is often very handy).

ᔦ **IRREGULARITIES & DISPUTES** If the dealer exposes a card when dealing to himself or to an opponent, the non-dealer has the right to instantly end the hand and score the offending dealer -1 point. The non-dealer will also automatically deal the next hand. If the non-dealer decides to continue play, the misdealt card (or cards) is put back into the deck and the entire deck is reshuffled. No other penalties apply.

If the misdeal results in one player having too few cards or in the stock having too few cards at the end of the hand, the offending dealer scores -1 point and the affected player plays on with a short hand. If the misdeal leaves a player with too many cards, the offending dealer scores -1 point, the excess cards are added face up to the table, and the game continues. On the very next deal, the dealer must also short his hand by the number of cards dealt in excess.

If a player uses a card to incorrectly capture another card (for example, incorrectly pairing 9♦ on the table with 6♦ from the hand), the offending card must be trailed immediately. If a player makes a build that on her next turn she cannot win, the opponent scores 1 point. The build remains on the table and may still be won by either player.

- -

VARIATION 1: DRAW CASINO

This straightforward variation of the standard two-player game is more of a novelty. That said, in China it is the most popular version of the game played today. There is only one round of dealing: four cards to each player and four cards to the table. The remaining stock cards are placed on the table. In all subsequent rounds, players draw one card from the stock after their turn, so they always maintain a four-card hand. In all other respects, the game is identical to the standard version.

- -

VARIATION 2: ROYAL CASINO

Once you've mastered the basic game, give Royal Casino a try. It plays exactly like standard Casino, except that face cards now have point values, which greatly expands your building and pairing opportunities.

Face cards have the following values when combining and building them: kings are 13, queens 12, jacks 11. Aces are now worth either 1 (as in the standard game) or 14, determined at the discretion of the players. Set aside the rules against using face cards in builds and multi-card pairing. In Royal Casino, you may use a queen in your hand to capture two or more queens on the table. You also may use a queen (with a face value of 12) in your hand to combine with 10♦, 2♣ on the table, or to combine with 9♥, 2♦, A♠ (playing A♠ as 1 point). Alternatively, you may combine A♠ in your hand with Q♣, 2♥ on the table (playing A♠ as 14 points).

- -

VARIATION 3: SPADE CASINO

Here's another good way to add zing to a standard Casino game. The idea is to make spades more valuable, which increases the risks for players who use spades in builds and combinations.

All spades are worth 1 point when tallying scores, except for J♠ (worth 2 points), and the Little Casino (2♠, worth 2 points). The Big Casino (10♦) is now worth 3 points. Players still earn 1 point for capturing a majority of spades. In each hand there are 26 total points at stake (not counting points for sweeps). Games of Spade Casino are typically played to 61 points.

- -

VARIATION 4: THREE-HAND CASINO

Compelling three-player games are hard to come by, and it's a shame that Three-Hand Casino is not more widely played. The game has plenty to recommend it, especially if your threesome is looking for a game that balances skill, strategy, and cutthroat play. Who knows, maybe Three-Hand Casino is due for a comeback.

There are no partnerships. Instead, each player vies against the other two to score the greatest number of points. The rules are exactly like the standard two-player game, the only difference being that a hand ends after four rounds instead of the standard six, due to the greater number of cards in play (sixteen in the first round, twelve in each of the three subsequent rounds).

The player to the left of the dealer always plays first, and the deal rotates clockwise after each hand. Games of Three-Hand Casino are typically played to 15 points (short game) or 21 points (standard game).

VARIATION 5: FOUR-HAND CASINO

Four-Hand Casino is usually played when four die-hard Casino players gather and nobody is willing to sit out for a game. Skip ahead to Contract Bridge, Four-Hand Bezique, or Partnership Klaberjass if you crave more action.

Choose teams by dealing out the cards; the first two players to draw aces are partners, and they sit opposite each other. The game is played exactly like the standard two-player game, the only difference being that a hand ends after three rounds instead of the standard six, due to the number of cards in play (twenty in the first round, sixteen in each of the two subsequent rounds).

The first player to capture a card collects all the cards for that team. At the end of each hand, the cards and points of each partnership are pooled, and scores are awarded accordingly. There's not much intrateam strategy in the game. Players can try to create builds for their partner to capture, but since table talk is not allowed, this is not an easy thing to pull off.

VARIATION 6: SCOPA

Naysayers may argue that Scopa is not a variation of Casino but a stand-alone game in its own right. Scopa and Casino are very similar, the main differences being the deck (forty cards instead of fifty-two), scoring values, and the fact that some elements of Casino (primarily building) are not allowed.

Scopa may be played by two or three players. Start with a standard fifty-two-card deck, and remove all 8s, 9s and 10s, for a total of 40 cards. When combining cards, the following values are used: numbered cards are worth their face value, aces are worth 1, kings 10, queens 9, jacks 8.

All players start with three cards (not the usual four), with four cards on the table. When players empty their hands of cards, three additional cards are dealt to each player until the stock is exhausted.

SCORING The goal of Scopa is the same as in Casino, namely to capture cards from the table and thereby earn points:

CARD	POINTS
Most cards (21 or more); no points for a tie	1
Most diamonds (6 or more); no points for a tie	1
Sette Bello (7♦)	1
Primiera (see below)	1

As in standard Casino, 1 point is awarded for a sweep (capturing all the cards on the table in a single turn).

Scopa also has a unique scoring feature called *Primiera,* earned by the player who has the most points after adding up their highest-value cards in each of the four suits. Primiera scores are calculated at the end of each hand on the following basis: 10 points for face cards, 12 points for 2s, 13 points for 3s, 14 points for 4s, 15 points for 5s, 16 points for aces, 18 points for 6s, 21 points for 7s. To determine who wins the Primiera point, each player adds together the scores of their single highest card in each suit. For example, player one's highest-value cards in each suit are 7♦, A♥, 5♣, J♠; player two holds 6♦, J♥, 4♠, 6♣; player three has 7♥, 7♣, Q♦. Player three is immediately disqualified because only three suits are represented (this example assumes player three has won no spades). Player two scores 60. And player one scores 62, thereby winning the 1 Primiera point. No Primiera point is scored if there is a tie.

Scopa is won by the first player to score 11 game points. As in Casino, it is allowed to "call out" early, with identical penalties for making a false claim.

HOW TO PLAY Scopa is played identically to Casino, with the following exceptions. You may capture only a single combination per turn, not multiple combinations. So if the table cards are 5♥, 5♦, 6♣, 4♠, a king captures either the 5♥-5♦ combination or the 6♣-4♠ combination, but not both.

Similarly, your 7♥ may capture either 4♥-3♦ or pair with the 7♦, but you may not do both in the same turn. In fact, in this example you are forced to capture the pair rather than the combination—in Scopa, if you have both a pair and a combination available, you must always choose the pair.

CRIBBAGE

DIFFICULTY *medium*	TIME LENGTH *medium*	DECKS 1

Cribbage requires skill, a healthy dose of strategy, and a pinch or two of luck—a heady brew that can sustain the interest of card players for hours on end. The game takes a few hands to master. But don't let this put you off. Cribbage is a superb two-player game.

One important element of the game is the board. Cribbage boards are typically made of wood and have small pegs that simplify score tracking. A Cribbage board is not required, but it makes scoring a lot easier.

∾ **HOW TO DEAL**   Start with a standard fifty-two-card deck. Cards rank high to low from king down to ace. Face cards are worth 10 points, aces are worth 1, and all other cards are worth their ***index value***. Deal each player six cards, one at a time and face down. No other cards are dealt.

Each player looks at her cards and then nominates two cards to place face down in the center of the table. This is the *crib*, an extra hand of four cards that always belongs to the dealer. Once the crib is established, the non-dealer cuts the deck, and the dealer turns up the top card from the lower portion of the deck. This is the *turn-up card,* which is used by both players as a fifth card in their hand. If the turn-up card is a jack, the dealer scores 1 point for His Heels (see scoring, below).

∾ **SCORING**   The goal in Cribbage is to be the first player to score 121 points (in tournament play, if a player wins with 121 points before his opponent scores 61 points, a double-game score is earned). Players earn points for scoring the following combinations:

FIFTEEN   Score 2 points for any card combination that adds up to 15 points.

PAIR   Two cards of the same rank earn 2 points. In the matching phase, players earn points if they pair an opponent's card. For example, if player one throws 9♦ and player two throws 9♣, player two earns 2 points for the pair.

MULTIPLE PAIRS Three cards of the same rank are worth 6 points, because they can be combined into three sets of pairs. For example, 4♥, 4♦, 4♣ in your hand may be combined into three pairs of fours (4♥-4♦, 4♥-4♣, 4♦-4♣) for a total of 6 points. With four cards of the same rank, you earn 12 total points for making six sets of pairs. Multiple pairs also may be played in the matching phase. For example, player one throws 5♥ and player two throws 5♣ for 2 points. If player one replies with 5♦, he earns 6 points for three sets of pairs (5♥-5♣, 5♥-5♦, 5♣-5♦). If player two miraculously follows with a fourth card of the same rank, she earns 12 points.

RUN At minimum, a run is three cards in sequence, regardless of suit. So 5♥-6♦-7♦ earns a player 3 points, while a run of four cards is worth 4 points. If a player has a pair of cards in the run, multiple runs may be scored. For example, the hand 3♥-4♦-5♥-5♣ is worth 8 total points for the two three-card runs (3♥-4♦-5♥ for 3 points; 3♥-4♦-5♣ for 3 points), plus a pair of fives for 2 additional points. A quadruple run (for example, 9-9-10-10-J) scores 16 points.

In the matching phase, players earn points for runs even if the cards are not played sequentially. For example, if player one throws 5♣ and player two throws 7♥, then player one may throw any 6 to earn 3 points for a run. The run is not allowed if a nonsequential card is thrown into the mix. So in this example, the run is not scored if the cards are played in the following order: 5♣, 7♥, J♦, 6♣.

FLUSH At minimum, a flush is four cards of the same suit, regardless of rank. So the hand 3♥-7♥-10♥-J♥ is worth 4 points (1 point for each card in the flush). If the turn-up card is also a heart, the hand is worth 5 points. Flushes are earned only for cards held in your own hand. Flushes may not be earned during the matching phase, and four-card flushes in the crib do not earn any points. However, if the crib cards are of the same suit *and* if the turn-up card matches that suit, then the crib owner earns 5 points for a crib flush.

HIS NOBS This oddly named bonus (worth 1 point) is earned by any player who holds a jack of the same suit as the turn-up card.

HIS HEELS Another oddly named bonus (1 point), this time earned by the dealer when she happens to turn up a jack.

GO POINT A player pegs 1 "go" point when his opponent cannot play a card without taking the total over 31 points; or 2 "go" points for himself when he scores exactly 31 points and forces his opponent to begin play back at zero.

LAST POINT The player who throws the last card in the matching phase earns 1 point.

∾ **HOW TO PLAY** Each hand of Cribbage is divided into two phases, the *matching phase* and the *showing phase*.

MATCHING PHASE Once the crib is established and the turn-up card is settled, the game starts with the non-dealer leading a single card from her hand, face up, and announcing the card's rank out loud (for example, if you play 5♥, announce "five"). Players then alternate throwing cards face up on the table, in an attempt to earn points by combining their cards plus their opponent's into pairs, runs, fifteens, and "go" points.

For example, if player one throws 7♦ and player two throws 7♥, player two pegs 2 points for a pair. If player one replies with 7♠, she pegs 6 total points for creating three sets of pairs.

Alternatively, if no pairs, runs, or fifteens are scored, then the player who cannot play a card without going over 31 total points sacrifices a "go" point to his opponent. For example, if player one leads 10♥, player two follows with Q♠, and player one replies with 8♦, then player two either must throw a three (thereby pegging 2 points for hitting 31 exactly); or throw an ace or a two, keeping the total below 31 points; or, if she cannot play a card without exceeding 31 points, peg 1 "go" point to her opponent. In the latter case, the count begins again at zero and the next card is led by player one.

The player who throws the last card in the matching phase scores 1 point.

SHOWING PHASE Once each player has exhausted his four cards, each "shows" and scores his cards in the following strict order: non-dealer, dealer, dealer's crib.

The turn-up card is used by both players as a fifth card in their hands. For example, assume the non-dealer holds J♠-J♥-Q♠-K♥ and the dealer holds 5♦-6♦-7♦-J♦. If the turn-up card is 5♠, the players score the following:

Non-dealer scores 12 total points for two runs (J♥-Q♠-K♥ for 3 points; J♠-Q♠-K♥ for 3 points), one pair (J♠-J♥ for 2 points), and making fifteen twice (J♠-5♠ for 2 points; J♥-5♠ for 2 points).

Dealer scores 16 total points for two runs (5♦-6♦-7♦ for 3 points; 5♠-6♦-7♦ for 3 points), one flush (5♦-6♦-7♦-J♦ for 4 points), one pair (5♦-5♠ for 2 points), and making fifteen twice (5♦-J♦ for 2 points; 5♠-J♦ for 2 points).

SCORING THE CRIB After the matching and showing phases are finished, the dealer turns up the crib cards and pegs points for any pairs, multiple pairs, runs, flushes, and fifteens it contains, using the turn-up card as a fifth card in the hand. For example, if the turn-up card is Q♠ and the crib contains 5♥-5♦-3♣-7♥, then the dealer earns 2 points for a pair (5♥-5♦), and 8 points for making fifteen four times (Q♠-5♥ plus Q♠-5♦ plus 7♥-3♣-5♥ plus 7♥-3♣-5♦).

∾ **HOW TO WIN** There are two critical decisions a player must make in Cribbage: which two cards to throw into the crib, and which card to lead with in the matching phase. The crib decision is usually straightforward if you're the dealer. Look at your six cards and determine which four have the best odds of earning points for pairs and runs. As the dealer, you ultimately will earn any points in the crib, so it's OK to throw a pair into the crib if it means you keep a run of three or more together in your hand. When in doubt, keep a run, and hope the turn-up card will add to it.

The decision is more complicated for the non-dealer. You must strike a balance between keeping the best four cards possible in your hand and being careful not to throw useful point cards into the dealer's crib.

There's no more frustrating hand to be dealt when you're the non-dealer than 3♥-3♦-5♥-5♦-6♥-7♠. You hate to throw any points into the dealer's crib. Yet there's no other choice, so minimize the pain by throwing 3♥-3♦ into the crib (a gift of 2 points to the dealer) and keep the other four cards, since they have a much greater scoring potential.

꙾ POINTS OF ETIQUETTE   Etiquette matters in Cribbage. There are not many rules, so novice players owe it to themselves to commit the following to memory.

After playing a card, always announce the current card total. It is rude to do otherwise. For example, if you throw 8♦ on 10♥, say "eighteen."

Similarly, announce what you're scoring as you play. If you throw 5♦ on J♥, say "fifteen for 2 points." If you throw 9♣ on 7♦-8♥, say "24 for a run of three."

Table talk is not allowed in Cribbage. So do not discuss or drop hints about cards you hold, cards in the crib, points of strategy, etc.

If a player forgets to peg a score she is entitled to, or simply doesn't add her points properly, once the next card is played, the opponent may declare *muggins* and take the unearned points as her own.

- -
VARIATION 1: CRIBBAGE 1/11

Once you get the hang of Cribbage, try this deceptively simple variation in which aces may be counted as 1 or 11 in either the matching or showing phase. For example, the hand A♠-3♥-4♣-5♦ is normally worth 3 points for the 3♥-4♣-5♦ run. In Cribbage 1/11, the hand is worth 5 points: 3 for the run plus 2 for fifteen (A♠-4♣).

- -
VARIATION 2: REVERSE CRIBBAGE

This is played exactly like the standard game. The only difference is that the first player to score 121 points loses rather than wins. And yes, it is much harder than it sounds not to score points, especially if you're the dealer. This is a superb variation for veteran Cribbage players who love the basic game but are looking for new challenges.

- -
VARIATION 3: THREE-HAND CRIBBAGE

This is an excellent game for three players and requires no extra learning or effort, as long as you're already familiar with the basic two-hand game. The game is played exactly like the standard game, with the following exceptions.

Instead of four cards, all players are dealt five, and one card is dealt to the crib. Each player then throws one card into the crib, so each player (as well as the crib) holds four cards.

In the matching phase, the only difference is that in the case of a go point being earned, the next round is always opened by the first player unable to play a card in the previous round. The player to the left of the dealer determines the turn-up card, and also opens. When scoring during the showing phase, the order is always clockwise, starting with the player to the left of the dealer.

- -
VARIATION 4: FOUR-HAND CRIBBAGE

The main argument against four-hand cribbage is that few opportunities exist to work collaboratively with your partner. There is no bidding, no trump, no dummy hand—none of the features common to more sophisticated four-player partnership games.

The game is played exactly like the standard two-hand game, except that partners sit opposite one another, and instead of four cards, all players are dealt five. Each player then throws one card into the crib, so all players (plus the crib) have four cards.

The player to the left of the dealer determines the turn-up card and leads the first round. In the case of a go point being scored, the first player unable to play a card in the previous round always leads the next round. Each team combines its score during the game. When scoring during the showing phase, the order is always non-dealing team, dealing team, dealing team's crib.

- -
VARIATION 5: TABLETOP CRIBBAGE

This is a *no-peekie* offshoot of Cribbage (think of it as standard Cribbage minus the matching phase) and uses most of the same scoring rules. The game is best for two players sitting side-by-side (not across from each other). Deal twelve cards to each player, face down in a pile, and do not look at any cards. Take the next card and lay it face up in the middle of the table. Put a marker (penny, beer cap, matchstick, etc.) on top of it. No other cards are dealt.

Tabletop Cribbage uses a five-by-five layout of cards. The object is to play point-earning cards in rows (if you're the non-dealer) or columns (if you're the dealer). The non-dealer leads, and plays a card in any empty slot. The only restriction is that the card must touch the edge of an existing card on the board, either to the side, top or bottom, or diagonal edge.

Columns—Scored by Dealer

▾	▾	▾	▾	▾
Empty Slot	Empty Slot	Empty Slot	Empty Slot	Empty Slot
Empty Slot	Empty Slot	Empty Slot	Empty Slot	Empty Slot
Empty Slot	Empty Slot	Turn-Up Card Marker	Empty Slot	Empty Slot
Empty Slot	Empty Slot	Empty Slot	Empty Slot	Empty Slot
Empty Slot	Empty Slot	Empty Slot	Empty Slot	Empty Slot

Rows—Scored by Non-Dealer

Each player alternates taking a card from his hand (remember, players are not allowed to look at their cards) and playing it on the board. No points are scored until all twenty-four cards have been played. The non-dealer always counts points first. Each row or column is treated like a standard hand of Cribbage, scoring points for pairs, runs, and/or fifteens. Only five-card flushes are allowed. No points are awarded for His Heels or His Nobs.

CUARENTA

DIFFICULTY *low*	TIME LENGTH *short*	DECKS 1

The name means "Forty" in Spanish, which is how many points you need to win. The game is popular throughout South America, but in Ecuador it has been elevated to a national pastime. The rules are simple enough, and once you master them, it's a fast-paced, think-on-your-feet kind of game.

∾ **HOW TO DEAL** Start with a fifty-two-card deck, and remove all 8s, 9s, and 10s for a total of forty cards. Aces are always low in Cuarenta. Deal five cards to each player, face down, in a single batch. The remaining cards are set aside for later use. The deal alternates after each game.

∾ **SCORING** The first player to score 40 points wins the game. Points are awarded for cards captured during play and for the following special circumstances:

At the start of the game, any player dealt four-of-a-kind immediately wins the entire game.

At the start of the game, any player dealt three cards of matching suit proclaims a *ronda* (round) and earns 4 points.

A player earns 2 points, called a *caída* (fall), for capturing by matching (not by adding or sequencing) the card just played by an opponent. If you're lucky—or clever—enough to capture part of an opponent's ronda, and if you declare this before the next hand is dealt, score yourself 10 points!

If you clear the pot of cards, it's called a *limpia* (clean) and is worth 2 points. You cannot earn a limpia if you have 38 or more points.

At the end of the game, a player who captures twenty cards earns 6 points, plus 1 point for every two additional cards captured. If both players capture more than twenty cards, the non-dealer earns 6 points and no other points are awarded. If neither player captures twenty cards, the player with more cards earns 2 points.

∾ **HOW TO PLAY** The player to the left of the dealer places one card on the table, face up. The opponent may capture this card three different ways:

MATCHING Play a card of equal rank (e.g., 4 on a 4) and capture both cards.

ADDING Play a card that adds up to the value of one or more *non-face* cards in the pot. For example, if 2, 3, 6 are in the pot, playing 5 will capture the 2 and 3. Aces are valued as 1 point. Face cards have no point value and may not capture or be captured in this manner.

SEQUENCING When capturing by matching or adding, capture any other cards in the pot that are in unbroken ascending rank. If the pot contains 3, 4, 5, 6, Q, for example, your 4 captures the 4 (for the match) as well as the 5 and 6 (for sequencing).

You may not capture more than once per turn, so if the pot contains A-3-4-7, you may play a 4 either to capture the 4 (for the match) or to capture the A and 3 (for adding), but not both. Either way, you may capture a sequence, if it's available. If you fail to capture all cards you are entitled to—usually by not seeing a sequence opportunity—your opponent may point this out before playing a card and capture the card(s) for herself.

Deal five more cards to each player once both players' hands are empty; continue until the stock is exhausted (in a two-player game this means four total deals). Any cards left in the pot between deals stay in the pot and are available for subsequent capture, but you may not score a caída using cards from a previous deal.

∾ **STRATEGY TIPS** Playing to an empty pot is dangerous, since it is relatively easy for your opponent to score a caída. A good defensive move is to lead with one card in a pair of cards, to minimize the chances of your opponent capturing it on a match.

The four-person partnership version of Cuarenta is played exactly as above, with just two slight differences. Partners sit opposite each other, and only two deals per game are possible (as opposed to four).

Gin Rummy

The history of this game is legendary. In 1909, Elwood Baker, a Whist teacher based in Brooklyn, New York, invented this variation of the already famous game of Rummy. Elwood originally called the game Gin, playing on the hard-alcohol heritage of Rummy (which was originally called Rum).

In the 1940s, the game was adopted by Hollywood, popularized in film and on radio, and grew into a nationwide fad under the name "Gin Rummy." It remains one of the world's truly great two-player card games. Though it's easy to learn, there's plenty of strategy and skill required. Gamblers are also fond of the game, since its scoring system readily lends itself to betting.

∾ **HOW TO DEAL** Use a fifty-two-card deck, and deal ten cards to both players, one at a time and all face down. The remaining cards are the stock; the topmost stock card, turned face up, is known as the **upcard**. In Gin Rummy, kings are always high and aces are always low. A game typically lasts for twenty or thirty minutes, depending on how many individual hands are dealt.

∾ **SCORING** The goal is to be the first player to earn 100 points. Face cards are worth 10 points, aces are 1, and all other cards are worth their **index value**.

The first player to score 100 points earns an additional game bonus of 100 points, plus each hand he won during the game retroactively receives a 25-point "line" bonus.

∾ **HOW TO PLAY** The game always starts with the non-dealer, who chooses whether or not to take the upcard. If the non-dealer decides not to take it, the dealer then has the option. If both players decline the upcard, the non-dealer takes the topmost stock card into her hand, making eleven cards total.

The non-dealer must then discard one card of her choosing, leaving it face up on top of the existing upcard. The game alternates back and forth between dealer and non-dealer.

The goal is to organize your ten cards into any combination of the following hands. It doesn't matter which hands you end the game with, as long as all ten cards belong to a sequence or a set:

SEQUENCE   Three or more cards of matching suit, in ascending rank. For example, 5♠-6♠-7♠ is a valid sequence. *Continuous ranking* is not allowed, and aces are always low.

SET   Three or four cards of matching rank. For example. J♠-J♣-J♥ is a valid set.

KNOCKING   Any cards in your hand that are not part of a set or sequence are considered unmatched. At any time, if the value of your unmatched cards is less than 10 points, you may knock. This forces a showdown with your opponent, to determine who is holding the fewest unmatched cards.

When knocking, turn your discard face down and place the cards in your hand face up, organized into sets and sequences. Your opponent does the same. If you're the knocker, your opponent can try to play his unmatched cards onto your sets and sequences, thereby minimizing his own unmatched cards.

Either way, add up the total of your unmatched cards, subtract your opponent's unmatched cards, and score yourself the difference. If your unmatched cards, for example, are 6♦ and 3♣ (9 total points) and your opponent is holding, unmatched, K♣, 8♦, 5♦, 4♥ (27 total points), score yourself 18 points ($27-9 = 18$).

If you're the knocker and your opponent holds *fewer* points in unmatched cards, your opponent scores the difference plus 25 points for a so-called *undercut*. This is the danger of knocking too early, without holding a gin.

GIN   If you knock while holding no unmatched cards, you have what's called a *gin.* Score yourself 25 points plus the sum of your opponent's unmatched cards.

∾ **STRATEGY TIPS** Veteran players agree: The only reason to take a card from the discard pile (rather than drawing a fresh card from the stock) is to complete an existing set or sequence.

Most players aim to create two sets and one sequence, and this strategy is effective. Improve your odds of achieving this by holding onto unmatched low cards (A, 2, 3, 4). Be sure to dump unmatched 10s and face cards after five or six turns, to avoid holding too many points in unmatched cards.

The real skill in this game is keeping track of the discards. And it's a good idea to knock as early as possible. Earning bonus points for gin is icing on the cake—it shouldn't be your primary goal.

∾ **IRREGULARITIES & DISPUTES** A *shutout* happens when a player scores 100 total points before her opponent wins a single hand. In this case, the winning player's score is doubled and the game bonus increases to 200 points. A *draw* happens when only two cards remain in the stock and neither player has knocked. The hand is instantly dead. All cards are shuffled and redealt.

In case of a misdeal, the hand is instantly dead. Score the non-dealer 10 points and redeal. In case of an illegal knock (e.g., the knocker has more than 10 points in unmatched cards), the opposing player may choose to continue with the knock, or force the offender to continue playing with his entire hand exposed.

VARIATION 1: OKLAHOMA GIN

This game is played exactly like the basic game, with a few twists. The rank of that first upcard determines the points required to knock: face cards leave it at the usual threshold of 10 points, aces require a gin hand to knock, and all other cards set a new threshold (e.g., an upcard of 7 means a player must have seven or fewer points in unmatched cards to knock). Finally, if the first upcard is a spade, scores for that hand only are doubled (not including any bonuses for undercutting or for gin). Games of Oklahoma Gin are typically played to 150 points.

VARIATION 2: THREE-HAND GIN RUMMY

Enthusiasts of Gin Rummy have discovered an elegant—and very rewarding—way for managing three players who each want a piece of the action. Before any cards are dealt, each player draws a card from the deck. High card means you play alone against the other two players. Second-highest card denotes the "on deck" player. If the lone player wins, she maintains her position and another hand is dealt. If the lone player loses, the person on deck becomes the new solo player, and her teammate moves to on deck.

VARIATION 3: FOUR-HAND GIN RUMMY

This is not your typical partnership game. Rather than playing as teams, partners play separately in head-to-head games with opponents. For example, if players A1 and A2 are teammates against players B1 and B2, the first hand pits players A1 vs. B1 and A2 vs. B2. Each plays a complete hand of Gin Rummy (so two decks are required). At the end of both games, the scores of both players are added up and then subtracted from the opponents' total. For example, if player A1 beats B1 by 17 points while player A2 loses to B2 by 12 points, team A wins the first hand by 5 points. After each hand, the players swap opponents and continue until one team scores 100 total points.

KLABERJASS

| DIFFICULTY *high* | TIME LENGTH *medium* | DECKS 1 |

Depending on where you grew up, you may know Klaberjass as Bella, Belotte, Clob, Clobber, Clabber, Klab, Klob, or Klabber. The game shares many characteristics with Bezique, Pinochle, and other melding and trick-taking games. What's unique is that players in Klaberjass "bid to win." Whichever player accepts trump is committed to winning the hand, so accept your trump suits wisely.

∾ **HOW TO DEAL** Start with one fifty-two-card deck, and remove every card between 2 and 6 so you're left with a total of thirty-two cards. In non-trump suits, cards rank in their natural order (A, K, Q, J, 10, 9, 8, 7). In trump, cards rank J, 9, A, K, Q, 10, 8, 7, so the jack and 9 of trump beat the ace of trump.

Players cut for deal, with the high card dealing the first hand. The deal alternates in subsequent hands. Deal six cards to both players, face down, in sets of three.

∾ **BIDDING** After each player has six cards, the dealer exposes the top card on the deck as the proposed trump suit and places it partly underneath the stock. The non-dealer may accept this suit as trump, or pass. If the suit is accepted, the non-dealer is said to have "won the bid" and is committed to winning the hand. If the non-dealer passes, the dealer decides whether to accept the trump suit (and commit to winning the hand) or to pass.

If the dealer also passes, the non-dealer is now free to declare any of the three remaining suits as trump (a definite advantage). The non-dealer also may pass (and should pass, if his cards are weak). Then it's back again to the dealer, who may either declare any of the three remaining suits as trump or pass. If the dealer passes now, the hand is dead and fresh cards are dealt.

Once a bid is made and the trump suit is chosen, the dealer gives each player three additional cards (for a total of nine each).

> **In Klaberjass, you risk victory or defeat on the basis of an incomplete hand. You must decide to accept or pass trump with only six of your ultimate nine cards.**

∾ **THE EXCHANGE**   Once the deal is complete, if the turn-up suit has been accepted as trump, either player holding the 7 of trump may exchange it for the turn-up card. No exchange is allowed if the original suit was not established as trump. The dealer now turns up the bottom card of the stock. This card is not in play, but it sometimes affects the players' strategy.

∾ **SCORING**   The goal in Klaberjass is to score 500 points, first by declaring the highest naturally dealt sequence of cards before the first trick is won, and then by winning tricks that contain high-value cards listed in the chart below. Players also earn points for playing a *Bella* (K, Q of trump; 20 points) and winning the final trick of the game (10 points).

KLABERJASS CARD VALUES	POINTS
Bella (K of trump, Q of trump)	20
Ace (trump & non trump)	11
King (trump & non-trump)	4
Queen (trump & non-trump)	3
Jack (trump)	20
Jack (non-trump)	2
10 (trump & non-trump)	10
9 (trump)	14
9 (non-trump)	0
8 (trump & non-trump)	0
7 (trump & non-trump)	0

Once all cards are played, the players tally points earned during the trick-taking phase. The player who did not win the trump bid tallies and scores points first, since her points are always valid.

The opposing player then tallies his points. Here's the rub: the winner of the trump bid only scores points if he surpasses his opponent's total. So if you won the trump bid, you must beat the other player's total score. If you have fewer total points, then all your points from the hand are added to the first player's score. In Klaberjass, you pay dearly if you win the trump bid and don't outscore your opponent.

> **FOR EXAMPLE** Player one wins the trump bid and ends the hand with 55 total points. Player two ends with 50 points. No penalties are levied, and each player keeps his or her points. However, if player one won the trump bid and ends with 55 points while player two ends with 70 points, player one's score for the round is 0 while player two's score is 125 points (70 + 55).

In the event of a tie, the disputed scores are set aside until the next hand is played. Whoever wins the subsequent hand wins all the points from the tied hand.

The only scoring complication is that while points are normally tallied at the end of a hand, the game officially ends the moment a player reaches 500 points. So you can win midhand, for example, by declaring a sequence or a Bella that pushes your score over the threshold. This is true even if you accepted the trump suit and would ultimately have lost all your points (had the hand been played to the end).

∾ **HOW TO PLAY** The non-dealer always leads the first trick. Once the opening card is played—but before the opponent plays a card—both players attempt to declare the highest sequence in their nine-card hands. Sequences are valued as follows:

> 50 points for a run of **four** in the same suit (e.g., K♣-Q♣-J♣-10♣)
> 20 points for a run of **three** in the same suit (e.g., Q♥-J♥-10♥)

For example, if player one is leading the first trick, he will play a card and then declare, "a run of three" and player two will attempt to declare a higher sequence. Only one player may earn points at this stage, so it is in player two's interest to match or beat player one's declaration. If player two counters, she might say "a run of three cards, king high," in the hopes of beating player one's lower three-card sequence. In the rare case where player one also has a three-card run to the king, player one will then reply, "trump?" Trump always wins.

Alternatively, if player two declares "a run of four" against player one's "run of three," then player two wins and becomes the sole declarer. Yet it's not as simple as all that! There are additional rules concerning the declaration.

The declarer's points are not scored until the declarer wins *at least one trick* during the hand. Though rare, it is possible for the declarer not to win a single trick. In this case, the declarer's score for the declaration is null and void.

The declarer may score any additional sequences in her hand. For example, if the declarer holds K♥-Q♥-J♥-10♥-10♣-9♣-8♣-8♦, she earns 50 points for the four-card run in hearts, plus 20 points for the three-card run in clubs.

If you are the declarer, you must show the winning sequence (plus any other sequence you wish to score) to your opponent, as verification. It's the polite thing to do.

Note that if neither player has a sequence to declare, the game proceeds to the trick-taking phase. Also note that sequences are always ranked using standard card rankings (A-K-Q-J-10-9-8-7), even if the sequence is in trump.

TRICK-TAKING PHASE After the declaration is complete, the rest of the tricks are played out, with the winner of the last trick leading the next. Tricks are won by the high card in the leading suit, or by the high trump played. In Klaberjass, you must follow suit if possible, or play a trump.

In addition to earning points by winning tricks containing the cards noted in the scoring table, you also earn points by playing a Bella over the course of two consecutive tricks. For example, let's assume hearts are trump. In trick number three, player one leads K♥ followed by player two's worthless 7♣. In trick number four, player two leads Q♥, declares "Bella," and scores 20 points *even if* player two wins the trick. A player is not required to win either trick containing the cards forming a Bella. And remember, the player who wins the last trick earns 10 points.

∾ **HOW TO WIN** It's always a good idea to save one high card to win the last trick (worth 10 points). However, do not sacrifice an opportunity to win the 9 or jack of trump. In the scheme of things, winning 10 points for taking the last trick rarely sways the outcome of a match.

You are under no obligation to declare a sequence at the beginning of the game, or even to declare a valid Bella in the trick-taking phase. Sometimes you don't want your opponent to know what cards you hold. At other times you may not want to earn points for your Bella; for example, if you accepted trump and are in danger of losing the hand.

If you are within 15 or 20 points of 500, it's a good idea to accept or choose trump in order to play a 9 or jack of trump, even if your hand is weak. When assessing the strength of your hand, it's more important to hold the jack of trump (and to a lesser extent the 9 of trump) than it is to be long in trumps. Holding the former, you're guaranteed 20 (or 34) points; holding the latter, you are guaranteed nothing.

∾ **IRREGULARITIES & DISPUTES** To score a Bella, you must declare it. Otherwise you cannot earn points for it. And no, you may not take credit for another player's Bella. If your opponent fails to declare it, those 20 points are simply lost.

If you have more than 500 points but fail to declare it, it's your loss. The game may end as soon as you achieve 500 points, but not if you fail to declare yourself the winner. If you declare yourself winner but don't have the necessary 500 points, the hand is played out and all your points are awarded to your opponent as a penalty.

If a player fails to follow the leading suit when he could have, or subsequently fails to play a trump when he could have, the offending player may fix the error without penalty before the next trick is played. Otherwise, all of the offending player's points in the hand are awarded to the opposing player as a penalty.

VARIATION 1: THREE-HAND KLABERJASS

This game's main difference is that, with three players, the trick-taking phase of the game is far more unpredictable. Three-hand Klaberjass also lends itself to alliances, backstabbing, and cutthroat competition. It is thoroughly expected that two players will gang up on the perceived leader in each hand—that's all just part of the game's thrill.

The game is played exactly like standard Klaberjass. The dealer gives each player six cards, in sets of three. The player to the left of the dealer is the first to accept the turn-up card as the trump suit, or to pass. If he accepts, he must end the game with a higher total score than either opposing player.

VARIATION 2: PARTNERSHIP KLABERJASS

Historically speaking, Partnership Klaberjass is the most popular version of the game. With four players in teams of two, the game plays like a simplified—but no less interesting—version of Contract Bridge, minus the complexity of bidding.

All players receive eight cards dealt in batches of three, two, and three. The dealer's last card is dealt face up and is the proposed trump suit for the hand. (After the first round of bidding, the dealer returns the exposed card to his or her hand.)

Bidding proceeds as in standard Klaberjass, with the player to the left of the dealer having the first opportunity to accept the trump suit or to pass. There's a third bidding option in Partnership Klaberjass, called a *Schmeiss*. If a player declares Schmeiss, she is signaling a weak hand to her partner. The partner may then decide whether to bid or to pass. If all four players declare Schmeiss, the hand is dead and fresh cards are dealt.

There is no trump exchange in Partnership Klaberjass. Instead, start with the declarations. The team with the highest sequence earns points for *all* sequences held by both partners. The losing team earns no points for its sequences.

There's a scoring twist in Partnership Klaberjass, a pair of moves called *Kontra* and *Rekontra*. If the non-bidding team believes the bidders will lose the hand, they declare Kontra, which doubles the points for the hand. If the bidders are feeling confident, they can reply Rekontra to double the points again (effectively quadrupling the points for the hand).

During the trick-taking phase, each team places the cards it has won in a single pile. These are tallied at the end of the game as in standard Klaberjass. Note that a Bella may be earned by combining a king and queen of trump from either partner's hand.

Partnership Klaberjass uses a different scoring system than the standard game. If the bidding team makes their bid (by having more total points than the non-bidders), they earn 1 point for a standard win, 2 points for a Kontra win, and 4 points for a Rekontra win. If the non-bidding team wins, they earn 2 points for a standard win, 4 points for a Kontra win, and 8 points for a Rekontra win. Games are typically played to 25 points.

PIQUET

DIFFICULTY *high*	TIME LENGTH *medium*	DECKS 1

Piquet is an aristocrat's game, with a noble pedigree stretching back for centuries. The game has hardly changed since it was first documented in the 1550s. Piquet is little known today except in France, where it is considered the national card game (psst! don't tell the French: The game was likely invented in Spain). Piquet rode a wave of popularity in England in the 1880s and '90s, but never established itself in the United States.

∾ **HOW TO DEAL**   Start with a fifty-two-card deck, and remove all 2s through 6s. This leaves thirty-two cards ranking (high to low) A, K, Q, J, 10, 9, 8, 7. Deal twelve cards to both players, three at a time and face down. Place the remaining eight cards in the center of the table, face down, to form the stock.

In Piquet, the dealer's hand is called *elder* and the opponent's hand *younger*. The deal rotates after each hand.

∾ SCORING   Games of Piquet are traditionally played to 100 points. However, the first player to reach 100 points does not automatically win the game. Instead, the current hand is played out and then the final points are tallied.

After cards have been exchanged, players battle to earn points in the *declaration phase* by declaring the highest cards in the following combinations:

CARTE BLANCHE   If either player is dealt no face cards, she earns 10 points.

POINT   The player declaring the most cards (minimum of three) in any single suit wins "point." That player scores 1 point for each card in the long suit. In case of a tie, players count the value of cards in their long suit (11 for ace, 10 for face cards, **index value** for all other cards), with the highest score winning. If the players are still tied, no points are awarded.

SEQUENCE   The player declaring the longest run of cards in the same suit earns points for the sequence as well as points for all other valid sequences in his hand. A three-card sequence earns 3 points, a four-card 4, a five-card 15, a six-card 16, a seven-card 17, an eight-card 18. In case of a tie, players compare the high card in each sequence. If the players are still tied, no points are awarded.

SET   The player declaring the best set—either three or four cards of the same rank—wins 3 points for each triplet, 14 for each foursome. A set of four always beats a set of three. If players have sets of equal length, the higher set wins (e.g., K-K-K beats 9-9-9). The player who wins set may also score points for other sets he may hold.

In the declaration phase, players can also earn points for the following penalties (or bonuses, depending on your perspective). If a player scores 30 points exclusively in the declaration phase before her opponent earns a single point, that player scores a bonus—called a *repique*—of 60 points.

The elder can earn a similar 30-point bonus—called a *pique*—by scoring 30 points in the declaration and/or trick-taking phase before the younger scores any points. Note that if the elder scores 29 points in the declaration phase and then earns 1 point for leading the first trick in the trick-taking phase, the elder earns a 30-point pique bonus but not a 60-point repique bonus.

The following points are also scored during the *trick-taking phase:*

LEADING TRICKS The leader of each trick earns 1 point.

WINNING A TRICK LED BY YOUR OPPONENT This earns you 1 point plus the lead of the next trick (which earns you a subsequent leading-trick point).

WINNING LAST TRICK The player who wins the last trick scores 1 point.

Players also earn 10 points for winning seven or more tricks, or 40 points for winning all twelve tricks.

∾ **HOW TO PLAY** A hand of Piquet is divided into three phases: first the exchange, then declarations, and finally head-to-head trick taking. Your strategy for each phase depends on whether you're the elder or the younger hand.

THE EXCHANGE Once both players are dealt twelve cards, both can improve their hands by swapping cards for cards in the stock. First, however, players should check for Carte Blanche. It is the players' choice whether to declare Carte Blanche before or after their opponent has exchanged cards.

If there is no Carte Blanche, the elder hand always exchanges first, with a *minimum* of one card and a *maximum* of five cards. Piquet has an interesting twist at this point: If the elder exchanges fewer than five cards, he is allowed to secretly examine the cards not taken. For example, if the elder exchanges two cards, he may look at the next three cards in the stock. This is part of the elder's overall advantage in Piquet.

The younger follows, exchanging up to as many cards as are left in the stock, or exchanging none at all (the younger is not required to exchange any cards). Here again Piquet offers an interesting twist: If the younger leaves any cards in the stock pile, she may decide to turn all remaining stock cards face up for both players to see. Sometimes it is to the younger's advantage to show these cards, sometimes not.

DECLARATION PHASE In this phase, players compete to earn points for holding the highest point, sequence, and set. Players also may earn bonus points for replique and pique. In Piquet, it is important to declare (and score) in the following order, with the elder always acting first: point, sequence, set.

The player with the most cards in a suit earns *point*. The typical interaction goes like this: The elder declares "five," indicating five cards in his or her long suit. The younger replies with a higher amount (such as "six"), or says "good" (thereby conceding the point), or asks "how much?" (this assumes a tie, in which case points must be calculated and compared). Either way, the winning point cards must be shown on request.

Next up is *sequence*, in which the player with the longest sequence of cards in the same suit (minimum of three) earns points as described in the scoring section above. Note that the player who wins sequence is also entitled to score all other valid sequences in her hand, even if these are of lower value than what was declared. The winning sequence (plus any other sequences scored) must be shown on request.

Last up is *set*, in which the player with the highest-value triplet or four-of-a-kind earns points.

TRICK-TAKING PHASE The elder always leads the first trick in the final phase of Piquet (and thereby automatically wins 1 point for first lead). The highest card in the leading suit wins the trick, and players are required to play a card in the leading suit if they have one. Otherwise it is OK to play a card from any other suit. The winner of each trick leads the following trick.

One point is awarded each time a player leads a trick; 1 point is awarded if a player wins a trick they did not lead; and 1 point is awarded to the player who wins the last trick in the hand.

∾ **HOW TO WIN**   With only thirty-two cards in play, and with each player holding twelve at the first deal, it is relatively easy to calculate which cards your opponent is likely holding. Certainly by the start of the trick-taking phase, experienced Piquet players know (usually down to the exact cards) what their opponent holds. And as in most worldly pursuits, knowledge is power.

In Piquet, the old adage also holds true: Loose lips sink ships! Do everything possible to prevent your opponent from guessing what cards you hold. Consider *sinking* (not declaring a possible scoring point, sequence, or set combination) if you think the combination can't win.

Piquet favors the elder hand, so your primary strategy as elder is to establish your long suit (or suits) by flushing out your opponent's **stopper** cards. Conversely, as younger, your strategy is more defensive. It is important to hold high-ranking stopper cards in your opponent's likely long suit or suits. It is also important to survey your twelve cards early, and decide where to fight and where to flee.

∾ **POINTS OF ETIQUETTE**   If you're contemplating a round of Piquet in France, where the game is still religiously played, following these points of etiquette will earn you a warm place in the hearts of your French competitors.

The rules of Piquet state that, upon request, a player must show a winning combination of point or sequence cards. However, this is never done—it is considered highly rude. Instead, an experienced Piquet player will only ask for the bare minimum required to confirm your winning cards. For example, if you score a tie on a sequence declaration, your opponent may ask to see only the highest card necessary to confirm the winning sequence. Or, if they are truly experienced, they may ask to see one of your discards as indirect proof.

Similarly, you are expected to provide information to your opponent where and when appropriate rather than to—how rude!—force your opponent to inquire directly. For example, if you and your opponent both declare five cards for point, the elder player will say something like "forty-seven" and the younger player should reply either "good" (conceding the point) or "forty-nine" (winning the point), but the younger should not reply "not good," since this would (unnecessarily) prompt the elder to inquire "how much?"

Never ask to see an opponent's foursome. It is simply not done. It is OK to inquire after an opponent's triplet; however, limit your inquiry to the cards' rank and not to the suits of individual cards.

- -

VARIATION: RUBICON PIQUET

Except in France, the traditional version of Piquet has been eclipsed by Rubicon Piquet. The games are identical in all respects except one. In Rubicon Piquet, there are only six total deals, alternating between each player three times.

At the end of six deals, a winner is crowned. Typical of Piquet, there are special rules for determining the final scores in a game of Rubicon Piquet. If both players earn more than 100 points, the winner scores 100 points plus the *difference* of the two scores. For example, if player one ends with 120 points and player two ends with 112 points, player one wins the game with a total of 108 points. Math alert! The winning score is 100 + (120–108). If either (or both) players score fewer than 100 points, the winner scores 100 points plus the *sum* of the two scores. For example, if player one ends with 85 points and player two ends with 70 points, player one wins the game with a total of 255 points.

RUSSIAN BANK

DIFFICULTY *medium*	TIME LENGTH *long*	DECKS 2

Solitaire connoisseurs will appreciate Russian Bank. The game follows a rough Solitaire framework, using tableau and reserve piles to build a set of foundation cards up by suit and rank. The twist here, of course, is that Russian Bank is highly competitive.

∾ **HOW TO DEAL** Each player starts with their own fifty-two-card deck (choose decks with different backings to tell them apart), and deals twelve cards, face down, as her stock, plus four face-up cards in the tableau, leaving room for two center columns, as shown below (F = foundations). Place the remaining cards face down in your reserve pile.

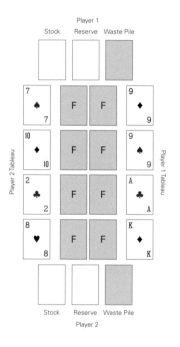

∾ **SCORING** The goal is to play *all* your cards (your stock, reserve, and waste piles) to your tableau or foundation piles. You also may load your cards onto your opponent's stock or waste piles (see below). The first player to rid himself of cards earns 30 points, plus 2 points for each card left in his opponent's stock, and 1 point for each card left in his opponent's reserve and waste piles.

HOW TO PLAY The game starts with player one moving any aces from his tableau to the foundations. Once a foundation has been seeded with an ace, you may then build on it *by suit* in *ascending* rank up to the king.

Next, player one turns up a stock card. If the card may be played to the foundations, it *must* be played to the foundations. Otherwise, use the card to build on your tableau in *descending* rank and in *alternating color*.

Thereafter, each turn follows the same rules of priority:

1. Turn up a stock card (unless one is already face up).

2. Any card that may be moved to the foundations *must* be. If both a stock and tableau card may be moved to the foundations, the stock card must move first.

3. Turn up a card from the reserve, and play it to the foundations or tableau. If the card is not playable, leave it face up in the waste pile.

Move cards in the tableau one at a time, not in groups. Fill tableau vacancies with any available card (following the rules of priority above), including the top card from another tableau pile.

During your turn, you also may *load* cards from your own stock, reserve, or tableau onto your opponent's stock or waste piles, by building up *or* down in rank and by suit. So if your opponent has 5♦ face-up in her stock, you may build 6♦, then 7♦, then 6♦ on her stock, forcing her to play these extra cards. And yes, it is OK to change directions mid-build.

Unlike most Solitaire games, you may not use any cards from your own waste pile. Instead, once your reserve is exhausted, turn the waste pile over (do not shuffle) to create a new reserve.

IRREGULARITIES & DISPUTES If either player builds incorrectly or does not follow the rules of priority, the error must be corrected only if it's noticed. Once the turn shifts, any errors stand.

SIXTY-SIX

DIFFICULTY *medium*	TIME LENGTH *medium*	DECKS 1

If you've played cards in Austria, you probably know this superb two-player game by the name of Schnapsen. The Anglicized name refers to the minimum points needed to win a hand. The game moves quickly, requires a good memory, favors skill over luck, and demands total concentration.

∾ **HOW TO DEAL** Start with a fifty-two-card deck, and remove all 2s through 8s. You're left with twenty-four cards ranking (high to low) A, 10, K, Q, J, 9.

Deal six cards to each player, face down in batches of three. Turn the next card on the deck face up (to determine trump suit for the hand) and set it aside. The remaining cards are the stock.

∾ **SCORING** The first player to earn 7 game points wins. You earn game points by being the first player in a hand to score at least 66 points from cards taken in tricks (see the scoring chart below). If neither player ***goes out*** and the hand is played out to the end, the player with the highest score earns 1 game point.

CARD	POINTS
Ace	11
10	10
King	4
Queen	3
Jack	2

If a player scores 66 points before an opponent scores 33 points, 2 game points are earned. If the opponent hasn't won even a single trick, 3 game points are earned. In case of a tie, the game point goes to the winner of the following hand.

In addition, if you're holding a king and queen of matching suit, you score 40 points (in trump) or 20 points (all other suits) by declaring a *marriage* and then leading either card. The player who wins the last trick of a hand scores 10 points, but only if the entire deck is played out and neither player closes.

In Sixty-Six, players are *not* allowed to write down or track their scores, nor to look back at tricks they have won. This makes it harder to "go out" with confidence.

∾ **HOW TO PLAY** The non-dealer starts the game by leading any card. At this early stage of the game, it is not required for the opponent to follow suit. However, the highest card in the leading suit (or the highest trump card) always wins the trick, and that player scores the point value of the two cards in the trick. The trick winner then takes a fresh card from the stock, followed by the trick loser.

Once either player wins a trick, he is allowed to exchange the 9 of trumps for whatever trump card was turned up at the beginning of the hand. Once the stock is exhausted, the game is said to be *closed*, and new rules come into play:

The last face-down card goes to the final trick winner, the face-up trump card to the trick loser.

Once the stock is exhausted, marriages are not allowed.

For the final six tricks, players must follow suit and win if possible; in other words, you must play a higher card of the same suit if you can.

Otherwise you must play—in order of priority—a lower card of the same suit, a trump, or a card from another suit.

Experienced players rarely let the game close on its own. As long as it's your turn, you may close the game at any point by placing the face-up trump card on top of the stock. Once the game is closed, follow the rules above for playing out the final five or six tricks (note that you still may score points for marriages, since the stock is not exhausted). After the final trick is taken and the last card played, if the player who closed the game does not have 66 points or more, her opponent earns 2 game points.

At any point in the game, if you believe your score is 66 points or greater, you can go out by simply saying so. The game immediately stops and points are tallied. Normal game points are awarded to the winner, unless they fall short of 66 points. In that case, their opponent earns 2 game points.

SPITE & MALICE

DIFFICULTY *low*	TIME LENGTH *medium*	DECKS 2

Back in the 1960s, Spite & Malice (also called Cat & Mouse) was among the most popular two-player games around. Sadly, Spite & Malice developed an unfair reputation as being a mere "kids' game" because it is both easy to learn and hugely entertaining to play. That said, if you're looking for a similar game requiring a bit more skill and strategy, try Russian Bank.

∾ **HOW TO DEAL** Start with two fifty-two-card decks, and shuffle them together. Deal twenty cards, face down, to each player's *pay-off* pile, plus a five-card hand (dealt face down) to each player. The remaining cards are the stock. In Spite & Malice, suits are irrelevant, aces are low, and kings are wild.

∾ **SCORING** The object of Spite & Malice is to be the first player to empty your pay-off pile into the center stacks. Though rare, it is possible for the stock to run out before either player wins. In this case the game is a draw.

∾ **HOW TO PLAY** Start by turning up the top pay-off cards; the highest card plays first. In the case of a tie, reshuffle the pay-off piles and try again.

Move aces to the center stacks as they become available, and then build the aces up by rank. Suits and colors do not matter. Kings are wild and may represent any card except an ace.

Play as many cards to the center as you like, using your topmost pay-off or side stack cards, or any card from your hand. (You may not move cards from your pay-off pile to the side stacks or move cards among side stacks.) If you play all five cards from your hand to the center stacks in a single turn, deal yourself five more cards from the stock.

When you're out of moves, signal the end of your turn by playing a card face up from your hand to your side stacks. You may have up to four side stacks. Once you reach this number, you must place your end-of-turn discards on top of an existing side stack. The problem, of course, is that the cards you're burying in the side stacks may not be played until the cards above them are played.

Whenever a center stack is built up to the queen (or to a king representing a queen), the entire stack is removed from the board and shuffled into the stock. This creates an empty space in the center stacks, which is filled with any available ace.

- -
VARIATION 1: CUTTHROAT SPITE & MALICE
The rules are identical to regular Spite & Malice, except that players are allowed to "load" cards onto their opponent's pay-off pile. "Loading" means to play a card from your hand or pay-off pile (not from your side stacks) that is one rank higher or lower than, and matching in suit to, your opponent's topmost pay-off

card. If that card is **6♦**, for example, you may load **5♦** or **7♦** on top of it. You are allowed to load as many cards as possible, and even to switch directions (e.g., play **6♦** on **5♦**, then play another **5♦** on the **6♦**).

- -
VARIATION 2: MULTIPLAYER SPITE & MALICE

This game is easily adapted to accommodate between three and six players. You need one deck of cards per player. All players are limited to four side stacks, but the number of center stacks varies by the number of players—four stacks for three players, five stacks for four players, etc.

OTHER VARIATIONS SUITABLE FOR TWO PLAYERS

Many of the three- and four-player games covered in the *Ultimate Book of Card Games* have variations specifically for two players. Here's a complete list:

.04 ~

Games Especially for Three Players

CHAPTER FOUR

Games Especially for Three Players

THREE IS THE CARD PLAYER'S FAVORITE NUMBER in most parts of the world. With three players, there is room for alliances (temporary two-on-one partnerships) and something called "imperfect" card knowledge—basically, you can know quite a lot about the cards held by your opponents, but not everything. In three-player games, there is no single player or partnership that knows how the cards are actually distributed.

The fact that Britain and the United States cannot take credit for the truly great three-player games is a legacy of the fifty-two-card deck, which reigns supreme in English-speaking countries. The fifty-two-card deck historically has favored the development of four-player games. In Italy, France, Germany, Spain, and China, decks of thirty-six or twenty-four cards are far more common and lend themselves to three-player games such as Skat and Seven Up.

1,000

DIFFICULTY *low*	TIME LENGTH *medium*	DECKS 1

This is an excellent three-player game that few people know how to play—not counting the Russian, Polish, and Lithuanian immigrants who brought the game to western Europe and the United States in the early twentieth century. It's likely that 1,000 is a simplified version of the German game Skat, but we'll pass no judgment on this heated historical argument. It's part of the "marriage" family of games, and offers plenty of action and competitive thrills.

∾ **HOW TO DEAL** Start with a fifty-two-card deck, and remove all cards except the following (listed high to low in rank, with corresponding point values), leaving twenty-four cards total:

CARD	POINTS
Ace	11
10	10
King	4
Queen	3
Jack	2
9	0

Deal seven cards to each player, and leave the three remaining cards face down on the table. This is the kitty.

∾ **SCORING** The first player to score 1,000 points wins. You earn points by capturing tricks that contain point cards, and by successfully declaring the following combinations (both cards must be in your hand when declaring):

K♥-Q♥ for 100 points

K♦-Q♦ for 80 points

K♣-Q♣ for 60 points

K♠-Q♠ for 40 points

At the end of each round, if the declarer's points total meets or exceeds his bid, the bid is added to the round score (e.g., if declarer bids 125 points and ends the round with 125 or more points, he scores his round points + 125). If the declarer does not meet the bid, the bid is *deducted* from his round score.

All other players score whatever points they won in the round, rounded to the nearest increment of five (e.g., if a player scores 51 points in the round, her final round score is 50; if she scores 53 points, her final score is 55).

∽ **HOW TO PLAY**   The game starts with a round of bidding. The player to the left of the dealer opens at 100 points and, moving clockwise, all players continue bidding in increments of five points (105, 110, 115, etc). Players are bidding on how many total points they think they will score in the round.

There are 120 point cards in each round, so bids above 120 can only be achieved by scoring at least one combination in the round. In fact, players may not bid more than 120 unless they are holding at least one combination *in* their hand.

Players may pass, but they may not re-enter the bidding later. Once two players in a row pass, the player with the highest bid becomes the declarer. The declarer turns up the kitty for all players to see and puts these cards into his hand. Now the declarer may—but is not required to—increase his bid, in increments of 5 points.

The declarer leads the first trick with any card; all other players *must* follow in suit (if they can). Otherwise, they play any card. The highest card in the leading suit wins the trick.

A unique feature of 1,000 is the ability to introduce a trump suit midgame. This happens when a player declares a king-queen combination, then leads one of the cards of said combination. The suit of the combination immediately becomes and remains trump until another king-queen combination is declared.

In the trick-taking rounds, once a trump suit is declared, any player who cannot follow the leading suit *must* play a trump. Tricks are won by the highest card in the leading suit, or by the highest trump card. If a player cannot follow suit and cannot play a trump, only then may they play a card from another suit. The round continues until all cards are played. The deal then moves clockwise.

- -

VARIATION: CUTTHROAT 1,000

Connoisseurs of 1,000 generally play the cutthroat version, which is exactly like the basic game but introduces three variants to the way the game is scored.

First up is the *barrel*. A player (or players) is "on the barrel" any time her cumulative score falls between 880 and 1,000 points. When this happens, her score is immediately reduced to 880 points. To get off the barrel in a subsequent round, the player must be the declarer and either score more than 120 points (thereby winning the game) or fail to meet her bid (thereby having points deducted, likely falling below 880 total points, and as a result falling off the barrel). If you're on the barrel and are not the declarer, any points you score in a round do not count. You may be on the barrel for no more than three rounds; after the third round, deduct 120 points from your score (thereby falling off the barrel).

Next up is the *zero play*. If a non-bidder fails to earn any points from tricks in three (not necessarily consecutive) rounds, 120 points is deducted from his score on the third instance.

Finally, the *forfeit play*. Before any cards are played (but after the kitty is reviewed), the declarer may forfeit the game. Each opposing player earns 60 points for a forfeit. You may forfeit as often as you like, but 120 points are deducted from your score on a third (and each subsequent third) forfeit.

8-5-3

DIFFICULTY *medium*	TIME LENGTH *short*	DECKS 1

8-5-3 offers the same thrills as Hearts, with an extra dimension of strategy and even more opportunities for brutalizing your friends. This game is not for the meek.

∿ **HOW TO DEAL** Start with a fifty-two-card deck, and deal sixteen cards, face down, to each player. The remaining four cards are set aside. The dealer reviews his or her cards, nominates a trump suit, discards any four cards (face down), and replaces them with the four cards originally set aside.

∿ **SCORING** The goal is to win tricks, and each player has a predetermined target: eight tricks for the dealer, five for the player to the dealer's left, three for the final player. At the end of each hand, players earn (or lose) 1 point for each trick above (or below) their target.

Games are played to 16 points. However, if a player wins twelve tricks in a single hand, the game is over and that player wins immediately.

∿ **HOW TO PLAY** The dealer leads the first trick with any card, and the other players must follow suit if they can. Tricks are always won by the highest card of the leading suit, or by the highest trump card. Aces are ranked high in this game.

Once the first hand is complete, the deal shifts clockwise and new rules are introduced. In the second hand (and all subsequent hands), the players who beat their targets in the previous hand may forcibly exchange cards with players who failed to meet their targets, up to the number of tricks by which their targets were missed. For example:

Assume player one beat her target, while player two lost by two tricks, and player three lost by one trick. On the next deal, player one exchanges two cards with player two and one card with player three. These cards are added to their hands and, for each card passed, they return face-down to player one the highest-ranking card in the same suit. So if player one passes 2♣ to player two, player two must return the highest club card in his hand. If the receiving player has no cards in the suit, the original card is returned.

Assume players one and two both beat their targets. On the next deal, both players pass cards to player three (the player with the highest target *for the upcoming hand* passes first), who returns the highest-ranking card(s) in the same suit(s). The number of cards passed equals the number of cards by which players one and two exceed their previous targets (e.g., if player two earned two tricks over the target, two cards are now passed).

Once the exchanges are complete, the dealer names trumps, discards four cards, and replaces them with the four set-aside cards. The game continues as before.

If the dealer of a new hand must exchange cards with other players and then picks a higher card of the same suit from the set-aside cards, the dealer must privately show (not give, just show) these higher-ranking cards to the appropriate player.

- -

VARIATION: 9-5-2

This is played exactly like the basic game, except for two rule changes. First, the targets are modified to nine tricks for dealer, five tricks for the player to the left of the dealer, two tricks for the final player. Second, the dealer is allowed to review the set-aside cards *before* deciding which cards to discard from her own hand. Games of 9-5-2 are played to 20 points.

BIG THREE

| DIFFICULTY *medium* | TIME LENGTH *short* | DECKS 1 |

Big Three is not well-known in Western card-playing circles, even though Da San (as it is known) is hugely popular in China. The rules of this Westernized version are identical. The only difference is the card rankings, which have been simplified.

∾ **HOW TO DEAL** Start with a fifty-two-card deck, choose a dealer to shuffle, and then place the deck face down on the table. Starting with the dealer, each player takes cards one at a time, moving clockwise, until all players have sixteen cards. The remaining four cards are left face down on the table.

Suits have no significance and cards rank (high to low) K-Q-J-10-9-8-7-6-5-4-3-2-A.

∿ **SCORING** Only the auction winner may gain and lose points. When any player runs out of cards, the round ends and the score is tallied. If the auction winner runs out of cards first, she earns the value of her bid multiplied by 2. For example, if the auction winner bids three and runs out of cards first, she scores 6 points (3 x 2). Otherwise, if either of the competing players runs out of cards first, the auction winner loses the amount of her bid multiplied by 2.

The scoring system is what drives the two-against-one component of the game. Only the auction winner earns or loses points, so the other two players form an ad-hoc partnership to stop the auction winner from being the first to run out of cards.

Games of Big Three are usually played to 20 points.

∿ **HOW TO PLAY** Once everybody has a sixteen-card hand, the player with 4♥ (or the lowest heart if 4♥ is not yet in play) starts an auction to decide who plays alone against the other two players. The possible bids are one, two, or three. The auction ends when somebody bids three, or when two players in a row pass. The winner of the auction takes the four remaining cards into his hand (for 20 cards total) and plays the hand against the other two players.

The person who opened the bidding (not necessarily the auction winner) plays first, and may make any of the following leads:

  Any single card
  Any pair
  Any triplet (e.g., 10-10-10)
  Any foursome (e.g., A-A-A-A)
  A run of three or more cards
  A run of three or more consecutive pairs (e.g., 4-4-5-5-6-6)
  A run of three or more consecutive triplets (e.g., 10-10-10-J-J-J-Q-Q-Q)
  A run of three or more consecutive foursomes

Note that aces, 2s, and 3s may not be used in runs or in runs of consecutive pairs, triplets, or foursomes.

Moving counterclockwise, the next player must beat the previous hand using the exact same number of cards and type of hand. If player one opens with 7-6-5, for example, player two may play only a higher run of three cards (e.g., 8-7-6), but not a run of four cards or anything else. If player two can beat the opening hand, it's player three's turn to play, using the exact same number of cards and type of hand.

Players are allowed to pass and then jump back in, but if two consecutive players pass, the cards on the table are turned face down and set aside. Whoever played the final hand in the previous round starts all over, playing a new combination of any type. The round continues until one player runs out of cards and scores are tallied.

VARIATION: FOUR-HAND BIG THREE

With four players, two teams are pitted against one another. Each player receives thirteen cards (there are no leftovers), and the highest bidder chooses any card *not* in his hand. The player holding that card becomes his partner, but does not disclose her identity until the nominated card is actually played.

All other rules are the same, except that three players in a row must pass in order to remove cards from the table and start a new hand. And when any player runs out of cards, that player's team wins and earns the bid amount multiplied by 2 (unlike the three-player game, a team isn't required to win the auction in order to score points at the end of each round.)

FIVE HUNDRED

DIFFICULTY *medium*	TIME LENGTH *long*	DECKS 1

The venerable United States Playing Card Company invented this game in 1904. Unlike many "invented" games from the twentieth century, Five Hundred has withstood the test of time because it is, simply, an excellent game. It evolved from Euchre, and shares some features with Bridge. For a time, it was among the most popular trick-taking game in the United States.

∾ **HOW TO DEAL** Start with a fifty-two-card deck, and remove all 2s thru 6s, then add one joker, for a total of thirty-three cards. Deal each player ten cards in batches of three, four, three, plus three face-down cards in the center of the table (this is called the *widow*).

∾ **CARD RANKINGS** The joker is always the highest trump. In suit bids, the jack of trump (called *right bower*) is the second-highest trump, followed by the jack of the suit matching the color of the trump (called *left bower*). So, if clubs are trump, the card rankings in trump are (high to low): joker, J♣, J♠, A♣, K♣, Q♣, 10♣, 9♣, 8♣, 7♣.

In non-trump suits, cards rank (high to low) from A to 7, not including the jack if it is left bower.

∾ **SCORING** If the bidder ultimately achieves his bid, he earns points as per the table below. If the bidder is able to win all the tricks in the round, he earns 250 points or the score from the table below, whichever is greater.

If the bidder is *set* and fails to achieve the bid, the value of the bid is subtracted from his score. Negative scores are permitted. The other players each score 10 points for every trick they individually won, regardless of whether the bidder wins or loses the bid.

The first player to score 500 total points wins the game. When two or more players score 500 or more points in the same hand, the bidder always wins (regardless of the final score). If neither player was bidding, the winner is the first player who crossed the 500-point threshold.

∾ **HOW TO PLAY** The hand starts with bidding. The player to the left of the dealer starts, and all other players have only one chance to increase the bid or to pass. When bidding, you must name a suit and a number of tricks that you're committing to win, as in "six hearts" or "nine diamonds."

A bid of 7♣ beats a bid of 7♠, for example, based on the point values in the following chart:

CONTRACT TYPE	6	7	8	9	10
Spades	40	140	240	340	440
Clubs	60	160	260	360	460
Diamonds	80	180	280	380	480
Hearts	100	200	300	400	500
No Trump	120	220	320	420	520

The hand is dead if all players pass, and the deal moves clockwise. Otherwise, the highest bid wins, and the opposing two players form a temporary partnership against the bid winner.

Experienced players usually add one final bid into the mix—a *nullo no-trump* bid. It's worth 250 points (and thus falls between 8♠ and 8♣ on the table) and requires the bidder both to play a no-trump game *and* to lose every trick. If a nullo no trump bid fails, the bidder loses 250 points, and the opposing players each earn 10 points for every trick they take.

TRICK TAKING The bid winner takes the three-card widow into her hand, discards any three cards face down, and leads the first trick. Thereafter, all players must follow suit if they can, or play any other card. Tricks are won by the highest trump played, or by the highest card in the leading suit. The winner of each trick leads the next trick.

Special rules govern the joker in no-trump games. First, if the joker leads a trick, the player must declare a suit, and all players must follow if they can. Second, the joker may be played mid-trick (and will automatically win the trick) only if the player in question cannot follow suit. Otherwise the jack may not be played.

∾ **HOW TO WIN** You have only one opportunity to bid, so it's appropriate to go a little beyond your comfort zone in order to win the bid. That said, don't make a suit bid without holding at least five trumps. And for no-trump bids, you really should have one *stopper* per suit—you can get away without a full set of stoppers if you hold the joker, but it is risky.

VARIATION 1: PARTNERSHIP FIVE HUNDRED

The partnership version of Five Hundred is played exactly like the basic game, with two exceptions. First, the deck: remove all 2s, 3s, and the black 4s, then add in one joker for a total of forty-three cards (players still receive ten cards each). Second, the scoring: partners pool all tricks and share a single score, and if either team scores -500 points, they immediately lose the game.

- -
VARIATION 2: TWO-HAND FIVE HUNDRED

This is exactly the same as the main game, with one exception: the deck is limited to twenty-five cards, comprising ace to nine in each suit, plus one joker.

- -
VARIATION 3: FIVE-HAND FIVE HUNDRED

This is an excellent five-player game, especially if all five players are hardcore lovers of the main game. There are only two rule modifications. First, a full fifty-two-card deck is used, plus one joker, for a total of fifty-three cards. Once a bid is made, the bid winner may select any other player to play as her partner. If the bid is for eight or more tricks, she may name two partners! Either way, the opponents play for themselves (and score individual points), while the bid winner alone scores points for winning or losing a bid (the bidder's ad hoc partners cannot win or lose points when they're partnered with the bidder).

SEVEN UP

DIFFICULTY *low*	TIME LENGTH *short*	DECKS 1

There's a hint of Hearts in this game, a taste of Bridge, and a strong flavor both of Setback and Briscola. This isn't to say Seven Up is a completely derivative game. It's an excellent and not-too-complicated game for three players.

∾ **HOW TO DEAL** Start with a fifty-two-card deck. Card rankings are standard, with aces always high. Deal six cards to each player, face down, and turn the next card on the deck face up. This is the proposed trump suit. If it's a jack, the dealer scores 1 point.

The player to the left of the dealer may accept or reject the proposed trump suit. If it's rejected, it's the dealer's decision whether to accept or reject the trump suit. If the dealer accepts, the player on the left scores 1 point and the game commences.

Otherwise, the dealer gives each player three additional cards, face down, and turns up another card as the trump proposal. If the proposed trump is the same as before, the dealer must give each player three new cards and try again with a new trump proposal. If it's a different suit, the suit is now trump and the game begins (if it's a jack, score the dealer 1 point).

All players must start with a six card hand, so all excess cards are discarded (players may choose their discards). At any point, if there are insufficient cards in the deck to continue dealing, all cards are thrown in, shuffled, and redealt by the same dealer.

∾ SCORING The object is to score points. In each round, a maximum of 4 points are awarded for:

HIGH POINT (1 POINT) to the player who captures the highest trump in play.

LOW POINT (1 POINT) to the player *dealt* the lowest trump card, regardless of who wins it in a trick.

JACK (1 POINT) to the player who captures the jack of trump.

GAME (1 POINT) to the player who scores the most overall points, based on the following values: score 10 points for each 10, 4 for aces, 3 for kings, 2 for queens, 1 for non-trump jacks.

In some games, the jack of trumps will not be in circulation, so only 3 points are awarded. If only one trump is in play, the card is both high and low. If two players tie for the game score, no point is awarded. The first player to earn 7 points wins the game.

∾ HOW TO PLAY Once a trump is established and all players have six cards, the player to the left of the dealer leads the first trick. Players must follow suit if they can, or throw a trump (trumps may be played at any time). If a player cannot follow suit and has no trump, then he may play any other card.

Tricks are won by the highest trump, or by the highest card in the leading suit. The trick winner leads the next trick. Scores are tallied when all cards are played. The deal rotates clockwise.

The first player to score 7 points wins. So, if two or more players are close to winning a game, points are counted out in order (high, low, jack, game). If the dealer has 6 points, she cannot win a game during the trump-selection phase; any points she might otherwise earn are simply ignored. And if a player fails to follow suit when he could have, he is scored -2 (if the jack of trumps is in play) or -1 (no jack in play).

- -
VARIATION: PARTNERSHIP SEVEN UP

Seven Up is a surprisingly good game for partnerships. The rules are identical to the main game, except that the partners' tricks are added together at the end of the game, and points are earned as a team (not as individual players).

SKAT

DIFFICULTY *high*	TIME LENGTH *long*	DECKS 1

Skat is a three-player trick-taking game. Despite the multitude of rules and variations inherent in Skat, the fundamental goal is simple. If you're the Player, you are trying to capture high-value cards in tricks and attempting to score the most points. Otherwise, you're trying to prevent the Player from scoring points. Remember this basic fact about the game and you're well on the way to mastering Skat.

> **Skat is one of the most popular card games in Germany, which reveals a bit about the national character when you consider that it is among the most complex, math-driven, rules-based games on the planet.**

If you're willing to persevere, Skat is full of rewards. No other three-player game comes anywhere near it in terms of variety of game play and overall strategy.

Skat was developed in Germany in the early nineteenth century, and it owes much to its predecessor, the less complicated but equally rewarding Schafkopf, which is covered below as a variation.

∾ **HOW TO DEAL** Start with a fifty-two-card deck, and remove all 2s through 6s, leaving thirty-two cards total. Players are dealt ten cards in batches of three, four, three. After dealing the first batch, leave two cards face down on the table—this is called the *skat*.

In Skat, the dealer is known as *endhand*, the player to the dealer's left is *forehand*, and the remaining player is *middlehand*.

∾ **HOW TO PLAY** Once the deal is complete, players bid for the right to select which version of Skat to play. In each round of Skat, four different games are possible, and card rankings vary, depending on which game is selected.

> **Suit games** feature trump (the suit changes from hand to hand) and, regardless of the trump suit, jacks are the highest trumps and rank as follows (high to low): J♣, J♠, J♥, J♦, followed by A, 10, K, Q, 9, 8 of trump. The remaining suits rank (high to low) A, 10, K, Q, 9, 8, 7.
>
> In **grand games,** only jacks are trump, ranking J♣, J♠, J♥, J♦. All other suits rank (high to low) A, 10, K, Q, 9, 8, 7.
>
> In **null games,** there is no trump, and suits rank (high to low) A, K, Q, J, 10, 9, 8, 7 (note how the 10 is back in its natural rank position).
>
> In **reject games** (which may be declared by the forehand only if both opponents pass without bidding), jacks are trump, the skat is not used, and the goal is to score as few points as possible.
>
> **BIDDING** Only the forehand and middlehand compete in the first stage of bidding. The middlehand bids first, and the forehand either may pass (thereby relinquishing the bid) or declare a "hold"—which reserves the forehand's right to match or improve on the middlehand's bid. In order to win the bid, the middlehand must outbid the forehand, whereas the forehand becomes the bidder if the bids are tied.

Next, the winner of the forehand-middlehand bidding goes head to head against the endhand. The endhand must bid higher in order to actually win the bid. Whoever wins both rounds of bidding is called the Player. The other two players are known as the Opponents.

The bids themselves depend on what suit-game combination you're hoping to play, though you don't actually choose a game to play until after the bidding is over.

Remember that you need to bid a *minimum* of two times the base value of the games below (e.g., 18, 20, 22, 24, etc.), and by bidding, you're agreeing to accept a contract of *at least* that value in game points. (Inevitably there is an exception to this rule: null games are considered "absolute" value, which is nothing you need to worry about—except that you're allowed to bid plain old 23, rather than two times 23, if you so desire.)

GAME	TRUMPS	BASE VALUE	GOAL
Suit Game (Diamonds)	Jacks + Diamonds	9	61 points or more
Suit Game (Hearts)	Jacks + Hearts	10	61 points or more
Suit Game (Spades)	Jacks + Spades	11	61 points or more
Suit Game (Clubs)	Jacks + Clubs	12	61 points or more
Grand Game	Jacks only	24	61 points or more
Reject Game	Jacks only	10	Win as few points as possible
Null Game	None	23	Win no tricks

A round of bidding, therefore, might look like this (with endhand ultimately becoming the Player with a winning bid of 24):

PHASE ONE:	PHASE TWO:
Middlehand: 18	Endhand: 23
Forehand: Hold	Forehand: Hold
Middlehand: 20	Endhand: 24
Forehand: Hold	Forehand: Pass
Middlehand: 22	
Forehand: Hold	
Middlehand: Pass	

You may bid in multiples of three or four times the base value, though in general, bids above 100 are rare.

THE SKAT Once the bidding is complete, the Player earns the right to select the game. This is Skat, so of course it's not as simple as that. The Player has two choices (*hand play* or *skat play*) that greatly impact the final outcome. If the Player chooses hand play, the Player does not look at the skat, but instead sets it aside. The skat is ultimately awarded as follows:

> In suit or grand games, the skat goes to the Player after the hand is over.
> In reject and null games, the skat is ignored.

In skat play, the Player *does* look at the skat, and then declares a suit game (naming the suit of choice), grand game, null game, or reject game. Thereafter, the Player takes the skat into his hand and discards any two cards back into the skat. These cards will, at the end of play, be added to the Player's point total (except in null and reject games, where the skat is ignored).

MULTIPLIERS At this point, the Player has an inkling about whether his bid is too low (because his cards are stronger than originally suspected). If so, he may declare an "open" game, whereby only the Player's cards are laid face up on the table for the opponents to see. The point benefit of playing—and winning—an open game comes later, when calculating the game score.

To increase the value of the bid even further, a Player may, before any cards are played, declare a *Schneider* (pledging to win 91 points in tricks) or a *Schwarz* (pledging to win *all* the tricks). These declarations may be invoked in conjunction with an open game, or on their own.

TRICK TAKING   The next step is to play some cards! The forehand leads (even if the forehand is not the Player) and the other players must always follow suit if possible. Otherwise, they may play a card from any suit, including trump. Tricks are won by the highest trump played, or else by the highest card in the leading suit. The trick winner leads the following trick.

Note that in suit games, a leading jack should be followed by the trump suit, not necessarily by the jack's own suit. This is because in suit games, jacks are always considered trump. In a diamond suit game, for example, a leading J♥ should be followed by a diamond, not a heart.

∾ **WINNING**   The hand ends once all cards are played and all tricks are taken. Now it's time to determine if the Player wins or loses his bid. In suit and grand games, the Player loses if the points earned in tricks (plus the two cards in the skat) contain fewer than 61 points, based on the following card values:

SUIT & GRAND GAMES	POINTS
Ace	11
10	10
King	4
Queen	3
Jack	2
9, 8, 7	0

A Player also loses by declaring a Schneider or a Schwarz and then failing to achieve it. The final way to lose is by "overbidding"—for example, if the value of the Player's game is less than his original bid. To determine if the game value is less than the original bid, a bit of math is required (the game value = the base value x the sum of all multipliers). If this total is less than the original bid, the Player loses. The base value depends on the trump suit:

GAME	BASE VALUE
Suit Game (♦)	9
Suit Game (♥)	10
Suit Game (♠)	11
Suit Game (♣)	12
Grand Game	24

To find the multipliers, simply add together the following multiplier scores if they apply to the current hand:

OUTCOME	MULTIPLIER SCORES
Game (always applies)	1
Matadors (with or against)	1 each
Hand Play	1
Schneider (declared)	3
Schneider (not declared)	1
Schwarz (declared)	5
Schwarz (not declared)	2
Schneider (declared), Schwarz made	4
Open Game	7

Matadors are trump cards in an *unbroken* sequence that are in, or missing from, the Player's combined tricks and skat cards. The unbroken sequence must always run highest to lowest from J♣, J♠, J♥, J♦, followed by the remaining trump cards. The matador count stops as soon as the sequence is broken.

If you're confused, let's assume diamonds are trump. If the Player holds J♣, J♠, J♥, A♦, K♦, he is "with three" matadors (J♣, J♠, J♥ in unbroken sequence). The A♦, K♦ may not be counted, since the J♦ is missing. Now assume the Player holds J♣, J♠, J♥, J♦, A♦, K♦; he is now "with five" matadors (J♣, J♠, J♥, J♦, and A♦ in unbroken sequence). Or, assume the Player holds J♦, A♦, 10♦, K♦, Q♦. He is now "against three," since the opponents must be holding J♣, J♠, J♥ in unbroken sequence.

The remaining multipliers are easy to calculate. If the Player declares and makes Schneider (91 points or more), the multiplier is calculated as follows: game (1), matadors (total with or against), and Schneider (announced, 3), for a total multiplier of at least 4 (or more, depending on the number of matadors). So if the base value was, say, 11 for a suit game in spades, and the multipliers add up to 5, then the game value is 11 x 5 = 55. And if the Player's original bid was less than 55, the game is lost!

Finally, you now calculate the Player's actual game score:

If the bid is successful and the game won, the Player scores the *game value* (which is likely higher than his original bid). For example, if the original bid is 40 and the final game value is 65, the Player earns 65 points for the win.

If the bid is unsuccessful, the Player loses the amount of the original bid (in hand play) or double the bid amount (in skat play).

∾ **NULL GAMES** Null hands have a fixed value. If the Player chooses a null game and wins no tricks, she earns a fixed number of points. Conversely, if the Player wins one or more tricks, she loses a fixed number of points.

NULL GAMES	POINTS WON	POINTS LOST
Null Game (Skat Play)	23	46
Null Game (Hand Play)	35	70
Null Open Game (Skat Play)	46	92
Null Open Game (Hand Play)	59	118

∾ **REJECT GAMES** In Reject games, the player who takes the fewest points in tricks scores 10 points (the skat is ignored). If the Player took no tricks at all, she scores 20 points.

∾ **IRREGULARITIES & DISPUTES** The most serious faux pas in Skat is discarding an incorrect number of cards to the skat. The penalty is an instant forfeit. Other serious misdemeanors include looking at the skat when you're not entitled to (penalty: you're barred from bidding in the hand and you must deduct 10 points from your score), and failing to follow suit when you could have (penalty: if it's the Player's error, he loses the game, if it's the opponents' error, the Player is awarded an automatic win).

- -
VARIATION 1: SCHAFKOPF

You could argue that Schafkopf is a game in its own right. Yet as an antecedent to Skat it shares many of that game's features—minus much of the complexity. The same thirty-two-card deck is used, but in Schafkopf, there is a permanent trump suit of fourteen cards comprising (high to low) Q♣, Q♠, Q♥, Q♦, J♣, J♠, J♥, J♦, A♦, 10♦, K♦, 9♦, 8♦, 7♦. In the non-trump suits, cards rank (high to low) A, 10, K, 9, 8, 7.

The initial deal is identical to Skat, with ten cards to each player, plus two cards to the "window" (formerly the skat). There's no bidding in Schafkopf. Instead, the player to the left of the dealer has the first chance to "take the window" and become the Player. If that player passes, the next player clockwise may elect to take the window, and so on. The Player takes the window cards and discards two cards back into the window. The other two players form a temporary partnership against the Player.

The player to the left of the dealer leads the first card, always. As in Skat, players must follow suit if they can. Also as in Skat, a leading trump—even if it's Q♣ or J♥—should be followed by another trump (e.g., by another queen, jack, or diamond).

The goal is to capture as many high cards as possible from tricks and from the two cards discarded to the window, based on the "Suit & Grand Card Values" defined above in Skat. If the Player wins a majority of points (scores 61 or more points) he earns game points as follows:

2 game points for scoring 61 to 90 points

4 game points for scoring 91 or more points (*Schneider*)

6 game points for winning all tricks (*Schwarz*)

Conversely, if the Player fails to win 61 or more points, the following penalties apply:

-2 game points for scoring 31 to 60 points

-4 game points for scoring less than 31 points

-6 game points for winning no tricks

The first player to earn 10 game points wins the match.

- -

VARIATION 2: THE LEAST

In this variation of Skat, if no players "take the window," the game is played out with slightly different rules, known as The Least. The goal is to score as few points as possible. The window is awarded to the winner of the last trick. Game points are awarded as follows:

If just one player wins no tricks, he scores 4 game points. If all players take one or more tricks, the player with the lowest point total scores 2 game points. If two players tie for low score, 2 game points are awarded to the player who did *not* win the last trick.

OTHER VARIATIONS SUITABLE FOR THREE PLAYERS

Many of the two- and four-player games covered in the *Ultimate Book of Cards* have variations specifically for three players:

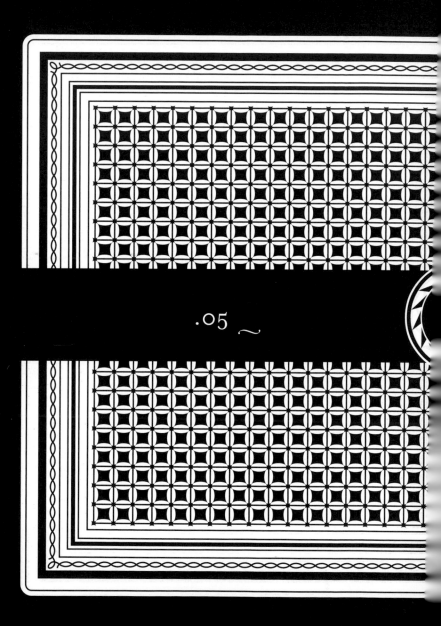

.05 ~

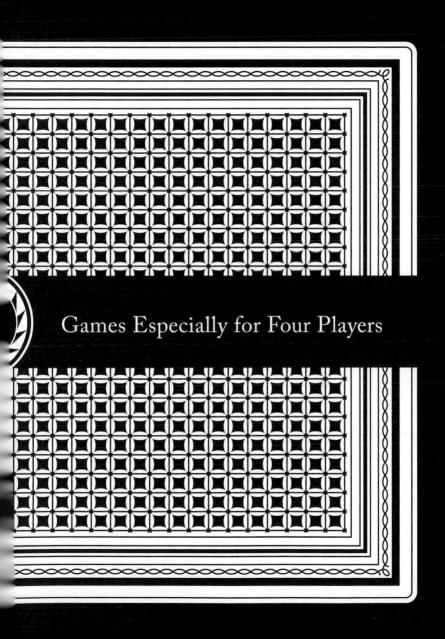

Games Especially for Four Players

CHAPTER FIVE

Games Especially for Four Players

THE WORLD OF FOUR-PLAYER GAMES IS DOMINATED by fixed-partnership games like Bridge, Canasta, Euchre, and Pinochle, which are covered in the following chapter. The games covered in this chapter are all games of *temporary* alliances. There are no permanent teams in Thirteen-Card Brag, Hearts, or Barbu; instead, you play alone or temporarily cooperate three-on-one or two-on-two, depending on the game.

Alliances (as opposed to fixed partnerships) make these four-player games easier to learn and play. You forsake some of the richness and subtleties of four-player partnership games, but sometimes this simplicity is exactly the point.

BARBU

DIFFICULTY *high*	TIME LENGTH *long*	DECKS 1

The modern game of Barbu mixes elements of Bridge and Solitaire, which makes it highly addictive. If you're wary of the complexities of Bridge, Barbu is a worthwhile substitute. The game has French roots (hence the name, which means "bearded" in French), but bears little resemblance to its eighteenth-century predecessor. Instead, a few obsessive Bridge players from Italy got hold of this game in the 1960s and gave it a complete makeover. Their rule modifications are now the rules of the game.

∾ **HOW TO DEAL**   Start with a fifty-two-card deck, choose a declarer at random, and deal thirteen cards face down to each player. Cards rank (high to low) from ace to 2. There are seven total "contracts" in Barbu, and each player must declare each contract once—for a total of twenty-eight hands per game. Each deal lasts seven hands and then moves one player to the left.

∾ **SCORING**   At the end of the twenty-eight-hand game, the player with the highest score wins.

∾ **HOW TO PLAY**   Once the cards are dealt, the declarer chooses a contract and leads the first card. The declarer must eventually play all seven contracts, but it's his decision as to the order. After the declarer has played all seven contracts, both the dealer and declarer shift one player to the left.

In Barbu, there are five *negative contracts* and two *positive contracts*. In negative contracts, there are no trumps. Players must follow suit if possible, otherwise any card may be played. The winner of each trick leads the next. In some contracts, there are restrictions on which card may lead a trick. The negative contracts are:

NO QUEENS   Players who "win" a queen in any trick score -6 points. Total point value for contract is -24 points.

NO TRICKS   Each trick taken is worth -2 points. Total point value is -26 points.

NO HEARTS Every heart is worth -2 points and A♥ is worth -6. Total point value is -30. Hearts may not lead a trick, unless the player has no other cards. Hearts won in tricks are set aside, face up, for all players to see.

NO KING OF HEARTS Only K♥ is worth points, in this case -20. Hearts may not lead unless the player has no other cards.

NO LAST TWO Only the last two tricks have point values; the penultimate trick scores -10 points and the last trick scores -20 points.

The positive contracts are:

TRUMP The declarer nominates a trump suit and leads the first trick. Players must always follow suit if possible. Tricks are won by the highest trump, or by the highest card in the leading suit. Barbu plays by strict trump rules. First, when trump leads, you must play your highest trump (unless your highest trump cannot win, in which case you may play any trump). Second, if a non-trump suit leads and you're *void* in that suit, you must play a trump (unless a higher trump has already been played, in which case you may play any other suit). Each trick is worth 5 points (for a total of 65 points), and the trick winner leads the next trick.

DOMINOES The declarer nominates a starting rank, along the lines of "dominoes from 7." The goal is to discard your entire hand first, by playing cards in ascending *or* descending rank, by suit, on the four *foundations*. For example, in "dominoes from 7," the declarer may lead 7♦ and 7♥, and then play 8♥ on 7♥. The following player throws 6♦ on the 7♦, 9♥ on 8♥, and starts a new foundation with 7♠. Ranking is continuous, so each foundation pile will contain thirteen cards total, organized by suit and sequence. Players must pass if they cannot play legally. The declarer is allowed to pass on his first turn, if he so chooses. Score 45 points to the first player to go out, 20 points to the second player, 5 to the third, and -5 to the last (for a total of 65 points).

After the contract is chosen, each player (starting to the left of the declarer) in turn is given a chance to *double* all, some, or none of the other players. A double is a polite way of saying, "I am going to beat your score!" When deciding whether or not to double, the only consideration is if your final score is likely to surpass the other player's score. The target of your double may also reply with a *redouble*, which is a polite way of saying, "Go ahead, I dare you to beat me!" A player wishing to double all other players declares "maximum."

In all cases, the declarer may double only players who have already doubled them. In each round of seven hands, every player is required to double the declarer at least twice. In the positive contracts, players may double only the declarer, not each other. Note that if one player doubles another, take the difference of their contract scores and add the sum to the player who did better and subtract it from the player who scored worse. When two players have doubled one another, take the difference of their contract scores and *double* it before adding and subtracting it from the players' scores.

∾ **SCORING** Mastering the scoring is the hardest part of Barbu. In the sample score sheet on the following page, hearts are trump (a positive contract) in Hand 1. Player two doubles player one, noted with a ⊛ symbol. The circle is to help track the fact that player two has made one of two obligatory doubles of declarer in the first seven hands; a **P2** notation is added to player one's column, to help track the fact that player one is being doubled by player two.

Now assume player one scores 40 points, player two scores 20 points, player three scores 5 points, and player four scores zero points.

If one of a pair of players doubles the other, calculate the difference between their hand scores, and add the difference to the player who scored better, and subtract the difference from the one who did worse. In the sample hand below, player two doubles player one, but player one scored 20 points better (40 − 20 = 20). So 20 points are added to player one's score and subtracted from player two's score.

If both players in a pair double each other, calculate the difference between their hand scores, double it, and add this amount to the player who scored better while subtracting the amount from the one who performed worse.

If a player did not double and was not doubled by another player, her score is simply noted on the score sheet. The "check" column is to verify that the total points awarded match the contract value.

The ◆ symbol in the sample score sheet indicates that a player has doubled all other players.

Hand	Player 1 Contract	Player 1 Doubles	Player 1 Score	Player 2 Contract	Player 2 Doubles	Player 2 Score	Player 3 Contract	Player 3 Doubles	Player 3 Score	Player 4 Contract	Player 4 Doubles	Player 4 Score	CHECK	
		PLAYER 1			PLAYER 2			PLAYER 3			PLAYER 4				
1	♥	**P2** 40 20	60		✽ 20 -20	0		5	5		0	0	65	65
2	No ♥	**P3** -6 12	6		◆ -6 0 12 -6	12		✽ -18 -12 -12	-42		0 6	6	30	30
3														
etc.														

BIG TWO

DIFFICULTY *low*	TIME LENGTH *short*	DECKS 1

This is a Westernized version of a popular modern Chinese card game. In China, the game is usually played for a small wager—say, 50 cents per player—which is won by the player who earns the least amount of points.

∾ **HOW TO DEAL** Start with a fifty-two-card deck, and deal thirteen cards, face down, to each player. Cards rank (high to low) 2-A-K-Q-J-10-9-8-7-6-5-4-3. There is also a hierarchy of suits (high to low): ♠, ♥, ♣, ♦. Thus 3♦ is the lowest card in the deck, 2♠ the highest. And rank is always more important than suit (e.g., 10♦ beats 9♠).

∾ **SCORING** The goal is to be the first player to empty his or her hand of cards. As soon as one player is out, the game immediately stops and scores are tallied. Players holding cards are scored 1 point per card (up to 9 cards) or 2 points per card (10–12 cards). If a player has not managed to play any cards, he is scored 39 points. A game of Big Two usually lasts until one player scores 50, at which point the player with the low score wins.

HOW TO PLAY The player holding 3♦ starts the game and must lead the card (face up in the center of the table), either on its own or in a valid combination. The valid plays in Big Two are:

SINGLE CARDS High card wins. Higher suit wins if cards are of equal rank.

PAIRS High pair wins. Higher suit wins if pairs are of equal rank.

TRIPLETS High triplet wins (e.g., 2-2-2 beats K-K-K).

FIVE-CARD HANDS All standard five-card poker hands may be played (see the Poker section), with subtle differences:

Despite 2s' high rank in most hands, the highest *straight* in Big Two is A-K-Q-J-10, the lowest is 5-4-3-2-A.

If two players have a *flush*, the highest suit wins, regardless of which cards are in either flush.

Standard *full house* rules apply.

You must include a fifth card with any *four-of-a-kind*. It has no impact on the outcome, though, as the higher foursome wins.

The highest *straight flush* is A♠-K♠-Q♠-J♠-10♠. If two players have straight flushes, the hand with the highest-ranked card (e.g., a high ace) wins. If there is a tie, the high suit prevails.

If you play a single card, your opponents must follow with a single card; if you play a triplet, opponents must follow only with a triplet. Play continues until three players in a row pass, at which point the trick winner sets aside the trick, face down in a single pile, and leads the next trick.

Note that players are never required to play a card, even if they can. And passing once does not mean you're out of the hand; players may jump back in on their next turn, if they can beat the cards on the table.

- -

VARIATION: THREE-HAND BIG TWO

This is virtually identical to the basic game except that all players receive seventeen cards, with the final card placed face up on the table. The player holding 3♦ leads and is required to take the extra card into her hand. The 3♣ starts the game if no player is holding 3♦.

Hearts

DIFFICULTY *medium*	TIME LENGTH *medium*	DECKS 1

Hearts is known as a "cutthroat" game for good reason. Its pleasure lies in pitting friend against friend in ruthless card combat; in overwhelming your good friends with unwanted point cards; in drowning your former friends in a deep pool of unwanted point cards; in repeatedly dumping into the hand of your now sworn enemies a heaping pile of unwanted point cards.

One reason for the ongoing success of Hearts is that the game has always favored players holding mediocre cards. In Hearts, low cards such as 2, 3, and 4 have the best chance of ducking tricks containing unwanted point cards. Another unique Hearts feature is that there is no winner, just a loser.

> **Hearts belongs to the illustrious family of negative, or reverse, card games. Unlike traditional card games such as Poker and Bridge, where winning hands or tricks is the goal, the original game of Hearts was called Reversis, and its object was to lose tricks instead of win them.**

∾ **NUMBER OF PLAYERS** Best for four, though three or five may play.

∾ **HOW TO DEAL** A standard fifty-two-card deck is used. In each suit the cards are ranked ace (high) to 2 (low).

Deal the entire deck. All players receive an equal number of cards, one at a time and face down. With three players there is one extra card; with five players, two extra cards. In either case, put the extra card(s) aside, face down. This is called the *kitty* and comes into play later.

❧ **PASSING CARDS**   After all players have received and organized their cards, all players must pass three cards—no fewer, no more, and typically cards that are unwanted—to another player. Players may not look at any cards passed to them until they pass three of their own cards to the appropriate player.

Cards are passed to the left in the first round, to the right in the second round. In three-player games, the third round is a *keeper*, which means no cards are passed. The cycle is repeated for the remainder of the game. In four-person games, cards are passed to the left; to the right; across; and the fourth round is a keeper. In five-person games, cards are passed to the left; two players to the left; to the right; two players to the right; and the fifth round is a keeper.

❧ **SCORING**   The object of Hearts is to *avoid* capturing tricks that contain point cards. Each card in the suit of hearts is worth 1 point. So players earn 1 point for every heart taken in a trick, up to a total of 13 points per round. In the most commonly played version of the game (see variations), the dreaded ♠Q is worth 13 points and the prized J♦ is worth *negative* 10 points.

Once all cards are played, add up your points and tally them on a public scorecard. Award 1 point for each heart taken and, if they are in play, 13 points for the ♠Q and -10 points for the J♦. Games last until a player scores more than 100 points (250 points for a longer game). At that point, the player with the highest score loses.

❧ **HOW TO PLAY**   After dealing is complete and all cards have been passed, the player with 2♣ starts the game. If no player has the 2♣ (because it is in the kitty), the player with 3♣ starts. Either way, the opening card is played face up in the center of the table.

Moving clockwise, the player to the left of the opener must play a card in the suit that leads (in this case, clubs). The trick is ultimately won by whoever plays the highest card in the leading suit. For example, if player one leads 2♣, player two might follow with K♣, and player three with 9♣. Player two wins the trick with the king, since it's the highest card in the leading suit.

The winner of the trick then takes the cards and places them face down in a pile (to be scored at the end of the round), and leads the next trick with the card of his or her choice. The cycle is repeated until all cards are played.

VOID IN A SUIT In Hearts, you must always play a card in the leading suit. However, if you are *void* (have no cards) in the leading suit, this is your opportunity to play, hurl, dump, and otherwise unload an unwanted card. Go ahead and dump the Q♠ or a high heart onto your unsuspecting opponent. For example, player one leads 7♦, player two throws 5♦, and player three (being void of diamonds) plays 8♥. Player one must take the trick because 7♦ is the highest card in the suit that led, and ultimately she scores 1 point for the heart.

The only exception is the opening hand: you may not play a point card (a heart, or Q♠ or J♦ if they are in play) on the very first round, even if you are void in clubs.

The winner of each trick is obligated to lead the next trick with a card of her choice. The only restriction is you may not lead with a point card (a heart, or the Q♠ or J♦ if they are in play) until *points have been broken*. Points are broken when a point card is legitimately played during a trick. Once this happens, players may lead tricks with point cards. The lone exception is when you have *nothing but* point cards in your hand. In this case, you have no choice but to open a trick with a point card.

WINNING THE KITTY In three- and five-player games, there will be an extra card or two left over from the deal. Set aside the card(s), face down, and award them to the first player who takes a point card. That player will put the card(s) face down in his pile, without showing it to the other players. If one or both of the cards is a point card, the player must add them to his score at the end of the round.

∽ **HOW TO WIN** When deciding which cards to pass, consider passing all your clubs or diamonds. This way, when somebody leads in your voided suit, you can reward them with a point card.

Unless you're trying to shoot the moon (see Variation 2), play your high cards as quickly as possible so you're not stuck winning a trick that contains an opponent's point cards. Another thing to avoid is suits where you have one high card and two or three mid-ranking cards. For example, holding Q♦, 9♦, 8♦, 7♦ means you will be forced to win at least one or two diamond tricks, which is never a good thing. Play the cards as quickly as possible or, better yet, pass three of these cards at the beginning of the hand.

While it may sound counterintuitive, always keep at least one high heart in your hand. Players especially should hold on to the A♥, since any player attempting to shoot the moon will ultimately fail if another player holds, and eventually leads, the A♥.

∾ **POINTS OF ETIQUETTE** Table talk is never polite, but in Hearts it is especially unforgivable. Knowing the location of the Q♠ or a few high hearts can influence the outcome of a game. Never discuss your hand or cards with other players.

Hearts is not a team sport. It is OK to work collectively to stop a player from shooting the moon. It is not OK to single out or gang up on a player.

The kitty cards should either be shared with all players, or with no players. It is not appropriate to show the kitty cards to some players but not to all. Tricks won should be placed, face down, in an orderly pile on the table. You are allowed to review the cards of the most recent trick taken by any player. Ask to see the relevant cards from their discard pile, but never touch another player's discard pile.

∾ **IRREGULARITIES & DISPUTES** If you fail to follow suit when able (for example, by playing a diamond on a leading club when you are not yet void in clubs), you may correct the error with no penalty before the next trick is played. Otherwise, if you are caught before the round is scored, charge yourself 13 points (26 points if the Q♠ is in play) and score all other players zero for that round.

If a player passes one or two cards but receives a full set of three, score that player a penalty of 10 points. The player whose hand is light on cards also should select an appropriate number of cards, face down, from the offending player's hand.

The players' scores at the end of each round should add to 13 (to 26 if the Q♠ is in play, to 16 if the Q♠ and J♦ are both in play). If the scores do not add up correctly, and if all players cannot agree on a solution, the amount in dispute should be charged as a penalty to all players. For example, if the scores add up to 24 instead of 26, all players receive a penalty of 2 extra points.

- -

VARIATION 1: BLACK MARIAH

This variant, in which the Q♠ is a point card worth 13 points, is so common that most modern Hearts players don't realize they're playing a variant of the original Hearts game.

With the Q♠ in play, game play is more strategic. Players must manage length in two suits and treat voided suits more suspiciously. As a point card, the Q♠ is subject to the rules of point cards and therefore may not lead a trick until points have been broken and may not be played on the very first round (even if you are void in clubs).

Hearts purists argue that a player holding the Q♠ must get rid of it on the first trick they legitimately can (by playing it as the first discard in a voided suit, or by playing it when an opponent leads A♠ or K♠). This is so the player holding the Q♠ cannot "choose" which opponent will receive the Q♠ and its 13 demoralizing points. This rule is hogwash, and misses the entire point of playing the modern form of Hearts. Whimsy, favoritism, and a thirst for revenge are the soul of the game.

> **STRATEGY TIPS** If you are dealt the Q♠, it is generally safe to hold the card if you are long in spades (e.g., holding 3 to 4 additional spades in 4- and 5-player games, 4 to 5 extra spades in 3-player games). Conversely, if you are dealt the Q♠ and have fewer than two additional spades, pass it! Get rid of it! Do not hold the Q♠!
>
> Try to avoid "queening yourself." This occurs when you are holding the Q♠, have no additional spades in your hand, and a dastardly opponent leads a

low spade. In this example, you have no choice but to play the Q♠ and to subsequently win the trick and its 13 points. The best defense here is a good offense: dump the Q♠ as early as possible, especially if you are not comfortably long in spades.

The only other way to avoid the self-flagellation described above is if the player next to you has only the K♠ or A♠ and is forced to play them because they, too, forgot or could not dump the high spade earlier in the round. Lucky you, unlucky them.

For players who aren't holding the Q♠, your strategy is simple: flush out the Q♠. It pays to lead a few low spades (not A♠ or K♠, obviously) in order to force someone else to play (and take) the dreaded Q♠.

- -

VARIATION 2: SHOOT THE MOON

Many players skip this variant until they are moderately skilled at Hearts. This is sound advice. Shooting the moon is confusing to novice players and adds little to the basic game. However, once you master Hearts, by all means introduce shooting the moon to your repertoire. It's rare that you can actually pull it off.

Normally players avoid taking point cards at any cost. In this variation, taking points is a good thing. However, you may not take some points, you must take all points. In other words, to successfully shoot the moon, a player must win all 13 hearts plus the Q♠ (if it is in play). When a player shoots the moon, he is scored zero points for that round, while all other players each receive 13 points (26 points each if the Q♠ is in play).

If you are playing the Jack of Diamonds variation, note the J♦ has no effect on shooting the moon. In rounds where a player successfully shoots the moon, the J♦ is irrelevant and no player scores the -10 point bonus typically associated with the J♦.

> **What's the most painful score in Hearts? That would be 25 points. It's a sure sign you attempted to shoot the moon but failed, by one card.**

STRATEGY TIPS The fewer players in a game, the easier it is to shoot the moon. But no matter how many players in a game, you need a specific type of hand to shoot the moon. Typically this means holding high cards (preferably the ace and king of most—if not all four—suits), plus one suit that is especially deep and long.

Strive to hold—or at least know the location of—the A♥, K♥, and Q♠. Managing these cards is critical to success.

Often you'll have a hand that *could* shoot the moon, but only if the game unfolds a certain way. In these instances, avoid taking the Q♠ or tricks stuffed with hearts early on. Don't commit to shooting the moon until you absolutely must.

VARIATION 3: JACK OF DIAMONDS

Some players live and die by how many points they earn in a game of Hearts. The more points they score, the worse they feel. This variation offers relief to point-averse players. The J♦ is a point card worth -10 points. The player who wins the J♦ during normal Hearts game play scores -10 points at the end of the round. The J♦ is subject to the rules governing point cards, and therefore may not lead a trick until points have been broken, and may not be played on the very first round (not that you would want to).

Don't miss the Q♠ forest for the J♦ trees. Time and time again, mediocre players will do everything possible to win the J♦, only to find themselves the unexpected recipient of the Q♠ to boot. Net result: 3 unwanted points.

If you are holding the J♦, consider passing it at the beginning of the round. Strangely enough, it is harder to throw yourself the J♦ than it is to win it from an opponent (as long as she plays before you in rotation, and not after). If you decide to pass the J♦, keep a high card in each suit for as long as possible, in order to capture the J♦ when it is finally played.

VARIATION 4: SPOT HEARTS

This variation is identical to the standard game, with one glaring exception: all hearts are worth their face value in points. Instead of each heart scoring one point (for a total of 13), 2♥ is worth 2 points, 3♥ worth 3 points, etc.; face cards are worth 10 points each; and A♥ scores 11 points, for a total of 95 points.

Games of Spot Hearts are played to 1,000 points. The score for shooting the moon is adjusted to 95 points. The Q♠ is adjusted to 50 points, though traditionally the Q♠ is not played as a point card.

- -
VARIATION 5: PARTNERSHIP HEARTS

It is possible to play Hearts in teams. The partnership version of the game, played exclusively by four players, is identical to the standard game. The only difference is that partners sit opposite one another and pool their tricks and any points scored. Although there is little scope for partners to play into each other's hands (table talk is not allowed), the partnership version of Hearts is still worthwhile for groups of four.

- -
VARIATION 6: CANCELLATION HEARTS

This variation is exclusively for groups of six or more.

Shuffle two fifty-two-card decks, and deal them out evenly to all players. Set aside any extra cards, face down, in a kitty (won by the first player who takes a point card). All standard Hearts rules apply, with the following exception: when identical cards are played in the same trick, they cancel each other out and have no impact on who wins the trick. For example, if two A♣ cards are played in the same trick, they cancel each other out. The trick goes to the player who threw the next highest card in the leading suit.

It is possible that no card can win the trick. For example, if A♣ opens followed by 10♥, Q♠, 8♥, 7♥, A♣, the two A♣ cards cancel each other out, and no other player can win. If this happens, set aside the trick and give it to the winner of the *next* trick. The player who opened the set-aside trick should open the next trick. If the final trick in a round is set aside, the cards are dead and simply not scored.

THIRTEEN-CARD BRAG

DIFFICULTY *medium*	TIME LENGTH *short*	DECKS 1

Card players from the United Kingdom know this game as Crash; in the United States it's called Thirteen-Card Brag. The rules are virtually identical. The concept here is beautiful in its simplicity: create as many three-card "brag hands" as possible, and hope to beat the corresponding hands of your opponents. A point is earned by the winner of each three-card hand.

Is this setup amenable to wagering? Absolutely! Brag is sometimes played for mere points and honor; however, it's more common to nominate a point target (say, 10 points) and a monetary value for hitting the target (say, 50 cents).

∾ **HOW TO DEAL** Start with a fifty-two-card deck, and deal all cards, one at a time, so all players receive thirteen. In Brag, 3s are high, followed by aces, kings, queens, etc.

∾ **SCORING** The game ends—and a winner is declared—the moment any player scores 11 points. If one player captures all 4 points in a hand, it's called a *crash* and earns the player 1 bonus game point (score 5 points instead of 4).

∾ **HOW TO PLAY** Each player organizes her cards into three-card brag hands, based on the hand values below, and places them face down on the table in high-to-low order (your best hand on the left, followed by your next-best, etc.). Set aside any cards not used to create a brag hand. Valid brag hands are (high to low):

PRIAL Three cards of the same rank (e.g., 7♥-7♦-7♠).

RUNNING FLUSH (also called a *trotter*) Three cards of matching suit in *descending* rank (e.g., 10♣-9♣-8♣). In Brag, the highest running flush is 3-2-A, followed by 2-A-K and A-K-Q. The lowest is 4-3-2.

RUN Three cards of any suit in *descending* rank (e.g., 3-2-A is the highest run).

FLUSH Three cards of matching suit (e.g., 8♥-5♥-2♥). Aces are the high card in flushes (not 3s), so A♦-7♦-2♦ beats K♣-5♣-3♣.

PAIR Two cards of the same rank. Always include a third card with your pair (e.g., Q♦-Q♣-10♥), because ties are broken by that third card. Aces are the high card in pair groupings, so A♦-A♣-10♠ beats 3♣-3♦-A♥.

All players turn up their leftmost brag hand; score 1 point to the player with the best hand. In case of ties—called *stoppers*—no point is awarded. Continue until all hands are revealed and all four game points are awarded.

∾ **IRREGULARITIES & DISPUTES** Players must always follow the high-to-low hand rankings when placing their brag hands on the table. They are immediately out of the hand if they make a mistake—say, by placing a flush hand before a run. The remaining players continue the hand. If you play fewer than four hands, there's no penalty, you simply will not compete in the later contest(s).

- -

VARIATION 1: NINE-CARD BRAG

It's common to wager in Thirteen-Card Brag; in this variation, it's more than common, it's required. Typical wagers are 25–50 cents per game.

The rules are similar to the main game, except the high card is 9, followed by A, K, Q, J, 10, etc. Each player is dealt nine cards. And before any three-card hands are played, players may declare:

Four-of-a-kind, in which case they win the pot and a new hand is dealt. The highest four-of-a-kind hand wins in a *showdown*.

Four pairs, in which case the hand is dead, all players must *re-ante,* and a new hand is dealt.

Otherwise, the game proceeds as normal, with players laying out three brag hands on the table and scoring 1 point to the winner of each. Unlike in Thirteen-Card Brag, you may play a "junk hand" (any three random cards) in this variant. The high card wins the point. A player must earn 2 points to capture the pot; otherwise the pot stays on the table, all players re-ante, and a new hand is dealt.

VARIATION 2: SIX-CARD BRAG

This is essentially the same game as Nine-Card Brag, with the following differ-ences. High card is 6, followed by A, K, Q, J, 10, etc. All players are dealt six cards, and four-of-a-kind immediately wins the pot. Otherwise, players create two three-card brag hands and lay them on the table. A player must win (or tie) both hands in order to win the pot. The pot stays; if not, players re-ante, and a new hand is dealt.

- -

VARIATION 3: SEVEN-CARD BRAG

Follow the rules of Six-Card Brag, and simply substitute 7 as the high card and deal seven cards to each player. With no four-of-a-kind, all players create two three-card brag hands, simply ignoring the extra card.

TIEN LEN

DIFFICULTY *low*	TIME LENGTH *short*	DECKS 1

Tien Len, the national card game of Vietnam, shares many traits with the Chinese game Big Two. The main difference is that Tien Len is universally played for a wager—whether large or small, this game functions best when all players have something at stake.

∾ **HOW TO DEAL** Start with a fifty-two-card deck, and deal all players thir-teen cards. Cards rank (high to low): 2-A-K-Q-J-10-9-8-7-6-5-4-3. There also is a hierarchy of suits (high to low): ♥, ♦, ♣, ♠. Thus in Tien Len, 3♠ is the lowest card in the deck, 2♥ the highest. And rank is always more important than suit (e.g., 10♠ beats 9♥).

∾ **SCORING** The object is to *avoid* being the last player holding any cards. This player loses the game and pays all the other players an agreed-upon stake (typically 25 cents).

∾ **HOW TO PLAY** In the first round, the player holding 3♠ leads the first trick—and *must* play this card either on its own or as part of a combination, face up in the center of the table. (In subsequent rounds, the winner of the previous round plays first and may lead with any card or card combination.) In Tien Len, the valid plays are:

SINGLE CARDS High card wins. Higher suit wins if cards are of equal rank.

PAIRS High pair wins. Highest suit wins if pairs are of equal rank.

TRIPLETS High triplet wins (e.g., 2-2-2 beats K-K-K).

FOUR OF A KIND High foursome wins.

SEQUENCES Three or more cards in ascending sequence. Ranking is not continuous. The highest sequence is 2♥-A♥-K♥. High card wins, or the high suit wins if the sequences are of equal rank.

DOUBLE SEQUENCES Three or more pairs in unbroken sequence (e.g., 5-5-6-6-7-7). High pairs win, or the high suit wins if there's a tie.

If you play a single card, your opponents must follow with a single card; if you play a triplet, opponents must follow only with a triplet. Players are allowed to pass and then jump back in on their following turn, as long as they can beat the cards on the table.

Play continues until three players in a row pass, at which point the trick winner sets aside the trick, face down in a single pile, and leads the next trick.

TWENTY DOWN

DIFFICULTY *low*	TIME LENGTH *short*	DECKS 1

This game is easy, fun, and thoroughly addictive—Twenty Down is the perfect antidote to some of the more complicated four-person games in this collection.

∾ **HOW TO DEAL** Start with a fifty-two-card deck, and remove all 2s through 6s, leaving thirty-two cards total. Card rankings are standard, with aces always high.

Deal two cards to each player. The player to the dealer's left selects a trump suit (based on the two-card hand), and then all players receive three more cards, for a total of five.

∾ SCORING All players start the game with 20 points and compete to be the first player to score zero points. Points are awarded for the following:

-1 points for each trick won, or -5 points if a single player wins all the tricks

+5 points if a player stays in but wins no tricks

All points are doubled if hearts are trump

If all players but one drop out, that player scores -5 points (-10 points if hearts are trump)

If two players score zero points on the same hand, the player with the lowest negative score wins.

∾ HOW TO PLAY The game starts with a round of drawing. All players may (but are not required to) discard a maximum of three cards and draw replacements from the top of the deck. Next, all players must decide if they are "in" or "out" of the hand, with two caveats. If the trump suit is diamonds, all players *must* stay in. The player who selected trump must also play. The player to the left of the dealer plays the first card, and all players who are "in" try to beat it. Players must follow suit if they can, otherwise they may play a trump or, if they have no trump, any other card. Tricks are won by the highest ranking trump card, or by the highest card in the leading suit if no trumps are played.

Scores are tallied once all cards are played, and a new hand is dealt. If no winner emerges after eight hands, on the ninth hand (and in all subsequent hands) hearts are always trump and no player is allowed to drop out.

OTHER VARIATIONS SUITABLE FOR FOUR PLAYERS

Many of the games covered in the *Ultimate Book of Card Games* have variations specifically for four players. Also take a look at the next chapter, which features four-player partnership games.

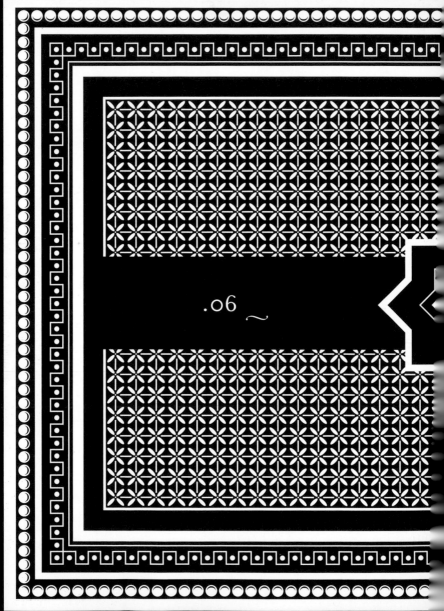

.o6 ~

Partnership Games

CHAPTER SIX

Partnership Games

DON'T BE SCARED OF PARTNERSHIP GAMES. It is true that these are games of considerable complexity and skill. And sure, some partnership games have accredited instructors, nationwide clubs, many libraries' worth of books written about them, their own cable TV shows, and weekly columns in the newspapers. On the face of it, it's easy to be intimidated.

But even the most complicated partnership game (that honor goes to Contract Bridge) can be conquered by first-time players without too much trouble. And once you've cracked open the door just a little, you'll discover an entire world of experienced players keen to mentor novice players.

Some of you will already be familiar with mainstream partnership games such as Bridge and Canasta. Likely you're in for a pleasant shock at the number of lesser-known—but hugely enjoyable—partnership games there are to sample: Pedro, Pinochle, Pisti, 18, Auction 45, Euchre, even Whist!

DIFFICULTY *high*	TIME LENGTH *medium*	DECKS 1

28 is hugely popular in India, especially in Kerala, and yet is almost completely unknown anywhere else. This is a shame, because it's one of the few trump-based partnership games where the trump suit is not exposed immediately.

∾ **HOW TO DEAL** Start with a fifty-two-card deck, and remove all 2s through 6s, for a total of thirty-two cards. Deal four cards to each player in a counter-clockwise direction. In each suit, cards rank (high to low): J-9-A-10-K-Q-8-7.

∾ **SCORING** Teams compete to be the first to score 15 total points. Points are awarded whether you succeed or fail to make a bid:

Bids of 19 or less, score 1 point if successful or -2 points for failing

Bids of 20 to 24, score 2 points if successful or -3 points for failing

Bids 25 or more, score 3 points if successful or -4 points for failing

∾ **HOW TO PLAY** The player to the right of the dealer opens the bidding. The minimum bid is 14 points, and bidding continues until three players in a row pass. You're bidding on how many total points your team thinks it will capture in tricks, based on the following card values: jacks, 3 points each; 9s, 2 points each; aces and 10s, 1 point each. In each hand, 28 total points are at stake, and so the maximum team bid is 28 points.

The bid winner nominates a trump suit by placing one card (of the proposed trump) face down on the table. The card is not shown to any other player until later in the game. The dealer then gives each player four more cards (for a total of eight). At this point the bid winner (or his partner) may increase his bid to a minimum of 24 or higher.

The player to the left of the dealer leads. All other players must follow suit if possible. The trick is won by the highest card in the leading suit, and the trick winner leads the next trick. The bid winner is not allowed to lead trump (the suit of which only he knows) unless he has no other cards in his hand.

If you cannot follow suit, you have two options: play a card from any other suit to the trick (and lose the trick), or, before playing a card, call for the trump suit to be exposed. In this case, the bid winner must expose the trump card, and the card is then added to the bid winner's hand. You must now play trump to the trick (if you have trump), or play a card from any other suit.

Once the trump suit is exposed, tricks are won by the highest trump or, if none, by the highest card in the leading suit. Players must still follow suit if possible, or play any other card (including trump). Trump, however, is not retroactive—any trump cards played prior to the exposure of the trump suit are given no special status.

If nobody calls for the trump to be exposed during the first seven tricks, the bid winner is required to expose trump in the last trick and then immediately to play it, since this is his last remaining card. Scores are tallied when all eight tricks are played. The deal rotates to the right.

- -

VARIATION: THREE-PLAYER 28

The three-player version of 28 follows the same rules as the basic game, except the thirty-two-card deck is reduced to twenty-four cards total (remove the 7s and 8s), and the minimum opening bid is 12 points (not 14). In each hand, the bid winner plays alone against the other two players.

400

DIFFICULTY *medium*	TIME LENGTH *medium*	DECKS 1

In Lebanon, 400 is the most common trick-taking game played. In some ways, the game is a mirror image of Spades, featuring a permanent trump suit (hearts in this case) and a single round of bidding. 400 has none of the complexity of Bridge or similar partner-based bidding games. For some players, this is a plus.

∾ **HOW TO DEAL** Start with a fifty-two-card deck, and deal thirteen cards to each player in batches of 1-2-2-2-2-2. Card rankings are standard, with aces always high.

∾ **SCORING** Scores are tracked for each individual player, even though 400 is a partnership game. The bid winner, if successful, earns the amount of her bid. A bid of 6, for example, scores 6 points; a bid of 8 scores 16 points (bids above seven are doubled—see below). The converse is also true. If you fail to make a bid, subtract the bid amount from your game score.

In order to win the game, a member of either team must score 41 total points, *and* her partner's score may not be negative. Otherwise, the game continues. If both teams earn 41 points or more in the same hand, the higher score wins.

∾ **HOW TO PLAY** Hearts are the permanent trump suit. Once all cards are dealt, bidding starts with the player to the right of the dealer and proceeds counterclockwise. Players bid only once. The minimum bid is 1, and your bid commits you to winning that number of tricks.

Bids from 1 to 6 are worth that amount; all bids 7 and above are doubled (e.g., a bid of 7 is worth 14 points). If the sum of all bids is 10 points or less, the hand is dead and new cards are dealt.

Otherwise, the player to the right of the dealer leads the first trick, and the other players must follow suit if they can. If they cannot, they may play any card including trump (permanently established in hearts). Tricks are won by the highest trump or, if none, by the highest card in the leading suit. Scores are tallied after all thirteen tricks are played, and the deal rotates counterclockwise.

- -

VARIATION: CUTTHROAT 400

The cutthroat element comes from modified bidding rules. All other rules are identical to the main game. Bids from 1 to 4 are worth their face value; bids 5 and above are worth double points. Players must bid a minimum of 3 (not 1) with scores between 30 and 39 points; a minimum of 4 with scores between 40 and 49 points (above 41 points, your partner must have a negative score, thus preventing your team from winning).

ALKORT

| DIFFICULTY low | TIME LENGTH short | DECKS 1 |

Alkort is an ancient Icelandic game, with roots at least into the early eighteenth century. It remains popular in Iceland, though nowadays a small wager is typically added between the teams (say, $1 per game) in order to enliven an otherwise straightforward trick-taking game.

∾ **HOW TO DEAL** Start with a fifty-two-card deck, and remove all 10s and 5s, leaving forty-four cards total. Deal nine cards to each player in batches of three. The eight remaining cards are the stock.

Card rankings are always (high to low) K♦-2♥-4♣-8♠-9♥-9♦, followed by aces, jacks, 6s, and the remaining 8s. All other cards have no ranking. If you lead with a non-ranking card, however, you will win the trick if only other non-ranking cards are played. The one exception is 7s; these *always* win when leading a trick, otherwise they are considered non-ranking.

∾ **SCORING** The goal is to capture tricks, and the first team to capture five earns 1 point. A bonus of 5 points is awarded if a team wins five tricks before their opponents win any tricks. An extra 1 point is awarded on top of that for each additional trick captured before the other team wins its first trick (for example, if Team 1 wins seven tricks in a row, they score 7 total points). Games are typically played to 15 points.

∾ **HOW TO PLAY** After the hands are dealt, a player holding only non-ranking cards may exchange from one to eight of his own cards with fresh cards from the stock. Otherwise the stock is not used. Partners show each other their highest single card. The player to the left of the dealer then leads the first card. High cards win the trick. If cards of equal rank are played, the trick is won by whichever card was played first. The round ends after all nine tricks have been captured.

AUCTION FORTY-FIVE

DIFFICULTY *medium*	TIME LENGTH *short*	DECKS 1

This is the most interesting—and challenging—of the Irish "Spoil Five" family of games, which includes Twenty-Five, Forty-Five, and Fifty-Five. The difference here is the team play, which adds a layer of mystery and mischief to the game. If you're new to two-player team games, Auction Forty-Five is a superb and easy-to-master introduction.

∾ **HOW TO DEAL** Start with a fifty-two-card deck, and deal five cards to each player in batches of 3-2. The remaining cards are the stock. Typically for Spoil Five games, the card rankings vary, based on whether the suit is trump or not:

NON-TRUMP SUITS (HIGH TO LOW)

Clubs & Spades: K-Q-J-A-2-3-4-5-6-7-8-9-10

Diamonds: K-Q-J-10-9-8-7-6-5-4-3-2-A

Hearts: K-Q-J-10-9-8-7-6-5-4-3-2
Note that A♥ is always the third-highest trump

TRUMP SUITS (HIGH TO LOW)

Clubs & Spades: 5-J-A♥-A-K-Q-2-3-4-6-7-8-9-10

Diamonds: 5-J-A♥-A-K-Q-10-9-8-7-6-4-3-2

Hearts: 5-J-A-K-Q-10-9-8-7-6-5-4-3-2

∾ **SCORING** Each trick is worth 5 points, and the first team to score 120 points wins. An extra 5 points are given to whichever team won the highest trump in play. If the bid winners meet or exceed their bid, they score the bid amount and nothing more (though they are eligible for the 5-point high trump bonus). Otherwise, the bid amount is deducted from their score. If a team successfully bids 30, they earn a double-point bonus of 60 points.

HOW TO PLAY The player to the left of the dealer opens the bidding. Players may pass, hold, or bid in multiples of 5, up to 30. A "hold" commits you to the previous player's bid. Players who pass are allowed to bid again on their next turn. The bid is won when three players in a row pass. The bid winner nominates a trump suit for the hand. Note that teams with a game score of 100 or more points are not allowed to bid less than 20.

Once a trump suit is named, each player starting to the left of the dealer may discard up to five cards, and replace them with fresh cards from the stock.

The player to the left of the bid winner leads. Players must follow suit if possible, otherwise they may play any card. Tricks are won by the highest trump, or by the highest card in the leading suit. The exceptions: You may play trump at any time, and when trumps lead, you are not required to play any of the three-highest trump cards unless a higher trump leads. For example, if hearts are trump and J♥ leads, you are required to play A♥ if that's your last trump card.

- -

VARIATION: FORTY-FIVE
This is the same four-player game as above, except bidding is tossed out. In its place? Once all cards are dealt, the dealer turns up the next card. This determines trump for the hand. And if it's an ace, the lucky dealer may swap the ace for any card in her hand. The team winning three or four tricks earns 5 game points (10 points, if they capture all five tricks). Games are played to 45 points.

BACK ALLEY

DIFFICULTY *medium*	TIME LENGTH *long*	DECKS 1

If you're a fan of Spades, you will immediately fall in love with Back Alley. Both games are partner-based trick-taking games. Back Alley's edge comes from its fixed-length deal of twenty-six hands. Your strategy varies drastically depending on the number of cards you're holding, which means Back Alley doesn't get stale.

∾ **HOW TO DEAL** Start with a fifty-two-card deck, and add two jokers. Nominate one joker as the "Big Joker" and one as the "Little Joker."

A complete game of Back Alley consists of twenty-six deals. Deal thirteen cards to each player in the first hand, twelve in the second, eleven in the third, etc., down to one card each in the thirteenth hand, and then back up to two cards in the fourteenth hand, three in the fifteenth, etc., until all twenty-six hands are dealt.

Card ranking is standard, with aces always high. The Big Joker is always the highest trump, followed by the Little Joker, then the ace, king, queen, etc.

∾ **SCORING** Teams that meet or exceed their combined bids score 5 points for each trick bid, plus 1 point for every trick above their bid. Otherwise, they lose the amount of their bid multiplied by five. In a board bid, tricks are worth 10 points each. If you're courageous enough to bid a "double board" or "triple board," you're committing to 15 and 20 points per trick, respectively. The non-bidding team earns 1 point for every trick they capture. The team with the highest score at the end of twenty-six hands wins.

∾ **HOW TO PLAY** After the first hand is dealt, the dealer turns up a card from the deck; its suit determines trump for the remaining twenty-five hands. If the turn-up card is a joker, there is no trump suit. In that case, the second joker is a "dead card" and should be replaced by a fresh card from the deck when it turns up.

After trump is established, a round of bidding starts with the player to the left of the dealer. Players may bid only once. The valid bids are pass, board (which commits you to win every trick in the round), or any whole number from one up to the number of cards dealt in the hand. If players from the same team bid, their individual bids are added together whether they like it or not! If all players pass, the hand is dead and the cards are redealt.

80 above-the-line bonus points for capturing those two extra tricks. If the contract was doubled or redoubled, you earn even more bonus points, depending on whether your team is vulnerable or not.

If your team is not vulnerable, score an above-the-line overtrick bonus of 100 points (doubled) or 200 points (redoubled).

If your team is vulnerable, score an above-the-line overtrick bonus of 200 points (doubled) or 400 points (redoubled).

If the declarer's team fails to make its contract, no below-the-line points are scored. However, the opposing team earns above-the-line bonus points as follows:

If the declarer's team is not vulnerable, the opposing team scores 50 points per overtrick or, if doubled, 200 points for the first overtrick and 300 points for each subsequent overtrick. If the contract is redoubled, the opposing team scores 400 points for the first overtrick and 600 points for each subsequent overtrick.

If the declarer's team is vulnerable, the opposing team scores 100 points per overtrick or, if doubled, 200 points for the first overtrick and 300 points for each subsequent overtrick. If the contract is redoubled, the opposing team scores 400 points for the first overtrick and 600 points for each subsequent overtrick.

When a team wins two games, they win the rubber and receive a 500-point "rubber bonus" if their opponents are vulnerable. Otherwise, they earn a rubber bonus of 700 points.

A typical Bridge game might be scored like so:

NORTH-SOUTH	EAST-WEST
40	–
500	–
–	40
60	120

The highest individual bidder leads. Players must follow suit if possible; otherwise they may play any card. Tricks are won by the highest trump or, if none, by the highest card in the leading suit. As in Hearts and Spades, players may not lead trumps until trumps have been broken or unless they bid a board, in which case they may lead trumps. If the Big Joker leads a trick, all other players *must* play their highest trump; if the Little Joker leads, they must play their lowest trump.

Bridge

If you are new to Bridge, you have a long road ahead of you. This is not intended to frighten you off. Instead, it's meant to manage your expectations. There are thousands—literally—of books dedicated to Bridge, and committed players can spend lifetimes mastering its nuances. That's because Bridge is complicated. And worst of all, you need at least four people to play a proper game of Bridge—not two, three, or five, but precisely four, preferably with similar amounts of playing experience.

Now for the good news. Even detractors acknowledge that Bridge is among the world's finest card games. If you commit time and mental energy to learning Bridge, after just a few hours you will be hooked. It's OK if you don't immediately understand every twist and turn. With even a rudimentary understanding of Bridge's rules and strategies, you will enjoy it.

⌘ A BRIEF HISTORY All Bridge games are descendants of Whist. In 1905, Whist enthusiasts in London, New York, and Boston codified a new form of the game, called Auction Bridge. In 1926, the millionaire Harold Vanderbilt tinkered with the game's rules on a Caribbean cruise and singlehandedly invented Contract Bridge. Enter Ely Culbertson and his wife (an Auction Bridge teacher), Josephine Dillon. They took Contract Bridge and turned it into an international phenomenon in the 1930s and '40s, making and losing many millions of dollars along the way.

Ely Culbertson, credited as the man who made Bridge, wrote no less than ten Bridge books, and transformed the game into a mainstream success. Culbertson was also a true character. In his autobiography, *The Strange Lives of One Man*, he writes, "This is the complete story of my life, told as candidly and as ruthlessly as I could. All the names and places, including the jails, mentioned herein are authentic."

Contract Bridge (sometimes called Rubber Bridge) is the quintessential version of the game, and it's the game described first below. Contract Bridge is a bidding and trick-taking game. At the start of each hand, the teams bid on how many tricks they think they can win. The team with the highest bid earns (or loses) points based on whether they achieve their bid. Over the years, other popular variations have evolved, including Duplicate Bridge (played at professional tournaments), Chicago Bridge (a simplified four-deal version), and Honeymoon Bridge (for two players).

∾ **NUMBER OF PLAYERS** Bridge is always played by four players divided into two teams. Partners sit facing one another, and are universally referred to as North, South, East, and West, based on their positions around the table. The teams, then, are North-South and East-West.

∾ **HOW TO DEAL** A standard fifty-two-card deck is used. Card rankings are standard, with aces always high. The suits rank (high to low) no trump, spades, hearts, diamonds, clubs. *No trump* (abbreviated **NT**) means there is no trump suit, and it acts like a fifth suit for the purposes of bidding. Spades and hearts are *major suits* and score higher contract values than diamonds and clubs, which are *minor suits*.

All dealing is clockwise. Deal thirteen cards to each player, one at a time. It's important to have a second deck of cards at the ready, shuffled by the dealer's partner. At the end of one hand, the alternate deck is used to deal the next, to speed the game along.

BIDDING Most of Bridge's complexity is in the bidding. At its simplest, bidding determines the minimum number of tricks a team must win, as well as the trump (or no trump) suit for the hand.

Bids always assume a base of six, so that a bid of 1 commits you to winning seven tricks, a bid of 2 commits you to winning eight tricks, etc. Since suits are ranked in Bridge, a bid of 2♥ beats a bid of 2♦ or 2♣, but loses to a bid of 2NT, 2♠, or to any bid of three or higher.

The dealer always opens the bidding, which then proceeds clockwise around the table. The dealer may *pass* or make a bid at any level. The bid is intended to communicate information about the dealer's hand to his or her partner (more on bidding strategies later). Either way, the next player either must pass or beat the dealer's bid. For example, if the dealer opens with 2♦, the next player must bid 2♥ or more, or pass.

Players may also *double* an opposing team's bid, which effectively doubles the point value of the previous player's bid and is used to punish a team for overbidding. For example, if North opens with 2♦ and East replies with an aggressive bid of 4♠, South may double. This means South believes East has overreached and is likely to lose the bid of 4♠.

A team that's been doubled may then *redouble* the bid. This is akin to a double-dare, and it *quadruples* the points at stake. In the example above, West might redouble South's double of East's 4♠. Note that if the next player in rotation makes a higher bid, all doubles and redoubles are canceled. So in the example above, if North replies to West's redouble with a bid of 4NT, the doubles and redoubles are ignored and East must decide whether to *overcall* (e.g., make a higher bid, in this case any bid of five or more) or to pass.

A typical bid can be diagrammed as follows, starting at North and with East-West ultimately winning the contract at 4♥:

NORTH	EAST	SOUTH	WEST
Pass	1♥	1♠	2♦
2♠	Double	Pass	4♥
Pass	Pass	Pass	--

Players who pass are allowed to rejoin the bidding on their subsequent turns. The bidding ends when three players in a row pass. The winning bid is called the **contract**, and the player who opens the bid in the *winning suit* is the **declarer**. In the example above, even though West makes the highest hearts bid, East is the declarer because East opened bidding in hearts.

BIDDING STRATEGY Players always start by calculating their hand's point value. This is a simple two-step process:

First, calculate your *high-card points*: 4 points for an ace, 3 for a king, 2 for a queen, 1 for a jack. There are 40 total high-card points in a deck, so you're in a decent position if you hold more than 10 points.

Next, calculate your *long-suit points*. Score yourself 1 point for each card in a suit *longer* than four cards. For example, if you hold six diamonds, score yourself 2 long-suit points.

So, the hand A♠-K♠-10♠-5♠-Q♥-J♣-10♣-8♣-5♣-3♣-2♣-K♦-5♦ contains 13 high-card points plus 2 long-card points, for a total of 15 points. The rule of thumb for bidding in Bridge is:

Pass with fewer than 12 points.

With 13 or 14 points, bid at the one level in your longest suit.

With 15 or more points and a balanced hand (e.g., you have at least two cards in every suit) bid **1NT**.

Once the bidding starts, *short-suit points* are added to your score if and when your partnership finds a *suit fit*. This helps you decide whether to bid or not for a slam or a game (see next page). The rule of thumb for determining suit fit: You must hold four or more cards in the suit bid by your partner (e.g., your partner opens 1♠ and you have four-card support in spades). In this case, give yourself the following short-suit points:

5 points for a **void** (no cards) in any suit.

3 points for a **singleton** (just one card in a suit). Don't score yourself high-card points *and* singleton points. A singleton K♦, for example, scores 3 points for high card or 3 points for the singleton, but not both!

1 point for a *doubleton* (just two cards in any suit).

Whenever possible, teams try to make the following contracts to earn bonus points at the end of the hand:

SMALL SLAM This is a bid of 6♠, 6♥, 6♦, 6♣, or 6NT. You may lose only one trick to your opponents. Teams should hold at least 33 to 36 points to bid a small slam.

GRAND SLAM This is a bid of 7♠, 7♥, 7♦, 7♣, or 7NT, and requires a team to win every single trick! To bid a grand slam, teams should hold at least 37 points between them.

It's OK if you cannot secure a slam contract. It just means you're not eligible for bonus points (or liable for penalty points) at the end of the hand.

One final note: There are numerous systems for bidding in Bridge, known as *bidding conventions*. If you're interested in learning a specific bidding method, such as the popular Blackwood Convention, visit a Web site like the American Contract Bridge League (www.acbl.org).

∾ **HOW TO PLAY** The player to the left of the declarer leads the first trick, and as soon as the first card is played, the declarer's partner turns over his cards, organized into columns by suit. This player is known as the *dummy*, not because they're a dull knife or a dim bulb, but because the dummy plays no role in the hand from this point forward.

Instead, when it's the dummy's turn in rotation to play a card, the *declarer* chooses which card to play. The dummy sits back, refills players' drinks, and otherwise stays out of the way. The dummy is not allowed to discuss strategy or offer any advice to any player.

A typical Bridge hand, therefore, can be diagrammed as follows, with the North-South team having won the bid against the West-East team. In this example, South is declarer and North is dummy:

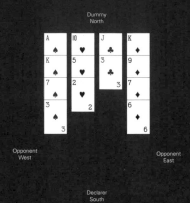

Opponent
West

Opponent
East

Declarer
South

If West opens with 8♦, for example, the declarer plays a card from the dummy's hand and the turn shifts to East. All players *must* follow suit if possible; otherwise they may play any card in any other suit, including trump. Tricks are won by the highest trump played or, if none, by the highest card in the leading suit. The winner of each trick leads the next trick.

Table position is important in Bridge. In the example above, assume that hearts are trump and that South knows (based on how East-West interacted during the bidding phase) that East holds a strong hand of diamonds. In this case, South will try to *finesse* a trick by leading, say, 9♦ from the dummy (South does this by having the dummy win a trick, in order to lead the next).

If East holds A♦, J♦, 10♦, 5♦, they're in a pickle. Against a lead of 9♦, East could play A♦ to guarantee winning the trick. But this is a risky move: against A♦, South will inevitably play a low diamond, resulting in East *overplaying* (a nice way of saying "wasting") the ace. Yet if East plays J♦ instead, South might play Q♦ and win the trick. And any play that captures a trick with a low card—against an opponent holding a higher card in the same suit—is called a *finesse*. It's a thing of beauty when it works, unless of course you're on the losing end of it.

scoring In Bridge, teams compete to win **rubbers**, which consist of three *games*. Whichever team wins two out of three games wins the rubber. It takes 100 points to win a game. Points are awarded as follows (for each trick in excess of six):

> 20 points per trick for contracts in clubs or diamonds. A successful contract of, say, 3♦ earns 60 points (three tricks x 20 points each).

> 40 points per trick for contracts in spades or hearts. A successful contract of 2♥ earns 80 points (two tricks x 40 points each).

> 40 points for the first trick and 30 points for all subsequent tricks in no-trump contracts. A successful contract of 2NT earns 70 points (1 x 40 points plus 1 x 30 points).

Keep score on a piece of paper divided into two sections: *above the line* and *below the line*. Successful contracts are scored below the line and count toward winning a game. Bonus scores for **overtricks** (tricks in excess of the contract) and **undertricks** (tricks shy of the contract) are scored above the line and do not count toward a game.

Double all above-the-line points when the contract is doubled; quadruple the points when the contract is redoubled. And don't forget to score an extra bonus of 50 above-the-line points to the declarer's team if they succeed in making a doubled contract.

BONUS POINTS In each rubber, teams that have won a game are considered *vulnerable*, while teams that have not are *not vulnerable*. Points for slam contracts are as follows:

> If your team is not vulnerable, score an above-the-line bonus of 500 points for a small slam, 1,000 points for a grand slam.

> If your team is vulnerable, score an above-the-line bonus of 750 points for a small slam, 1,500 points for a grand slam.

The declarer's team also scores an above-the-line bonus for each overtrick earned, using the same point values as the contract bids. For example, a successful 2♥ contract with 2 overtricks (e.g., your team won ten total tricks in the hand) scores 80 below-the-line points for the 2♥ contract plus

In the first hand, North-South wins a 3♦ contract and captures eleven total tricks, for a score of 60 below the line and 40 above the line for overtricks. In the second hand, East-West fails to make a doubled contract of 3♥ by two tricks. So North-South scores 500 above-the-line points (on a doubled contract that's 200 points for the first undertrick, 300 points for the second undertrick).

In the third hand, East-West wins a contract of 3♥ and captures ten tricks, for a total of 120 points below the line and 40 points above the line for one overtrick. This earns East-West the game and makes them vulnerable in the next game. The total points at the end of the first game are 600 points for North-South, 160 points for East-West.

VARIATION 1: CHICAGO BRIDGE

The rules of this variation are identical to Contract Bridge. The main difference is that a rubber lasts for four deals—no more, no less. The idea here is to simplify and speed up the normal Contract Bridge game. In Chicago Bridge, vulnerability is "assigned" (since it's unlikely to develop on its own in just four hands) as follows:

Deal 1: North deals, neither team vulnerable

Deal 2: East deals, North-South vulnerable

Deal 3: South deals, East-West vulnerable

Deal 4: West deals, both sides vulnerable

If both teams pass on the bidding, the hand is dead, and cards are shuffled and redealt by the very same dealer. Game bonus is 500 points (vulnerable) or 300 points (not vulnerable). Partial scores are carried over until a team wins a game, at which point the partial score is erased. In Hand 4 only, score either team a bonus of 100 points if they earn a partial score.

VARIATION 2: DUPLICATE BRIDGE

Most players agree that luck plays a small but crucial role in Contract Bridge. That's because a mediocre team dealt good cards will usually beat a better team holding mediocre cards. The luck of the draw has an impact. This is not the case in Duplicate Bridge, where hands are replayed by different sets of players to eliminate the luck factor.

Duplicate Bridge is typically played in Bridge clubs, since you need specialized equipment (sixteen "boards" that are numbered sequentially, each containing four pockets labeled N, S, E, W to stash the pre-dealt Duplicate Bridge hands) and large numbers of Bridge players (eight players for two teams of four, or twelve players for a three-table game). If you're new to Bridge and aspire to club play, learn more about Duplicate Bridge at the American Contract Bridge League (www.acbl.org).

- -
VARIATION 3: HONEYMOON BRIDGE

Bridge is best played by four people. That said, there is a semi-enjoyable two-player version called Honeymoon Bridge. The two players sit next to each other, and one of them deals out four thirteen-card Bridge hands. The hand opposite each player is their own personal dummy hand, which should not be looked at until after the bidding. The bidding alternates between the two players until one player passes. At this point, the two players review their own dummy hands but still keep them concealed until after the first card is played. Lead from the hand that is to the declarer's left (either dummy or player, whichever is appropriate). Then turn over both dummy hands and follow the normal rules of Contract Bridge. Each player pulls cards from his own dummy when it's his dummy's turn.

- -
VARIATION 4: CUTTHROAT BRIDGE

The three-player version of Bridge follows the Contract Bridge rules, with only a few exceptions. Deal four thirteen-card hands (one to each player plus a dummy hand); bidding is opened by the dealer. Once two players in a row pass, the declarer automatically plays with the dummy hand against the two other active players. The player to the declarer's left leads the first card, after which the dummy hand is turned up. The rest of the game proceeds as normal.

Each player keeps her own separate score. If the declarer makes the contract, she earns the standard points. If the declarer fails to make the contract, the two opponents *each* score for undertricks. If either opponent has honors, both score it. The rubber bonus is 700 points if neither opponent has won a game, otherwise the bonus is 500.

VARIATION 5: AUCTION BRIDGE

Auction Bridge, popularized in the early 1900s, put the nail in the coffin of Whist and was the very first version of modern Bridge to have mainstream success. There are no differences at all in the way Auction Bridge and Contract Bridge are played—the only difference is in scoring. In Contract, overtricks do *not* count as below-the-line points towards game; in Auction Bridge, *all* the declarer's tricks are scored below the line and count towards game score, which means the declaring team can afford to be less accurate in their bidding.

In Auction Bridge, each *odd trick* (the number of tricks more than six won by the declarer) scores towards game, even if the tricks were not contracted. The trick values are as follows:

	NORMAL	DOUBLED	REDOUBLED
No Trump Contract	10	20	40
Spades Contract	9	18	36
Hearts Contract	8	16	32
Diamonds Contract	7	14	28
Clubs Contract	6	12	24

So a contract of, say, 3♦ is worth 21 below-the-line points on its own (3 x 7 = 21). However, if the declarer wins ten total tricks on a contract of 3♦, he instead scores 28 below-the-line points. The first team to score 30 points below the line wins the game. The first side to win two games earns a 250-point rubber bonus.

If the declarer makes a doubled contract, he scores above-the-line bonuses: 50 points for the contract, plus 50 points for each overtrick won in excess of the original contract. Redoubled contracts score 100 points for contract, 100 points for overtricks. Score a 50 point above-the-line bonus for small slams, 100 points for grand slams.

When the declarer loses the contract, the opposing teams scores 50 points above the line for each undertrick (100 points per trick if the contract is doubled; 200 points per undertrick if the contract is redoubled).

The side holding the majority of honors earns above-the-line bonus points, regardless of which team is the declarer. In trump contracts, the honors are A, K, Q, J, 10; in no-trump contracts, the honors are all four aces. The honors bonus is:

  30 points: three honors
  40 points: four honors, divided
  50 points: five honors, divided
  80 points: four trump honors in one hand
  90 points: four trump honors in one hand, fifth honor in partner's hand
  100 points: four aces in one hand for no trump contracts
  100 points: five honors in one hand

CANASTA

DIFFICULTY *high*	TIME LENGTH *medium*	DECKS 2

In the 1930s and '40s, Rummy was the second-most popular card game in the United States (after Bridge). In the 1950s, Rummy fell from favor and was overtaken by two of its offspring, the games of Gin Rummy (invented in Brooklyn, NY) and Canasta (invented in Uruguay).

Canasta is not one game, it is an umbrella term for a family of games. Most are team-based, although variations such as Two-Hand and Three-Hand Canasta, as well as Oklahoma Canasta, ditch team play for individual play. The "classic" version described here dates from the 1940s. It is still played, though nowadays it's more likely you'll encounter the Samba or Bolivia variations.

∾ **HOW TO DEAL** Start with two fifty-two-card decks plus four jokers (108 cards total). There are no card rankings, since sequences have no value in Canasta. Jokers and all 2s are wild. Deal eleven cards to each player. Set the remaining cards face down in the center of the table (this is the stock), turn up a card from the stock, and place it face up on the table (this is the discard pile).

∾ **SCORING** Going out is important, but it is not the game's primary objective; the true goal is to score as many points as possible through melding. Cards have the following values in Canasta:

CARDS	POINTS
Joker	50 points each
A, 2	20 points each
K, Q, J, 10, 9, 8	10 points each
7, 6, 5, 4, 3♠, 3♣	5 points each

Once the game ends, teams calculate their scores like so: game bonuses plus the value of all cards melded, minus the value of all cards still in hands.

GAME BONUSES	POINTS
Going Out	100
Going Out "Concealed"	200
Each Red 3	100
All Four Red 3s	800
Each Mixed Canasta	300
Each Natural Canasta	500

You also earn points for each red 3 played on the table (800 points total if you meld all four). If your team didn't meld, then each of your red 3s scores -100 points (-800 points if you happen to hold all four).

Keep in mind that any points scored in a natural or mixed canasta are added to the card values; for example a natural canasta of seven 8s is worth 500 points for the canasta, plus 70 points for the seven 8s, for 570 total points.

Going out *concealed* means you go out in a single turn, including playing your mandatory canasta. In other words, to earn this bonus, you may not have melded or added any cards to your partner's melds, and you must play a canasta in your final turn. Also keep in mind that if you go out concealed and your partner has not yet melded, you must also meet the initial melding requirements!

Games of Canasta are typically played to 5,000 points.

∾ **HOW TO PLAY** The player to the left of the dealer starts by drawing a card (either from the stock or the top card in the discard pile); making melds; and then discarding one card from the hand, face up, on top of the discard pile. The turn then proceeds clockwise.

To create melds, players take cards from their hand and place them on the table, face up, in sets of three or more cards of equal rank (e.g., 5♥-5♦-5♠ or 9♦-9♣-Joker). Keep in mind:

Melds must have at least two *natural* cards.

Each team may not meld more than one set of the same rank; instead, additional cards must be melded onto the original set.

Each team may build on their own existing melds, for example, adding 5♣ to an existing 5♥-5♦-5♠ set. They may never build on the opposing team's melds.

A set of three of four *black* 3s (e.g., 3♠-3♠-3♣) without wild cards may be melded on a player's last turn, on which they go out. Otherwise, black 3s may not be melded. Moreover, if a player discards 3♠ or 3♣, the next player may draw only from the stock (he may not take the discarded black 3).

Red 3s are bonus cards; if you have one, place it face up on the table on your next turn and take a replacement card from the stock.

INITIAL MELD REQUIREMENTS   The first meld made by either team must meet a minimum value, based on their score at the start of the hand:

Scores below 0 must meld at least 15 points

Scores from 0 to 1,495 must meld at least 50 points

Scores from 1,500 to 2,995 must meld at least 90 points

Scores of 3,000 or more must meld at least 120 points

Bonuses do *not* count toward initial meld requirements. So any points you may earn from a canasta or a red 3 does not count; even with a seven-card canasta in hand, you may not meld it if the value of the cards within the canasta do not meet or exceed your initial meld requirements.

∾ **DISCARD PILE**   You may not take the topmost discard without also taking the entire discard pile. In fact, to take a card from the discard pile, you must meld the pile's topmost card in the very same hand, either to create a new set (containing at least one natural card, in addition to the discard) or to build on an existing set (again, the existing set must contain at least one natural card). As long as you meet these requirements, you may meld as many cards as you like from the discard pile. Any cards not melded go into your hand.

The discard pile is considered *frozen* against either team if they have not yet melded an initial set, or against both teams whenever the discard pile contains 3♥, 3♦, or a wild card. When the pile is frozen, it may be taken only if the top card is immediately melded with a *natural* set of equal rank from your hand. For example, if the pile is frozen and the top card is 8♣, you may take the discard pile only if you play a new set of natural eights including the 8♣.

∾ **CANASTAS** A canasta is a meld of seven or more cards of equal rank (e.g., 8♥-8♥-8♣-8♣-8♦-8♦-8♠). The canasta is *natural* when it contains no wild cards, otherwise it is considered *mixed*. A mixed canasta may contain no more than three wild cards. Teams are not allowed to go out until they meld one canasta.

When a canasta is played, place the cards in a pile, and put a red card on top if it's natural, a black card on top if it's mixed. Continue building natural cards onto the canasta; you may also build wild cards as long as you don't exceed the three-wild-card maximum.

∾ **GOING OUT** Once your team has at least one canasta, you may go out by melding all your cards or by melding all but one and discarding the last card. Remember that players going out are allowed to meld black 3s on that final turn. You may also complete the required canasta and go out on the same turn.

If you go out, all cards in your partner's hand count against your total score— so it's not always wise to go out too quickly. If you are able to go out but are unsure if it's a good time (e.g., your partner may be holding high-point cards such as jokers and aces), you are allowed to ask your partner, "should I go out?" You may ask this question only immediately after drawing from the stock or taking the discard pile, and before making any melds (not including the required meld of the top discard, if applicable). Your partner answers "yes" or "no," and the answer is binding. If your partner says "yes," you must go out.

If the stock is exhausted and neither team has gone out, play continues as long as all players take the previous player's discard and meld it. In other words, players *must* take the discard if the pile is not frozen and if the discard matches any previous meld of that player's side. The game ends when a player is allowed to draw from the stock but cannot because the stock is empty.

∾ **IRREGULARITIES & DISPUTES** You lose 100 points any time you are forced to retract a card from the table—for example, if you mistakenly meld an invalid card, or if you accidentally expose a card from your hand during melding. If you play a meld that does not meet the initial melding requirements, your minimum initial score is increased by 10 points as a penalty. If you fail to declare a red 3—assuming you had a valid chance to declare it—you lose 500 points.

VARIATION 1: SAMBA CANASTA

Samba is team-based and closely follows the rules of the standard game. Start with three fifty-two-card decks, add six jokers (162 cards total), and deal each player fifteen cards. When drawing cards from the stock, players *always* take two cards and *always* discard only one.

In Samba, you may meld sequences of cards (8♣-7♣-6♣). Aces are always high, and 4 is the lowest card you may legally meld in a sequence. A seven-card sequence is called a *samba*, and it may not contain any wild cards. When melding sets, no more than two wild cards are allowed.

You may add natural cards from your hand to an existing canasta, but you may not take the top discard for this purpose. You and your partner may, however, meld more than one set of equal rank and use these cards to create canastas. So you may also mix and meld two sequences of cards to create a samba, as long as no more than seven cards are involved (e.g., you may not create a samba from a sequence of four with another sequence of four).

You are only allowed to take the topmost card in the discard pile in two situations: you immediately meld it with two natural cards of equal rank from your hand, or you immediately meld it with an *existing* sequence of fewer than seven cards. In the former scenario, you take the entire pile into your hand; in the latter, you take only the top card and leave the remainder of the discard pile "as is."

The initial melding requirements in Samba are:

Scores below 0 must meld at least 15 points

Scores from 0 to 1,495 must meld at least 50 points

Scores from 1,500 to 2,995 must meld at least 90 points

Scores from 3,000 to 6,995 must meld at least 120 points

Scores of 7,000 or more must meld at least 150 points

To go out, each team must meld a minimum of two canastas or sambas. The bonus for going out is 200 points. Sambas are worth 1,500 points. The bonus for declaring all six red 3s is 1,000 points. All other scoring is the same. Games of Samba are typically played to 10,000 points.

- -
VARIATION 2: BOLIVIA CANASTA

This is exactly like Samba Canasta, except that three or more wild cards may be melded on their own. And if you meld seven wild cards, it's called a *bolivia* and scores 2,500 points. The initial melding requirements are standardized at 150 points. When going out, a team must have at least one canasta and one samba. Games are played to 15,000 points.

- -
VARIATION 3: BRAZILIAN CANASTA

Brazil meets Bolivia in this screwball Canasta variation. Follow the rules of Bolivia and score bonuses of 2,000 points for a bolivia and 1,500 points for a samba. However, if you have melds on the table that are incomplete versions of the bolivia or samba (for example, if you meld six wild cards but not the seventh), deduct 1,000 points each from your score if the other team goes out.

The discard pile may not be taken to make the initial meld, and the initial meld requirements are steep: below 6,995 points you must meld 150 points; from 7,000 to 7,995 you must meld a canasta; from 8,000 to 8,995 you must meld a canasta within a meld of at least 200 points; and above 9,000 you must meld a natural canasta. Games are played to 10,000 points.

VARIATION 4: JOKER CANASTA

This is another team-based variation. Deal thirteen cards to each player. The discard pile is always frozen and may be taken only with a natural pair (you must meld the top card immediately with two natural cards of equal rank from your hand). You may meld wild cards as canastas, and each team needs two canastas to go out. Canastas, though, may never contain more than seven cards total.

The initial meld requirements are 100 points for scores below 2,995 points; 130 points for scores between 3,000 and 4,995; 150 points for scores above 5,000.

Black 3s function exactly like red 3s but are scored separately. The first 3 you declare in either color is worth 100 points; 300 points for the second; 500 points for the third; and 1,000 points for the fourth. The score for 3s is automatically subtracted from your game score, unless your team melds at least one canasta. If you hold seven 2s, score your team 4,000 points. Four jokers and three 2s are worth 3,000 points. Games are played to 8,500 points.

VARIATION 5: MEXICANA CANASTA

Follow the basic Canasta rules with the following twists. Start with three fifty-two-card decks plus six jokers (162 cards total). Deal thirteen cards to each player. The first member of each team who melds draws thirteen cards from the stock and adds them to his hand. The discard pile may not be taken when the top card is a 7. A canasta of 7s is worth 1,000 points. To go out, a team must meld two canastas and declare as many red 3s as they have canastas.

VARIATION 6: HAND & FOOT CANASTA

Here's another team-based variation, but unlike standard Canasta, this game only lasts for four deals (one by each player). Start with five fifty-two-card decks plus ten jokers (270 cards total), and deal each player two thirteen-card hands; the first is called the *hand*, the second is called the *foot*. The foot may not be played (or looked at) until the hand is played out. The remaining cards are the stock.

All players take two cards from the stock, and then discard only one. When picking up the discard pile, you may only take up to seven cards—and you may not take any cards at all if the top card is a 3. If you have not met your initial melding requirements, only the top discard counts against your minimum. And if the top discard is wild, you may pick up that card only with a matching set of wild cards from your hand.

Melds are known as either *clean* (no wild cards), *dirty* (up to two wild cards), or *wild* (nothing but wild cards). To go out, each team must have at least one wild meld. Seven-card melds are called *piles*—stack them in a neat pile, and top it with a red card (for a clean pile), a black card (for a dirty pile), or a joker (for a wild pile; use a 2 if it contains no joker).

In order to go out, a team must meld at least two dirty piles, two clean piles, and one wild pile with exactly seven cards in each. Each player also must have played at least one turn from his foot. If you meld all cards from your hand, immediately pick up your foot and continue play. Otherwise, meld all cards from your hand but one, discard it, then pick up the foot and use it on your next turn.

If you are going out, you must ask your partner's permission and, if it's given, meld all your remaining cards, or all but one and discard the last card. If your partner says "no," you must wait until the next turn to go out.

Card values are the same as those in standard Canasta. Bonus points are as follows:

    1,500 points for each "wild pile"

    700 points for each "clean pile"

    300 points for each "dirty pile"

    100 points for each red 3

    100 points for going out

The game lasts four rounds only, so each player deals once. The initial melding requirements are: 50 points in Round 1; 90 points in Round 2; 120 points in Round 3; 150 points in Round 4.

VARIATION 7: OKLAHOMA CANASTA

Rummy meets Canasta in this superb—and popular—Canasta variation. There are no teams here. Instead, two to five players compete as individuals. Two decks are used, plus one joker (105 cards total), and all players are dealt thirteen cards.

The standard rules of melding apply, but in Oklahoma Canasta you may also meld sequences of three or four cards. Aces are played high or low in sequences. Another key difference from standard Canasta is that melds may not grow to more than four cards.

The joker and all 2s are still wild. The only difference is that—as in Rummy— you must nominate a suit and rank when playing a wild card. Other players may subsequently take the joker into their hand (not the 2s, just the joker), as long as they swap it with the nominated card.

The Q♠ may be discarded only on your last turn (e.g., you may not discard Q♠ as long as you can discard any other card). Each player calculates score by adding the value of the cards melded and subtracting it from the value of the cards left in her hand. The player who goes out earns a 100-point bonus. Card values are:

CARDS	POINTS
Joker Melded	100
Joker Left in Hand	200
2 Melded as 8 through King	10
2 Melded as 3 through 7	5
2 Left in Hand	20
Q♠ Melded	50
Q♠ Left in Hand	100
Ace	20
K, Q, J, 10, 9, 8	10
7, 6, 5, 4, 3	5

Games are typically played to 1,000 points, and the winner earns a 200-point bonus (used for multigame campaigns).

VARIATION 8: TWO-HAND CANASTA

Follow the rules of the basic game, but obviously there is no team play—players compete head to head. Deal fifteen cards each, and always draw two cards from the stock (but still discard just one). Players may not go out until they have melded at least two canastas.

VARIATION 9: THREE-HAND CANASTA

In Three-Hand Canasta, everybody plays for themselves. However, in each round, two players form a temporary partnership against the *lone hand*. Deal thirteen cards each, and always draw two cards from the stock (but discard just one). Players may not go out until they have melded at least two canastas. The first player to take the discard pile becomes the lone hand. The others play in temporary partnership and may combine melds and work together. If a player goes out before the discard pile is taken up, that player is by default the lone hand.

The initial meld requirements are player specific, so each player is likely to have a different point requirement. The players each have a column on the score pad—the lone hand scores his own points, the opposition scores their total points. However, red 3s only score for the individual players and not for the ad hoc team.

Once the stock is exhausted, the round ends once the player who drew the last card of the stock discards. If the stock is empty and the discard pile was never taken, there is no lone hand, and each player earns his individual score. Games are played to 7,500 points.

Euchre

Euchre is a quintessentially American game, even though it is played throughout English-speaking countries and owes many features to ancient German trick-taking games. The first references to Euchre came from the Pennsylvania Dutch; thereafter it moved up the East Coast and into the American Midwest, where it is still among the most popular and commonly played games.

There is no global standard for Euchre. The game is played differently in Canada, Britain, Australia, and even within the United States. The rules below cover the four-player partnership version of Euchre, a.k.a. "standard" Euchre, sometimes called North American Euchre.

☙ **HOW TO DEAL** Start with a fifty-two-card deck, and remove all 2s through 6s, for a total of thirty-two cards. Deal each player five cards in batches of 3-2. The dealer finishes by turning up the bottom card of the deck (this is the turn-up card).

☙ **CARD RANKINGS** The jack of trump (called *right bower*) is always the highest-ranking trump, followed by the jack of the suit matching the color of the trump (called *left bower*). So, if clubs are trump, the card rankings are (high to low): J♣, J♠, A♣, K♣, Q♣, 10♣, 9♣, 8♣, 7♣. In non-trump suits, cards rank (high to low) from A to 7, not including the jack if it is left bower.

The left bower is considered trump in all aspects. When clubs are trump, for example, the J♠ may not follow a spade lead (unless you are void in clubs and intentionally mean to trump the spade lead) and, when J♠ leads a trick, clubs must follow (not spades).

∾ SCORING The goal is to score 5 game points. Points are awarded for winning at least three of the five tricks in each round. If the *making* side (see below) wins three or four tricks, they score 1 point; if they win all five tricks, it's called a *march* and earns 2 points (a lone maker scores 4 points for march).

The making team is *euchred* if they fail to win at least three tricks. The defending team earns 2 points for a euchre. A lone defender scores 2 points for three or four tricks, 4 points for a euchre.

∾ HOW TO PLAY Starting to the left of the dealer, each player has an opportunity to accept or decline the proposed trump suit (indicated by the suit of the turn-up card). Players say either "I order it up" to accept (dealer's partner says "I assist" to accept), or "pass." The dealer alone accepts trump with a proclamation of "I take it up." If the turn-up is accepted, the game starts immediately and the dealer is allowed to swap a card in her hand for the turn-up.

If all players pass, the turn-up card is placed face down and the player to the left of the dealer nominates any suit as trump (except the suit just passed on), followed by all players having a chance to accept or decline the newly proposed trump suit. If no player accepts the trump suit in the second round, the dealer must choose trump.

Whichever player accepts trump is called the *maker*; the opposing team is called the *defenders*. If the maker has a strong hand, he may declare "I play alone," which automatically **force-folds** his partner. If this happens, either partner on the defending team may reply "I defend alone," which force-folds the defending partner.

The first trick is led by the player to the left of the dealer, no matter which player is the maker. The only exception is if the maker is playing alone—in this case, the first trick is led by the player to the left of the maker. All other players must follow suit if possible; otherwise they may play any card. Tricks are won by the highest trump played or, if none, by the highest card in the leading suit. The trick winner leads the next trick.

HOW TO WIN You should "go for maker" when holding any three trump cards. It's more risky—but still common—to go for maker holding an ace and king. In games where the score is 4-1 or 4-2 in your favor, it's worth going for maker even with a weak hand. At worst, you lose 2 points; at best, you win or prevent the defending team from winning with a lone-player bonus.

Never hold off playing a winning card on the assumption that the card will be even more useful later. And never ever play a higher card than your partner, or trump a trick that your partner is already winning.

IRREGULARITIES & DISPUTES The worst transgression in Euchre is failing to follow suit when you can. There is no penalty if you fix the error before the next trick is played. Otherwise, the cards remain as played and score -2 points for the penalty. Table talk is off-limits. If you break this taboo by discussing strategy or your cards, the opposing team may name a suit for your team to lead on the next hand! If you accidentally pass or bid out of turn, your team loses the right to bid on the hand.

- -
VARIATION 1: 24-CARD EUCHRE
This is the most common form of Euchre played in the American Midwest. The rules are identical to the standard game. The main difference is the deck: start with fifty-two cards, and remove all 2s through 8s, for a total of twenty-four cards. Games are typically played to 10 points.

- -
VARIATION 2: 25-CARD EUCHRE
This is the version of the game most commonly played in Britain. The rules are essentially identical to 24-Card Euchre, except that one joker—called *best bower*—is added to the deck. The best bower is always the highest trump, ranking above right bower. When the jack is the turn-up card, hearts are the proposed suit.

- -
VARIATION 3: HASENPFEFFER EUCHRE
Follow the rules for 25-Card Euchre, but deal each player six cards. The last card, left face down on the table, is the *widow*. The player to the left of the

dealer starts a round of bidding. All players bid only once, from 1 to 6, and highest bid wins. If all players pass, the bid is forced at 3 to the player holding the joker.

The bid winner takes the widow, names a trump suit, replaces the widow with any card from her hand, and leads the first trick. Games are played to 10 points. If the bidding team achieves their bid, they score 1 point for each trick won. Otherwise, they lose the amount of their bid.

VARIATION 4: THREE-HAND EUCHRE
Got three players? You can play Euchre (follow the standard rules) with two simple modifications. The trump maker always plays alone against the other two players, who form a temporary partnership as defenders. And the maker scores 3 points for a march while the defenders each score 2 points for euchres.

VARIATION 5: SIX-HAND EUCHRE
Two teams of three compete head to head here. Start with the thirty-two-card Euchre deck and add one joker (which is always the highest trump). If a maker wants to play alone, the maker's two partners discard their hands face down, and the lone maker can ask either one for a card. A card is given—without discussion or consultation—from the partner to the maker, and the maker discards a single card in return. A march and a euchre score 3 points instead of the standard 2; for a lone maker, the scores are 6 points each, instead of the standard 4. Games are played to 10 points.

VARIATION 6: CALL-ACE EUCHRE
This is an old-fashioned version of Euchre, and rarely played. Don't let that stop you—it's plenty of fun and can be played by four to six players. Follow the standard rules, but once a maker is selected, he nominates any suit (trump or not), and the player holding the highest card of that suit secretly becomes the maker's partner. It's secret because the maker's partner does not announce herself. It will simply become obvious at some point during the round.

There are two exceptions. First, the maker may declare "I play alone," and play without assistance. Second, the maker plays alone if he happens to hold the highest card in the nominated suit. Again, this isn't known immediately—the maker may think he has an anonymous partner in the game, but he does not! When the maker has a partner, score points for the making team and the defending team exactly as in the standard game. When the maker has no partner, each defender scores her own points. In games of five or six players, a team that scores a march earns 3 points.

PEDRO

| DIFFICULTY *low* | TIME LENGTH *medium* | DECKS 1 |

Pedro evolved from the older Italian game of Briscola. While you could argue that Pedro is merely a simplified version of Briscola, that's not giving Pedro its due. The game is fast-paced, competitive without being ruthless, and makes an excellent introduction into partnership trick-taking games.

∾ **HOW TO DEAL** Start with a fifty-two-card deck, and deal nine cards to each player, in batches of three. Card ranking is standard, with aces always high.

The 5 of trump is called *pedro*; the *low pedro* is the 5 of the suit of matching color (e.g., when clubs are trump, 5♣ is pedro, 5♠ is low pedro). The low pedro acts as a trump, ranking below the pedro but above the 4 of trump. When hearts are trump, for example, cards rank (high to low): A♥-K♥-Q♥-J♥-10♥-9♥-8♥-7♥-6♥-5♥ (Pedro)-5♦ (Low Pedro)-4♥-3♥-2♥.

∾ **SCORING** The goal is to score 62 points. In each hand a total of 14 possible points are awarded to the team who captures:

CARDS	POINTS
Pedro	5
Low Pedro	5
Ace of trump	1
Jack of trump	1
10 of trump	1
2 of trump	1

The opponents of the bidding team add any points won to their score. The bidding team does the same if their bid is achieved; otherwise, the bid amount is deducted from their score. It is called *bidder goes out* when both teams each have 55 or more points. On the next hand, the bidding team wins if they achieve their bid. Otherwise, the hand is scored as normal.

∾ **HOW TO PLAY**   Each player has one opportunity to bid or pass, starting from the left of the dealer. Bids are from 7 to 14 points, and the highest bid between partners wins out. The dealer is forced to play a bid of 7 if all other players pass.

The bid winner names a trump suit (she may not consult her partner). Once trump is settled, all players discard all *non-trump* cards from their hands. Each player states how many cards he needs to create a six-card hand (players holding six or more trumps keep them all), and receives the appropriate number of replacements from the deck. The dealer always goes last and is allowed to "rob" the deck—to look at the deck and take all remaining trump (in some cases, the dealer may end up with more than six cards in his hand). If the deck is short of trump, the dealer may take any other cards as replacements.

The bid winner leads the first trick. Players must follow suit (if possible) or play trump. If you can do neither, only then it is OK to play cards from another suit. Tricks are won by the highest trump or, if none, by the highest card in the leading suit. The trick winner leads the next trick.

If any player starts the round holding more than six cards, she dumps all excess cards on the first trick. This way, at the start of the second trick, all players are holding five cards. When dumping excess cards, it's customary to place them in a stack with the card on top played face up to the trick, and the excess cards hidden from view. You are not allowed to dump any point-earning trumps as excess.

Remember that low pedro counts as a trump when leading tricks. So, when hearts are trump, a player leading 5♦ (low pedro) is leading a heart, and hearts must follow. Scores are tallied once all cards have been played. Deal rotates to the left.

VARIATION 1: KING PEDRO

This could easily be called "Pedro Gone Wild." The main difference between the games is points, which are bigger and badder in King Pedro. The king of trump is worth 30 points, which increases the possible points per round from 14 to 44. The 2 of trump is won by the team that plays it, whereas the other trumps are won as usual by the team capturing them in tricks.

Deal twelve cards to each player, and deal four cards face down to the kitty. The highest bidder names trump and takes the kitty. All players reduce their hands to six cards and dump any excess trump in the first trick-taking round. When trumps are led, players must follow suit. When non-trumps are led, players may play any card (including trump). When a player has no more trumps left, he must declare "I'm up!" and throw down his hand. He's out of the game until the next hand is dealt.

The object is to score 200 points, and to do this on a bid you've just won. You cannot win the game unless your team is the bid winner, even if your score is above 200 points.

VARIATION 2: CINCH

Cinch retains many of Pedro's basic features, and varies mainly in the method of scoring. Follow the standard Pedro rules, with the following exceptions. The 5 of trump is called *right pedro*; the 5 of the suit of matching color is the *left pedro*.

The goal is to score 51 total points. A team that achieves its bid scores the bid amount minus the opposing team's score. For example, a bid of 8 scores 2 points (8 − 6 = 2), a bid of 10 scores 6 points (10 − 4 = 6). It's possible for a successful bid to result in points for the opposing team. For example, a bid of 6 scores 2 points for the opposing team (6 − 8 = -2 points, scored as +2 to the opposing team). If a team fails to make their bid, the opposing team scores the points they won plus the amount of the bid.

In Cinch, bids are from 1 to 14 points, and the bid is won when three players in a row pass. If all players have passed, the dealer names a trump suit but is not required to play for a specific bid target.

Once trump is settled, all players discard non-trump cards as usual. In the rare case when a player is initially dealt more than seven trumps, he must dump trump in order to create a six-card hand. If the deck has more trump than the dealer can use to make a six-card hand, the dealer leaves the unused trump on the table, face up, for all players to see.

PINOCHLE

DIFFICULTY *high*	TIME LENGTH *medium*	DECKS 1

Pinochle is a family of games, much like Solitaire and Canasta. The most popular form of the game—and the one described first below—is Four-Hand Pinochle (Single Deck), which uses a single deck of Pinochle cards. The game is sometimes called Partnership Auction Pinochle, because it is played by two teams competing head to head.

Pinochle is an American invention. It evolved on the East Coast in the 1850s and '60s from the French game Bezique and the German game Skat. Pinochle remains extremely popular, both in its four-player and three-player incarnations.

∾ **HOW TO DEAL** Start with a forty-eight-card Pinochle deck. Note that Pinochle decks are not the same as standard fifty-two-card decks. You can buy a Pinochle deck, or create your own as follows: take two fifty-two-card decks with the same design backings, remove all 2s through 8s, and shuffle the cards together. This results in a forty-eight-card deck with duplicates of every card. In Pinochle, cards rank (high to low) A, 10, K, Q, J, 9.

The dealer gives each player twelve cards, face down. The dealer may choose to deal cards one at a time or in batches of two or three, as long as the deal is consistent throughout the game.

∾ **SCORING**   Teams score 1 point for every "counter" (every ace, 10, or king) won in hand play; there are 24 total counter points. Whichever team wins the last trick earns 1 bonus point.

To calculate each team's total score, follow this formula: melding points + counter points = total score. For the bid winners, if their total score is greater or equal to their bid, the total is officially added to their game score. If their total score is less than their bid, they are *set* and the bid value is subtracted from their game score (meld and counter points are simply discarded). For the opponents, their total score is added to their game score as long as they earn at least one counter point. Otherwise, their meld points are discarded.

Games of Pinochle are typically played to 250 points. If both teams score 250 points in the same hand, the highest overall score wins.

∾ **HOW TO PLAY**   Start with a round of bidding (or auction) with the player to the left of the dealer. The minimum bid is 15 points and must be raised by one or more points by subsequent players. A bid winner emerges after three players in a row pass. The bid winner then nominates a trump suit for the round.

The bid itself is an estimate of how many points you may possibly meld, plus the number of "counters" (aces, 10s, and kings) you may win during the hand play. If all players pass, the dealer is forced to bid the minimum 15 points.

Next, the partner of the bid winner selects four cards from her hand and passes them to the bid winner, face down. The bid winner reviews the passed cards and then reciprocates by passing back four (inevitably mediocre) cards to his partner. The non-bidding team does not pass cards.

∾ **MELDING**   The next step is scoring melds. Each player lays his melds directly in front of him on the table. Partners add their resulting scores together, and all melds are picked up and returned to their original hands. Valid Pinochle melds are:

RUN (15 POINTS)   A-10-K-Q-J, the jack must be trump

DOUBLE RUN (150 POINTS)   A-A-10-10-K-K-Q-Q-J-J, both jacks must be trump

PINOCHLE (4 POINTS) Q♠-J♦

DOUBLE PINOCHLE (30 POINTS) Q♠-Q♠-J♦-J♦

ACES AROUND (10 POINTS) Four aces, one from each suit

DOUBLE ACES AROUND (100 POINTS) All eight aces

KINGS AROUND (8 POINTS) Four kings, one from each suit

DOUBLE KINGS AROUND (80 POINTS) All eight kings

QUEENS AROUND (6 POINTS) Four queens, one from each suit

DOUBLE QUEENS AROUND (60 POINTS) All eight queens

JACKS AROUND (4 POINTS) Four jacks, one from each suit

DOUBLE JACKS AROUND (40 POINTS) All eight jacks

MARRIAGE (2 POINTS) K-Q of same suit (not trump)

TRUMP MARRIAGE (4 POINTS) K-Q of trump suit

ROUND ROBIN (24 POINTS) A marriage in every suit

9 OF TRUMP (1 POINT) Each 9 of trumps scores 1 point

Partners may not pool cards together or meld on each other's cards. However, within their own hands, players may meld the same card more than once, as long as the melds are of different types. For example, the jack of diamonds may be used in a run, a Pinochle, and Jacks Around; however, a king and two suited queens do not count as two marriages.

∾ **HAND PLAY** After all melds are scored and returned to the hands, the bid winner leads the first trick with any card. Subsequent players must play a higher card in the same suit. If they cannot, their options are (in order of priority):

Play any lower card in the same suit

Play trump and beat any trumps already played

Play any lower trump

Play any other card

> *Shooting the moon* is a good way to increase the value of your Pinochle hand. Once all melds are scored but before hand play starts, the bid winner may declare "shoot the moon," and thus commit the bidding team to win each and every trick in hand play. They score 25 bonus points if successful. If they fail, it's equivalent to a set: the value of their bid is deducted from their game score, along with a -25 point penalty, and their melds and counter points are discarded.

Tricks are won by the highest trump or, if trumps were not played, by the highest card in the leading suit. If duplicate cards are played, the trick is won by whichever card was played first. When a trick is won, remove it from the table and place the cards face down in front of the trick winner. Trick winners lead the following trick. Scores are tallied once all cards are played. The deal rotates clockwise.

∾ **IRREGULARITIES & DISPUTES** If any player bids out of turn, the bid is void and his team may not bid again in the round. Any time a card is accidentally exposed during play, it is left face up on the table and *must be played* at the first possible opportunity. In hand play, if any player fails to follow suit, play a higher trump, etc., there is no penalty if the error is detected and corrected prior to the start of the next trick. In all other cases, the offending team stops earning counter points the moment the error is detected. The offending team keeps any counters already scored, but does not receive credit for any new counters earned, even if that means forfeiting their meld points.

- -
VARIATION 1: FOUR-HAND PINOCHLE (DOUBLE DECK)
Some Pinochle players prefer double-deck games because of the increased melding possibilities. This game is played exactly like the single-deck version above, with just a few key differences. The first is the deck. You need either two standard Pinochle decks with all 9s removed, or four standard fifty-two-card decks with all 2s through 9s removed, shuffled together. Either way, the final deck should contain eighty cards, have only cards ranking A, 10, K, Q, J, and have four identical copies of each card. All players are then dealt twenty cards.

There are no changes to the bidding rules, except that the opening bid must be at least 50, you bid by 1s until you reach 60, and bids above 60 are in multiples of five. The bid winner must hold at least a marriage in his nominated trump suit; otherwise he is set.

Games are typically played to 500 points. Valid melds in double-deck Pinochle are:

Runs (A-10-K-Q-J of same suit) earn 15 points. Score 150 points for two runs, 225 points for three runs, 300 points for four runs.

Aces (one each of different suits) earn 10 points. Score 100 points for having two each of different suits, 150 points for having three each of different suits, 200 points for having all 20 aces.

Kings (one each of different suits) earn 8 points. Score 80 points for having two each of different suits, 120 points for having three each of different suits, 160 points for having all 20 kings.

Queens (one each of different suits) earn 6 points. Score 60 points for having two each of different suits, 90 points for having three each of different suits, 120 points for having all 20 queens.

Jacks (one each of different suits) earn 4 points. Score 40 points for having two each of different suits, 60 points for having three each of different suits, 80 points for having all 20 jacks.

Pinochles (Q♠-J♦) earn 4 points. Score 30 points for two Pinochles, 60 points for three Pinochles, 90 points for four Pinochles.

Marriages (K-Q of same suit) earn 2 points each in non-trump suits, 4 points each in the trump suit.

- -
VARIATION 2: THREE-HAND PINOCHLE
This game is much more than simply "Plan B" whenever three Pinochle players can't find a fourth player. In fact, if ever a vote were held for Best Three-Hand Card Game Ever Invented, Three-Hand Pinochle (sometimes called Auction Pinochle or Cutthroat Pinochle) just might win. Follow the rules for the standard game, with the following modifications.

A forty-eight-card Pinochle deck is used (A-10-K-Q-J-9). Players are dealt fifteen cards each, and three cards are dealt on the table, face down, to a *widow* hand. Three-Hand Pinochle is typically played for money. All players start with an equal number of chips, typically along the lines of: 20 white chips (worth 1 unit each), 18 red chips (worth 5 units each), 5 blue chips (worth 10 units each). It's up to the players to decide how much a "unit" is worth (5 or 10 cents per unit is fairly common). Before cards are dealt, all players typically ante 5 or 10 units.

Bidding starts at 20. The bid winner exchanges three cards with the widow hand. The bid winner is allowed to forfeit the game *before* picking up the widow, but must pay a penalty to the pot of the bid value (see below; if the base unit = 10 cents, a bid value of 1 = 10 cents). The bid winner may also forfeit *after* looking at the widow; in this case he payed the pot and each player the bid value.

Only the bid winner melds in Three-Hand Pinochle. If the bid winner meets or beats his bid, the other players each pay him the bid value. If the bid value is 35 or greater, the bid winner is also paid the bid value from the pot. All bid values are doubled when spades are trump.

BID	BID VALUE
20 to 24	1
25 to 29	2
30 to 34	4
35 to 39	7
40 to 44	10
45 to 49	13
50 to 54	16
55 or more	20

The bid winner must win at least one counter in hand play, otherwise he is set. In some cases, the bid winner must also earn counters in order to make his bid. Either way, the opponents' goal is to prevent the bid winner from making the bid. Hand play stops the moment the bid winner makes his bid or is set. At that point, scores are tallied and all payoffs made. The deal rotates to the left, and the game continues until one player is out of chips (at which point the earning are divided between the other two players, depending on how many chips each is holding), or until a time limit passes (say, 30 or 45 minutes).

PISTI

DIFFICULTY *low*	TIME LENGTH *medium*	DECKS 1

Besides being the national card game of Turkey, Pisti (pronounced pishti) is one of the few partnership games where both the suits themselves and the hierarchy of cards within each suit are irrelevant. If anything, Pisti resembles a game such as Snap, but with room for a lot more strategy.

∾ **HOW TO DEAL**   It's traditional to deal (and play) in a counterclockwise direction. Start with a fifty-two-card deck, and deal four cards face down to the kitty, plus a batch of four cards to each player. Turn up the bottom card of the deck for all players to see. The remaining cards are the stock.

∾ **SCORING**   The goal is to be the first team to score 151 points. Points are awarded for the following cards captured during play:

CARDS	POINTS
10♦	3
2♣	2
Aces	1
Jacks	1

In addition, the team capturing a majority of cards (twenty-seven or more) scores 3 points. If both teams capture twenty-six cards, no points are awarded.

A *pisti*, worth 10 bonus points, is scored when the pile contains just one card that is captured by a card of equal rank. When a jack captures a lone jack, the pisti bonus is doubled to 20. You may score a pisti at any point in the game except on the very first and very last cards played. Turn the capturing card face up in your pile as a way to remember your pisti bonus—and to deflate your opponents' morale.

∾ **HOW TO PLAY** The dealer turns up one of the kitty cards to start a discard pile (turn up a second kitty card if the first is a jack).

Starting to the right of the dealer and moving counterclockwise, each player tries to capture the discard pile for her own team. You capture the pile by playing a card matching the rank of the topmost discard (7 captures 7, queen captures queen, etc.). Playing any jack captures the entire pile, regardless of the topmost discard's rank. Place captured cards in a pile, face down, in front of either team member. If you cannot capture the pile, play a card from your hand onto the discard pile. The next player now must match the card you've just played in order to capture the pile.

When the discard pile is captured for the first time, the winning team also takes the remaining face-down kitty cards; you may look at the kitty cards (the opposing team may not) before placing them in your capture pile. The next player in rotation then throws a card from her hand to start a new discard pile, and play continues in a counterclockwise direction.

When all players are out of cards, deal another batch of four cards to each player (do not deal any additional kitty cards). With four players, there are enough cards for three rounds. The exposed stock card is always dealt to the dealer on the last hand.

At the end of the game, the remaining cards in the discard pile are taken by the team who most recently captured a pile. Scores are tallied, and the deal moves to the right.

- -
VARIATION: TWO-HAND PISTI
Two-Hand Pisti is a surprisingly decent game for two players. The rules are identical to the main game. The only difference is there are six rounds (instead of three).

ROOK

DIFFICULTY *low*	TIME LENGTH *medium*	DECKS 1

The Parker Brothers' game company was founded in 1883; their first commercial success came in 1906 with the publication of the card game Rook. It took America by storm and was, at least until the release of Monopoly in 1935, the Parker Brothers' most profitable invention. The original game was played with a deck of fifty-seven cards; nowadays a standard fifty-two-card deck is used, with the addition of one joker.

∾ **HOW TO DEAL** Start with a fifty-two-card deck, and add one joker (the "rook"). Deal each player thirteen cards, and place the final card face down on the table. Card rankings are standard, with ace always high. The joker acts as the lowest card in the trump suit, below the 2 of trump.

∾ **SCORING** The object is to score 1,000 points. If the bid winners meet or exceed their bid, they score the value of the original bid. If they fail, they lose the value of the original bid.

Cards have the following values: 20 points for the joker, 15 points for each ace, 10 points for each 10 and king, 5 points for each 5. The other cards have no value. So a deck contains 180 total points, not including a 20-point bonus for winning the last trick and a 100 point bonus if a team wins all thirteen tricks.

∾ **HOW TO PLAY** The game starts with a round of bidding, starting from the left of the dealer. Players may either pass or bid from 70 (the minimum) upward in increments of 5. The bid is won when three players in a row pass. If all four players pass, the hand is dead and new cards are dealt.

The bid winner is allowed to swap any card in her hand with the face-down card on the table. The discard is part of the other team's hand, and counts toward their points. Each player then passes three cards to the left on the first deal, to the right on the second deal; the third deal is a keeper with no cards passed, and the cycle starts again. The bid winner then declares a trump suit—and she may not look at any cards being passed to her until after she nominates trump.

The player to the left of the dealer leads the first trick. All other players must follow suit if they can; otherwise they may play any card. Tricks are won by the highest trump or, if none, by the highest card in the leading suit. The trick winner leads the next trick. Once all cards are played, scores are tallied and the deal rotates left.

- -

VARIATION 1: 200

The mechanics of the game are identical to standard Rook. However, you play with fewer cards: take a fifty-two-card deck, and remove all 2s, 3s, 4s, and 6s, for a total of thirty-six cards. There is no joker.

Deal each player nine cards (there is no kitty). Bidding starts at a minimum of 50 points. The deck contains 100 total points: 10 points for each ace and 10, 5 points for each 5. The other cards have no value. There is no bonus for last trick or winning all the tricks.

Games are played to 200 points. Unlike in standard Rook, the bid winners keep all the points they earn in tricks as long as they meet their bid. The opposing team similarly keeps all the points they score in tricks, *unless* their cumulative score is more than 100 points. When this happens, at least one partner must participate in the bidding for his points to count. Otherwise his points are ignored.

- -

VARIATION 2: CALL PARTNER ROOK

Unlike standard Rook, the "call partner" version dispenses with fixed teams. Instead, in each hand the bid winner nominates a trump suit, and then selects any card not in his hand. Whichever player holds this card becomes the temporary partner of the bid winner.

The twist? The identity of this partner is held in secret and not disclosed, at least until it becomes obvious during the course of play. At the end of the hand, the nonbidding players each score whatever points they won in tricks. If the bidding team meets or exceeds their bid, they each score the amount of the bid. If they fail, they each lose the amount of the bid.

SPADES

DIFFICULTY *low*	TIME LENGTH *medium*	DECKS 1

There are strong hints of Bridge, Whist, and Hearts in the game of Spades. And yet, perhaps surprisingly, the game seems to have evolved on its own in the American South circa 1930. Over the years, Spades has come and gone, and come back again in terms of popularity. It's possibly the easiest of all partner-based trump-taking games, largely because the trump suit is always spades.

∾ **HOW TO DEAL** Start with a fifty-two-card deck, and deal thirteen cards to each player. Card rankings are standard, with aces always high.

∾ **SCORING** The objective is to be the first team to score 500 points. Points are awarded for meeting or exceeding your team's bid. Score ten times the bid value plus 1 point for each extra trick (known as ***overtricks***). If you and your teammate, for example, bid a total of seven and ultimately capture eight tricks, you score 71 (the bid of 7 x 10, plus 1 for the overtrick). You should avoid taking too many overtricks—each time a side accumulates ten overtricks, 100 points are deducted from their score.

If you fail to meet your bid, you lose ten times the bid value. If you successfully bid nil (see following page), score your team 100 points. If you bid nil but fail, subtract 100 points from your team's score. If you ***shoot the moon***, your team scores 200 points (for making it) or -200 points (for failing).

∾ **HOW TO PLAY** Spades are always trump. Each hand begins with a round of bidding, starting from the left of the dealer. You and your partner are bidding on how many total tricks you may win. This is not competitive bidding—you are not required to bid higher than the previous bid. Instead, each player bids once—and only once—and the bids are added together. For example: North opens with 3, East bids 1, South bids 4, West bids 3. The final bids are North-South for 7, East-West for 4.

A player may also bid *nil*, which means they cannot win a single trick. If your partner bids nil, you still must try to win the amount of your own bid. A team may also *shoot the moon* by bidding thirteen tricks.

The player to the left of the dealer leads the first card, which may be any suit except spades. All other players must follow suit if they can. Otherwise, they may play any card. Tricks are won by the highest spade or, if none, by the highest card in the leading suit. The trick winner leads the next trick.

Spades may not lead a trick until they are "broken"—that is, until a spade is played on another suit (because the player had no cards in the suit that was led), or because the trick leader has no other cards except spades in his hand. When all cards are played, scores are tallied and the deal rotates clockwise.

VARIATION 1: THREE-HAND SPADES

It is possible to satisfy a Spades craving with only three players. Each plays for herself and starts the game with seventeen cards (instead of thirteen). The extra card is set aside and does not count. The player holding 2♣ leads the first trick. All other rules are identical to the main game, except scoring for overtricks, which count against your bid. For example, if you bid six and win seven tricks, you subtract the overtrick from your initial bid (6 − 1) and then multiply by 10 (5 x 10) for a final score of 50.

VARIATION 2: SIX-HAND SPADES

Spades makes a good six-player game. You compete in three teams of two, and two fifty-two-card decks are used (104 cards total). All other rules are identical to the basic game, except that when two identical cards are played in the same trick, the second (more recent) card wins.

WHIST

| DIFFICULTY *low* | TIME LENGTH *medium* | DECKS 1 |

Without rugby, there would be no American football. Without cricket, there would be no American baseball. Without Whist, there would be no Bridge, Contract Bridge, Auction Bridge, or any of the other Bridge-derived games that evolved from their common ancestor Whist.

In the eighteenth and nineteenth centuries, when Whist was at the height of its popularity, few people would have called it a simple game. Yet Whist is a simple game. This is surprising when you consider the complexity of its offspring.

∽ **HOW TO DEAL** Start with a fifty-two-card deck, and deal thirteen cards to each player. The final card is turned face up for all players to see and fixes trump for the round. The trump remains on the table until the dealer's first turn, at which point the dealer returns the trump card to his own hand. Card rankings are standard, with aces always high.

∽ **SCORING** Teams compete to be the first to score 7 points. Points are awarded only to the team winning more than six tricks, and 1 point is awarded for each trick in excess of six. If your team wins eight tricks, for example, you score 2 points $(8 - 6 = 2)$.

∽ **HOW TO PLAY** The player to the left of the dealer leads the first trick with any card. All other players must follow suit if they can; otherwise they may play any card (including trump). Dealer: Don't forget to pick up (and/or play) the trump card just before playing your very first card.

Tricks are won by the highest trump played or, if none, by the highest card in the leading suit. The trick winner leads the next trick. Scores are tallied after all thirteen tricks are played. The deal rotates left.

VARIATION 1: BRITISH WHIST

In Britain, where Whist is still very popular, it's far more common to play to 5 game points (instead of 7). Otherwise, the rules are identical.

VARIATION 2: HONORS WHIST

The nineteenth-century version of Whist typically awarded points for *honors*—the A, K, Q, J of trump. Any team that captures all four honor cards scores a bonus of 4 points, or a bonus of 2 points for capturing three of the four honor cards. When scoring points at the end of the hand, honor points are tallied *after* the normal trick scores. This means the team scoring for tricks wins, in cases where both teams score 5 points or more in the same hand. The final restriction is that a team that starts the hand with a score of 4 cannot earn any points for honors in that hand.

OTHER PARTNERSHIP GAME VARIATIONS

Many of the games covered in the *Ultimate Book of Card Games* have variations specifically for four players and two-team partnerships. Here's a complete list:

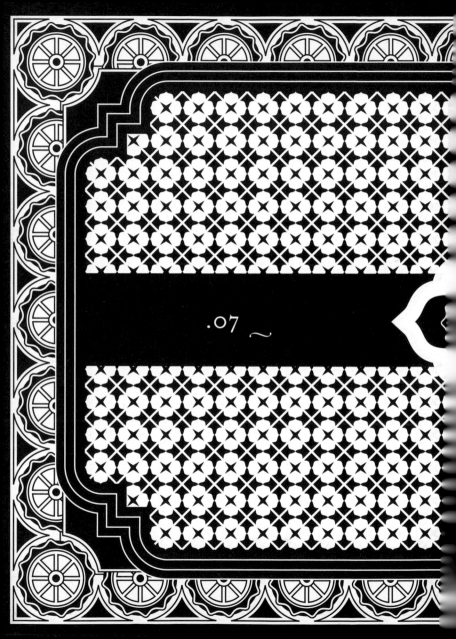

.07 ~

Multiplayer Games

CHAPTER SEVEN

Multiplayer Games

IT DOESN'T REALLY MATTER HOW MANY PLAYERS you bring to the table—the games in this chapter are highly adaptable. They also tend to favor "luck of the draw" over pure skill, because the number of cards dealt to each player is minimized (and, along with it, the role of strategy and long-term planning).

AGURK

| DIFFICULTY *low* | TIME LENGTH *medium* | DECKS 1 |

This game's name means "cucumber" in Danish, and there are variants of the game in both Finland and Sweden, also called "cucumber" in the local languages. Apparently the cucumber is bad luck in Scandinavia when it comes to cards— kind of like buying a "lemon" of a car in the United States.

∾ **NUMBER OF PLAYERS** 4 to 7

∾ **HOW TO DEAL** Start with a fifty-two-card deck, and deal seven cards to each player, face down. The remaining cards are set aside. Card ranking is standard, with aces always high.

∾ **SCORING** The goal is to avoid earning points. Points are scored by the player who wins the last trick of each seven-trick round. Points are determined by the value of the card that won the last trick: aces are 14 points, kings are 13, queens are 12, jacks are 11, and all numbered cards are worth their *index value*. A player who wins the last trick, say, with 10♠, scores 10 points. Note that scores may never drop below zero.

When a player scores 21 points, he "loses a life" (or "gets cucumbered"), and his score is reset to the next-highest score. For example, if player one has 16 points and player two scores 21 points, player two loses a life and her score is reset to 16. Player two continues playing until the second time she scores 21 points, at which point she is out of the game. Agurk continues until only one player is left.

∾ **HOW TO PLAY** The player to the left of the dealer leads the first trick. Simply place the card face up in front of you; everybody plays their cards the same way, and players may look at the cards in front of other players at any time.

The other players have two choices: meet or beat the rank of the previous card, or play their lowest-ranking card. If 7♥ leads, for example, the following player may play another 7, a higher-ranking card in any suit, or his lowest-ranking card in any suit. The highest card wins the trick. If cards of equal rank are played in the same trick, the most recently played high-card wins. Scores are tallied once all cards are played, and the deal shifts clockwise.

BRISCOLA

DIFFICULTY *low*	TIME LENGTH *medium*	DECKS 1

If you've spent any time in small Italian towns watching old men play cards, odds are they were playing Briscola. It's both the Italian word for "trump" and one of Italy's most popular card games.

Briscola is a simple multiplayer game, easy to learn and even easier to master. If you're not quickly charmed by Briscola, try Briscola Bastarda instead. The five-player variant (described on page 286) features a mystery card, an unknown partner, and three-against-two game play. Still not loving Briscola? That's OK, when all else fails, try the two-person game of Bura, which closely resembles this game but is more strategic.

∾ **NUMBER OF PLAYERS** 2 to 6

∾ **HOW TO DEAL** Start with a fifty-two-card deck, and remove all 8s, 9s, and 10s for a total of forty cards. For three-player games, remove one 2 from the deck, for a total of thirty-nine cards. For six-player games, remove all 2s from the deck, for a total of thirty-six cards. In Briscola, cards always rank (high to low) A, 3, K, Q, J, 7, 6, 5, 4, 2.

The dealer is chosen at random. Each player receives three cards dealt face down, one at a time. The dealer then turns over the top card to determine trump, and places that card at the bottom of the stock so that it remains partly visible.

∾ **SCORING** The goal is to win tricks that contain point cards. With 120 possible points in play (see scoring chart), the winner of each round is the player who scores 61 points or better. Briscola is typically played to the best of three or five games.

CARD VALUES	POINTS
Ace	11
3	10
King	4
Queen	3
Jack	2
7	0
6	0
5	0
4	0
2	0

∾ HOW TO PLAY The player to the left of the dealer leads the first trick, playing any card from her hand. The other players are not required to follow suit—with the caveat that a trick is won by the highest card of the leading suit, or by the highest trump played.

After each trick all players (starting with the trick winner) take an extra card from the stock. The trick winner leads the next trick.

The game continues until players first exhaust the stock and then play the remaining cards in their hands. At this point, the game ends, players tally their points, and the player with the most points wins.

- -
VARIATION 1: FOUR-HAND BRISCOLA
The four-player version is identical to the standard game, except that the players form two teams. The scores of each team are added together, and the team with the highest total score wins. If you're new to partnership games, here's

one small piece of advice: If your partner leads with a high trump, don't over-trump (play a higher trump). This will only make your partner sad and irritable.

- -

VARIATION 2: BRISCOLA BASTARDA

This Briscola variant is exclusively for five players. For added spice, there is a round of bidding, with the winner earning the right to declare the Briscola, or trump, for that round. The twist is that the player who declares trump does so by naming a card that may or may not be in his own hand. If the player calls a Briscola that he is already holding, the game is played four against one. If the player instead calls a Briscola he does not have, the player holding the Briscola is secretly partnered with the bidder and is not allowed to disclose her identity until the Briscola card is finally played.

Deal each player eight cards, so that all forty cards are in play. Starting with the player to the left of the dealer, each player is asked to declare how many points he or she will win in the hand. Each subsequent bid must be higher than the previous bid. Players who pass once are ineligible to bid again.

When all players but one pass, the highest bidder declares the Briscola, or trump card. You may select a card you already hold, or choose a card that will strengthen your hand. For example, if you are long in spades but lack the A♠, you could declare A♠ as the Briscola. This makes spades the trump suit and partners you with whichever player holds the A♠. The remaining three players form an ad hoc team with the goal of preventing the two-player partnership from winning points.

If the bidder calls a Briscola he or she already holds, then it's four against one (though other players may not realize this until the bidder actually plays the Briscola, since it's unclear who—if any—of the other players might also be holding the Briscola).

The rest of the game is identical to the standard version of Briscola, except when it comes to the final scoring. The bidder and the Briscola holder add their points together. If the total is greater than or equal to the original bid, the bidder scores 2 points, the holder scores 1 point, and the other three players each score -1 point. On the other hand, if the total score is less than the original bid, the bidder scores -2 points, the holder scores -1 point, and each of the three opposing players score 1 point.

If the bidder was playing alone (if she declared a Briscola that was already in her hand), the bidder wins or loses 4 points and all other players win or lose 1 point. Games of Briscola Bastarda are typically played to 15 points.

BULLSHIT

DIFFICULTY *low*	TIME LENGTH *short*	DECKS 1

Here's a game that rewards bald-faced lying and cuss words. How refreshing. If kids are playing, you can recast the game as "Cheat" (its name in England) or "I Doubt It!" (its name in Russia).

∾ **NUMBER OF PLAYERS** 3 to 10

∾ **HOW TO DEAL** Deal out a fifty-two-card deck to all players, face down. It's OK if some players have an extra card or two.

∾ **SCORING** The goal is to be the first player to lose all your cards.

∾ **HOW TO PLAY** The player to the left of the dealer goes first. Play, face down, as many aces as you have, and say something like "two aces" or "three aces." It is absolutely fine if you don't really have any aces—the name of the game is bullshit, and lying is an integral part of the game (in fact, it's the whole point of the game).

The next player follows with 2s, the next with 3s, etc., all the while increasing the number of cards in the discard pile. After kings are played, the next player starts again with aces, and the cycle is repeated.

At any point, a player may call "bullshit!" This is a less polite way of saying, "Pardon me, I have grave doubts that the cards just played match what you have declared." When bullshit is called, the cards in question are turned face up and one of two things happens.

If the challenge is fair and the cards are not what they were declared to be, the person who played the cards must pick up the entire discard pile. If the challenge is scurrilous and the cards are exactly as declared, the accuser must pick up the entire discard pile.

After a challenge, the next player in rotation picks up the game where it left off.

BUSCA

DIFFICULTY *low*	TIME LENGTH *medium*	DECKS 1

Busca is played in small towns and big cities across Italy. The game feels like a precursor to Hearts (substitute "cappotto" for "shooting the moon") and, like Hearts, makes an excellent three- or four-person game.

∾ **NUMBER OF PLAYERS** 3 to 5

∾ **HOW TO DEAL** Start with a fifty-two-card deck, and remove all 8s through 10s, leaving forty cards total. Cards rank (high to low) 3, 2, A, K, Q, J, 7, 6, 5, 4.

Deal cards in a counterclockwise direction to all players, face down, as follows: eight cards each for five players, ten cards each for four players, thirteen cards each for three players. (In three-player games, the extra card is given to the dealer, who then discards one card and sets it aside, to be given to the winner of the final trick.)

∾ **SCORING** The goal is to avoid scoring points. Aces are worth 1 point, and all 3s, 2s, kings, queens, and jacks are each worth ⅓ of a point. The game ends when a player's score hits or exceeds 31; at that point, the player with the *lowest* score wins.

At the end of the round scores are calculated as follows:

> The winner of the last trick scores the difference between 11 and the sum of the other players' scores.

All other players add up points taken in tricks and round down (e.g., 4⅓ points scores 4 points, 5⅔ points scores 5 points).

If a player manages to score all the points, it's called a cappotto and earns that player zero points and all other players 11 points.

∾ **HOW TO PLAY** The player to the right of the dealer leads the first trick. Any card may be played. The other players must follow suit if they can, or else they may play any other card. There is no trump. Tricks are won by the highest card in the leading suit. The trick winner leads the following trick. Scores are tallied once all cards are played and the deal rotates to the right.

FAN TAN

DIFFICULTY *low*	TIME LENGTH *short*	DECKS 1

Fan Tan is often played for money. It's a game that offers low-key entertainment with a hint of gambling. Try a wager along the lines of 10 or 20 cents per chip.

∾ **NUMBER OF PLAYERS** Ideal for 4 or 5; may be played by 3 to 8

∾ **HOW TO DEAL** Deal out a fifty-two-card deck to all players; don't worry if some players have an extra card. Rankings are standard, with aces always low.

All players start with an equal number of chips or markers (20 to 25 chips per player is a good start) and *ante* into the pot either one chip (if they have one less card than the majority of players) or two chips (if they have one extra card).

∾ **SCORING** The goal is to be the first player to run out of cards. When this happens, the other players count their remaining cards and put one chip per card into the pot. The winner takes all chips in the pot.

∾ **HOW TO PLAY** The player to the left of the dealer starts and must play a 7 or pass. If nobody can play a 7, the hand is dead, all players throw one chip into the pot as a penalty, the deal rotates left, and new cards are dealt (followed by yet another ante).

If any player can open with a 7 (or multiple 7s—play 'em if you got 'em), place the card(s) face up on the table. The other players in turn may play another 7 or play cards higher and/or lower in rank (and matching in suit) of the face-up 7. If 7♥ is played, for example, the next player may throw 8♥ (form a pile to the left of 7♥) and/or 6♥ (form a pile to the right of the 7♥). Players continue building up or down in suit until all thirteen hearts are played. The same process is followed for the other 7s in the deck.

∾ **IRREGULARITIES & DISPUTES** If players pass when they could have played a card, and this is later discovered, the offender must put three chips into the pot as a penalty. If the offending player could have played a 7 but did not, he or she must put three chips into the pot and give five chips to each player holding the 6 and 8 in the suit corresponding to the unplayed 7.

NAPOLEON

DIFFICULTY *low*	TIME LENGTH *medium*	DECKS 1

Napoleon was the emperor of France, king of Italy, and Protector of the Confederate of the Rhine. This game evolved in England (of course) as a tribute to the two generals—Wellington and von Blücher—who defeated Napoleon at the Battle of Waterloo in 1815, sparing England from French domination. Americans will recognize this game as a distant cousin of Euchre.

∾ **NUMBER OF PLAYERS** 2 to 6

∾ **HOW TO DEAL** Start with a fifty-two-card deck, and deal each player five cards in batches of 3-2. Card rankings are standard, with aces always high.

∾ **SCORING** If the bid winner makes the bid, she scores the points shown below. If she falls short, subtract the corresponding bid from her score.

There is no bonus for winning extra tricks. Games of Napoleon are typically played to 25 points.

∾ **HOW TO PLAY** Starting from the left of the dealer, each player has one chance to bid or pass. You're bidding on how many tricks you may win. Suits are not mentioned, and each bid must be higher than the previous one. The bids in Napoleon are (low to high):

THREE Bidder to win three tricks (3 points)

NO TRICK Bidder to lose all tricks (3 points)

FOUR Bidder to win four tricks (4 points)

NAP Bidder to win all five tricks (5 points)

WELLINGTON Bidder to win all five tricks; used to *overcall* when a previous player bids nap (10 points)

BLÜCHER Bidder to win all five tricks, may be bid only after other players have already bid nap and Wellington (20 points)

If all players pass, the hand is dead, the cards are reshuffled, and new hands are dealt.

The bid winner plays the first card, and the card's suit determines trump for the hand. All players must follow suit if they can; otherwise they may play any other card. Tricks are won by the highest trump, or by the highest card in the leading suit. The trick winner leads the following trick. Scores are tallied once all cards are played, and the deal rotates left.

OH HELL

DIFFICULTY *low*	TIME LENGTH *short*	DECKS 1

Despite being a simple game to learn, Oh Hell is surprisingly difficult to win. It's also a great game for spoilers—those people who get a thrill from sabotaging other people's hands.

✎ **HOW TO DEAL** Start with a fifty-two-card deck. In the first round, all players receive one card, in the second round two cards, etc. The number of rounds depends on the total number of players:

    3 players: 15 rounds
    4 players: 13 rounds
    5 players: 10 rounds
    6 players: 8 rounds
    7 players: 7 rounds

Card ranking is standard, with aces always high.

✎ **SCORING** Players who make their bid exactly score 10 points plus the value of the bid (so a successful bid of 2 scores 12 points). Otherwise no points are scored.

✎ **HOW TO PLAY** Once all cards are dealt, the dealer turns up a card from the deck to determine trump for the round. Next, the player to the left of the dealer opens the bidding. Players bid only once, from zero up to the total number of cards in the current round. The bid winner must win *exactly* the number of tricks bid—no more, no less.

After the bidding is complete, the player to the left of the dealer plays a card. Tricks are won by the highest trump (which may be played at any time), or by the highest card in the leading suit. The trick winner leads the next trick. The last trick of every round is always played "no trump," which means there is no trump suit. Scores are tallied once all cards are played. The deal rotates left.

PALACE

DIFFICULTY *medium*	TIME LENGTH *medium*	DECKS 1

The joy in this game is watching your opponents' hands swell with cards as you nimbly dump cards from your own hand. Watch out, though—this game is alternatively known as "Karma," because it's a fact of life (and of Palace) that what goes around eventually comes around.

∾ **NUMBER OF PLAYERS** 3 to 6

∾ **HOW TO DEAL** Start with a fifty-two-card deck (add one joker if six are playing). Deal each player a row of three face down cards, followed by three face-up cards (covering the face-down cards just dealt), followed by a three-card hand, dealt face down. The remaining cards are the stock.

Cards rank (high to low) 2-A-K-Q-J-10-9-8-7-6-5-4-3-2, with 2s playing both high and low.

∾ **SCORING** A player is out of the game once he plays all nine cards from his hand and the table. The last player holding cards loses.

∾ **HOW TO PLAY** All players review their three-card hands and may, if they desire, swap one or more with their face-up cards on the table.

The player dealt the first face-up 3 (if none, the first face-up 4, or 5, etc.) goes first and plays any card (or pair of cards) from her hand, face up, onto a communal discard pile. She then replenishes her hand to three cards by drawing from the stock.

The next player must match the number of cards played with cards of equal or higher rank. If a pair of 5s is played, for example, the following player must follow with another pair of 5s or any higher pair of cards. If he cannot, he picks up the entire discard pile and the next player in rotation starts a fresh discard pile by playing any card or pair of cards.

Once the stock is exhausted, play continues without drawing. If a player starts his turn with no cards (because he played them on the previous turn) and the stock is empty, only then may he play his face-up cards. If any of these cards are playable, they are placed on the discard pile and the turn rotates. If the cards cannot be played, one card goes into the discard pile, which the player must then pick up.

When a player has no more face-up cards, she plays *blind* from her set of face-down cards, simply choosing at random. If that card (or cards, if appropriate) cannot be played, it's taken back into the hand, along with the entire discard pile. The player must once again play cards from her hand on subsequent turns.

Palace does not have official variations, per se, though it's almost unheard of *not* to include the following rule variations in modern games:

Any 2 may be played on any card, and any card may in turn be played on any 2.

The discard pile is removed permanently from the game when any 10 is played on it. The same player is rewarded with another turn.

If four cards of the same rank are played, either as a foursome or built up in unbroken sequence on the discard pile, the discard pile is removed from the game, and the same player gets another turn.

PANGUINGUE

DIFFICULTY *high*	TIME LENGTH *medium*	DECKS 5

This is the granddaddy of all Rummy games. Invented by the Spanish, Panguingue (or "Pan" for short) flourished in America's nineteenth-century casinos and gambling halls. Given this gaming legacy, it's no surprise that Pan is still played for stakes—typically 10 or 25 cents per chip. If you're familiar with Rummy, you will quickly master Pan, and in doing so reconnect with a game that was once ubiquitous throughout the American West.

HOW TO DEAL You need at least five standard fifty-two-card decks to play (in casinos, eight decks are used). Remove all 8s, 9s, and 10s from each deck, and shuffle them together. Card rankings are (high to low) K-Q-J-7-6-5-4-3-2-A. With so many cards in play, the deck is typically divided into two equal sections: a head used for dealing and a foot that serves as a reserve in case additional cards are needed.

All players start with an equal amount of chips or markers (50 is a good number, each worth 10 or 25 cents) and *ante* one chip into the pot. Dealing in a counterclockwise direction, the dealer gives ten cards to each player, face down, in five batches of two. The dealer then sets the head face down on the table (this is the stock), and turns up the top card, placing it face up next to the head (this is now a discard pile).

SCORING The objective is to be the first player to meld eleven cards. That's all ten cards in your hand plus the final card drawn. The winner of each hand collects one chip—plus the total of all *conditions* (see next page) earned—from all active players, as well as the antes from players who dropped out of the game.

HOW TO PLAY All players have an opportunity to fold once all cards are dealt. If a player folds, he adds two chips to the pot as a penalty and removes his cards from the table.

For the remaining players, starting from the right of the dealer and moving counterclockwise, each turn consists of drawing a single card from the stock or taking the topmost card from the discard pile, melding as many cards as possible (or none), and finishing by discarding a single card face up onto the discard pile. In Pan, there are special rules for drawing cards.

A card taken from stock must immediately be melded; otherwise it must immediately be discarded (in other words, you cannot add it to your hand).

A card taken from the discard pile may be used only to increase a player's existing melds.

Players may build only on their own melds. Players may split one meld into two, or borrow a card (or cards) from existing melds to form new melds, as long as all resulting melds are valid. In Pan, the melds are as follows:

Sets are three or more cards of equal rank, from either the same or different suits. Two cards of matching suit and one of a different suit are not a valid set. A same-suit set may be increased only by adding cards of the same rank *and* suit (to the set 4♥-4♥-4♥, only another 4♥ may be added). A mixed-suit set may be increased by adding cards of the same rank, regardless of suit (to the set 7♦-7♥-7♣, any other 7 may be added).

Aces and **kings** (these ranks are called *non-comoquers* in Pan) may form sets regardless of suit (A♥-A♥-A♛ is a valid set)

A **sequence** is any three cards in consecutive rank and matching suit. In Pan, 7s and jacks are considered consecutive; however, *continuous ranking* is not allowed—ranking must stop at the king (going up) or the ace (going down). You may add to a sequence by adding cards in proper sequence and suit.

∾ CONDITIONS Certain melds are called "conditions," and result in immediate payment of chips from all active players. The conditions and payouts are below; note that all 3s, 5s, and 7s are known as *valle* cards; cards of other ranks are *non-valle* cards.

A set of valle cards not in the same suit (e.g., 3♦-3♣-3♠) earns one chip from each player

A set of valle cards in matching suit earns two chips from each player, or four chips if the suit is spades.

A set of non-valle cards in matching suit earns one chip from each player, two chips if the suit is spades.

A sequence starting with an ace or ending with a king earns one chip from each player, two chips if the suit is spades.

When cards are added to conditions, the player collects the value of the original condition for every additional card. And if players create a condition that did not exist before splitting a meld, the player earns chips as if the meld was entirely new.

∽ FORCING If the top card of the discard pile can be used by a player to build an existing meld, other players may demand that the player draw the card and use it in a meld. The idea is to force the player to make a discard they would not otherwise have made.

Rummy

Rummy evolved from a Spanish game called Conquian (Panguingue is the closest modern equivalent), and was first recorded in the American Southwest in the 1850s. Rummy has since split into two families of games, those emphasizing "going out" (Rummy, Continental Rummy), and those emphasizing melding (Rummy Five Hundred, Contract Rummy). Rummy was the most widely played game in the United States in the 1930s and '40s, after which it was eclipsed by two of its own offspring, Gin Rummy and Canasta.

∾ **NUMBER OF PLAYERS** 2 to 6

∾ **HOW TO DEAL** Start with a fifty-two-card deck, and deal cards one at a time, face down, as follows:

    With two players, ten cards each
    With three or four players, seven cards each
    With five or six players, six cards each

Set the remaining cards face down in the center of the table (this is the stock), turn up the topmost stock card, and place it face up next to the stock (this is the discard pile). Card rankings are standard, with aces always low.

∾ **SCORING** When a player goes out, she scores points for every card remaining in her opponents' hands, based on the following values: 10 points for each face card, 1 point for each ace, and **index value** points for all other cards. If the winner melded her entire hand in a single turn, she earns a *rummy bonus*, and all points are doubled. Games of Rummy are played to 50 or 100 points.

∾ **HOW TO PLAY** The player to the left of the dealer starts by drawing a card (either from the stock or the top card in the discard pile); making melds; and then discarding one card from the hand, face up, on top of the discard pile.

To create melds, players take cards from their hands and place them on the table, face up, in the following groupings:

SETS are three or more cards of equal rank (e.g., 5♥-5♦-5♠).

SEQUENCES are three or more cards of matching suit in unbroken sequence. Ranking is not continuous, so K♠-A♠-2♠ is not valid.

Players may also build on existing melds (both their own and other players'). For example, you may add 5♣ to an existing 5♥-5♦-5♠ set. When a player melds all cards in his hand, he *goes out* and wins the hand. Scores are then tallied. If the stock is exhausted before a player goes out, turn over the discard pile (do not shuffle) to form a new stock and continue play.

VARIATION 1: CONTRACT RUMMY

This is the most common—and popular—variation of the standard Rummy game. The general play is similar, but numerous modifications have been added over the years. Contract Rummy may be played by three to eight players. There are no teams; everybody plays for themselves.

DEALING With three or four players, use two fifty-two-card decks plus one joker (105 cards total). With five or more players, use three fifty-two-card decks plus two jokers (158 cards total). Aces rank both high and low, and jokers are wild. Games are always limited to seven rounds. Each player receives ten cards in the first four rounds, twelve cards in the remaining three rounds.

The player who goes out first wins the hand, and scores are tallied. The player with the lowest total score after seven rounds wins the game. The same card values apply in both Rummy and Contract Rummy, except for jokers (20 points) and aces (15 points).

HOW TO PLAY Standard Rummy melds are used, except that aces rank either high (A-K-Q) or low (3-2-A). Ranking is still not continuous, so K-A-2 is not valid. Jokers are wild and stand in for any card.

In each round, a different contract is required to go out (see chart). In Round 1, for example, a player must meld two sets to go out.

ROUND	REQUIRED CONTRACT
1	2 sets
2	1 set, 1 sequence
3	2 sequences
4	3 sets
5	2 sets, 2 sequences
6	1 set, 2 sequences
7	3 sequences

When two or more sequences are required, play two different suits. Or, if you play in the same suit, separate the sequences by at least one card (the two sequences may not be in continuous rank order).

DRAWING CARDS Contract Rummy places restrictions on drawing cards from the discard pile. At the start of player one's turn, for example, he or she must first decide to accept or decline the topmost card in the discard pile. If player one declines, player two may accept it. If player two declines, player three may accept it, etc. If player three accepts it, he or she must take both the discard and the topmost stock card. Player three may not discard and may not meld (since it is not player three's turn). Instead, player one takes a stock card (at this point player one may not take a card from the discard pile) and continues the turn.

MELDING All players must first meld the exact melds called for in the contract. Until a player melds, say, two sequences in Round 3, she may not meld anything else. Once a player meets the contract, she then may build on her own melds or the melds of other players. However she may not create any new melds.

JOKERS When melding with a joker, a player must state a suit and rank for the card. Any other player (assuming he has met his contract) may swap the actual card for the joker, and use the joker immediately or keep it in his hand.

- -

VARIATION 2: CONTINENTAL RUMMY

In the 1950s, Continental Rummy was all the rage in the United States. Then Canasta came along and knocked the game off its pedestal. Continental Rummy follows the basic rules of Contract Rummy, except that instead of playing seven rounds, there is only one round and the contracts are fixed.

Continental Rummy may be played by two to twelve players. With up to five players, use two fifty-two-card decks plus one joker (105 cards total); with six to eight players, use three fifty-two-card decks plus three jokers (159 cards total); with nine or more players, use four fifty-two-card decks plus three jokers (212 cards total). All players are dealt fifteen cards in batches of three. Aces may be played high and low. Both jokers and 2s are wild.

The one and only goal in Continental Rummy is to go out, all at once, with one of the three following hands:

Five three-card sequences

Three four-card sequences plus one three-card sequence

One five-card sequence, one four-card sequence, two three-card sequences

Sets are not valid in Continental Rummy, and players may not meld or build any other cards. You go out with the above hands in one fell swoop, or you don't go out at all.

In addition to the standard point scores, the following points are added to the winner's score, multiplied by the number of players in the game (see chart). With seven players, for example, the winner earns 7 points (1 point x 7 players = 7 points) plus any other relevant bonuses multiplied by the number of players. Games of Continental Rummy are typically played to 500 points.

BONUS PLAYS	POINTS
Winning the game	1
Each 2 melded	1
Each joker melded	2
Going out, drawing no cards	10
Going out, drawing one card	7
Going out, no wild cards melded	10
All melds are the same suit	10

VARIATION 3: RUMMY FIVE HUNDRED

Follow the standard rules of Rummy, but use a single fifty-two-card deck for three or four players, or two fifty-two-card decks for five to eight players. Rummy card rankings are used, except the ace may be played both high (A-K-Q) and low (3-2-A) in sequences. Deal all players seven cards.

In addition to taking a stock card or the top card from the discard pile, players have a third drawing option: to draw two or more cards (in order; you may not pick and choose) from the discard pile, as long as you immediately meld the last card taken in the pile. For example, if you pick up eight cards from the discard pile, you must immediately meld the eighth card taken. The other cards are placed in your hand or used to meld valid combinations.

When building a card(s) on an opponent's existing meld, place the card(s) in front of you so you can score it later. If a card may be built onto more than one of your opponents' melds, you must specify which one.

Players are not required to go out by discarding; as soon as one player has melded all her cards, the hand is over and points are tallied. There is no bonus for going out. All scores are simply the sum of all cards melded subtracted from the sum of all cards left in your hand. Aces score 15 points in all cases, except when they're the low card in a sequence (3-2-A), in which case they score 5 points. The first player to score 500 points wins the game.

VARIATION 4: KOON KAN

This variant adds heat to the standard Rummy game by pitting two players in head-to-head competition. Start by removing all 8s, 9s, and 10s from a standard fifty-two-card deck, leaving forty cards total. Aces may be played both high and low. Deal ten cards to each player and set the remaining cards aside as the stock. No card is turned up for the discard pile.

The goal is to meld eleven cards: ten in your hand, plus the final card drawn. The non-dealer starts by turning up the topmost stock card. This card must immediately be melded or discarded. The player may not place the draw card in his hand. On all subsequent turns, players either draw from the stock (immediately melding or discarding), or from the discard pile (immediately melding).

Koon Kan follows all other standard Rummy rules. The game is a draw if the stock is exhausted before either player goes out.

VARIATION 5: TONK RUMMY

Tonk Rummy is ideal for two or three players craving a little action—as in wagering action. Before the game starts, agree on a stake (anywhere from 50 cents to $5). The game's namesake—a tonk—doubles the stakes, so don't let the stakes get too out of control.

Deal each player five cards, set aside the stock, and create a discard pile. Players start by adding up the value of their hands: face cards are 10 points each, aces are 1, and all other cards are their *index value*. If a player's hand is worth 49 or 50 points, it's a *tonk*. Declare tonks immediately, and all other players must pay the winner a double stake. The game is a draw if two players have tonks.

A player may **knock** at the start of any turn. By knocking, she is betting that she has the *lowest* overall score in cards. If she's right, she is paid the basic stake. Otherwise, she pays the actual low-score holder double the stake, while all other players pay a standard stake.

Players who go out by melding earn the standard stake, unless they go out without a discard. This is another type of tonk and earns the winner double stakes from all players. The game is over if the stock runs out. If this happens, the player with the lowest overall score is paid the basic stake from all players.

This is a wildcard-laden version of standard Rummy, best for two to four players. The standard Rummy rules are followed, with a few exceptions.

Start with a single fifty-two-card deck for two players; two fifty-two-card decks for three or four players. The game has eleven total rounds, and dealing is progressive: players receive three cards in Round 1, four cards in Round 2, five cards in Round 3, etc.

The other twist is that each round features a different wild card, based on the number of cards dealt: in Round 1, 3s are wild; in Round 2, 4s are wild; etc. Wild cards may stand in for any card. When a player goes out, the other players have one final turn to meld cards. After that, scores are tallied and the deal rotates to the left. After Round 11, the player with the highest score wins.

SETBACK

DIFFICULTY *low*	TIME LENGTH *medium*	DECKS 1

Setback was invented by enthusiasts of Seven Up who wanted a simplified bidding and trump-nominating process. And whereas Seven Up is a three-player game, Setback may be played by up to seven players. The games are similar in most other respects.

∾ **NUMBER OF PLAYERS** 2 to 7; best for 4

∾ **HOW TO DEAL** Start with a fifty-two-card deck, and deal each player six cards, dealt three at a time. Card rankings are standard, with aces always high.

∾ **SCORING** The goal is to win as many points as possible in tricks. There are four total points in play:

HIGH POINT (1) to the player who captures the highest trump in play.

LOW POINT (1) to the player who captures the lowest trump in play.

JACK (1) to the player who captures the jack of trumps.

GAME (1) to the player who scores the most overall points, based on the following values: score 10 points for each 10, 4 points for aces, 3 points for kings, 2 points for queens, and 1 point for non-trump jacks.

If two players tie for game point, the point is not awarded. In some cases, the jack of trumps is not in circulation, in which case only 3 points are possible.

If the bid winner meets or beats his bid, he scores all points made. If he fails to meet his bid, the value of the bid is subtracted from his game score. Non-bidders keep any points scored. Games are typically played to 7 points.

∾ **HOW TO PLAY** The player to the left of the dealer opens the bidding. All players have one opportunity to bid or pass. The only valid bids are one, two, three, four, and pass.

The bid winner leads the first card, and that card's suit determines trump for the hand. Players must follow suit if possible (trumps may be played at any time); otherwise they may play any card. The trick is won by the highest trump card or, if no trumps are played, by the highest card in the leading suit. The trick winner leads the next trick. Scores are tallied when all cards are played. The deal rotates clockwise.

- -
VARIATION: PITCH

This is played exactly as the main game, with one crucial difference. Any player—as long as her score is not negative—may make a *pitch bid*. This promises four tricks and, if won, ends the game instantly. A player with a negative score may pitch bid, but if she wins the bid, she simply scores 4 points; it is not an automatic win.

TOEPEN

DIFFICULTY *low*	TIME LENGTH *medium*	DECKS 1

It's hard to know if Toepen is more enjoyable played as a drinking game (all losing players must drink!) or as a low-stakes gambling game (all losing players must pay!).

∾ **NUMBER OF PLAYERS** 3 to 8

∾ **HOW TO DEAL** Start with a fifty-two-card deck, and remove all 2s through 6s, leaving thirty-two cards total. Card rankings are (high to low) 10, 9, 8, 7, A, K, Q, J. Deal each player four cards. The remaining cards are placed face down in the center of the table.

All players start with an equal number of tokens or ***chips*** (10 is good for three to five players; 6 or 8 is better with six or more players). Players typically pay a small amount to "purchase" tokens, and the eventual game winner is awarded this buy-in money.

∾ **SCORING** The goal is simply to win the last trick. Doing so means the losing players each forfeit one token to the pot. The game ends when all players but one run out of tokens. In ***knock*** games, all losing players must forfeit the number of knocks + 1 (e.g., if two players knock, you eventually lose three tokens).

∽ **HOW TO PLAY**   Any player dealt only aces, kings, queens, and jacks may throw the cards in and take four replacements from the deck. There's a bluffing element here—you may attempt to exchange your hand even if it contains cards other than aces, kings, queens, and jacks. If nobody challenges, you're in the clear. If you are challenged, you either forfeit a token for lying or the challenger forfeits a token for doubting your integrity. You keep the new hand either way.

After the exchange of cards, the player to the left of the dealer leads any card. Players must follow suit if possible. Tricks are won by the highest card in the leading suit. Trick winners lead the next trick. Scores are tallied after a player wins the fourth and final trick. The winner deals the next hand.

A player may knock once all players are dealt cards. Knocking increases point scores. In response to a knock, other players may fold (drop their cards on the table, face down) and forfeit a token, or accept the challenge and continue play. Traditionally, players must make a snap decision whether to fold or to stay—if players hesitate at all, they are in. If a player folds on the second knock, she must forfeit two tokens, and three tokens on the third knock, etc. There's no limit to the number of knocks per hand; the only restriction is that the same player may not knock two times in a row. If a player knocks and all other players fold, the losing players forfeit their tokens as usual, and the winning player deals the next hand.

TWENTY-FIVE

DIFFICULTY *medium*	TIME LENGTH *medium*	DECKS 1

Twenty-Five is one of the most popular card games in Ireland. Once you master the novel ranking of cards within the suits, the game is easy enough to play and is highly dependent on the luck of the draw. Twenty-Five is part of a family of Irish-descended games called "Spoil Five"; try Auction Forty-Five if you enjoy this general concept but prefer games of skill to games of (mostly) luck.

❧ **HOW TO DEAL** Start with a fifty-two-card deck, and deal five cards to each player in batches of 3-2. The dealer turns up the top card, and this card's suit is trump for the hand. Confusingly, the card rankings vary based on whether the suit is trump or not:

NON-TRUMP SUITS (HIGH TO LOW)
Clubs & Spades: K-Q-J-A-2-3-4-5-6-7-8-9-10
Diamonds: K-Q-J-10-9-8-7-6-5-4-3-2-A
Hearts: K-Q-J-10-9-8-7-6-5-4-3-2.

TRUMP SUITS (HIGH TO LOW)
Clubs & Spades: 5-J-A♥-A-K-Q-2-3-4-6-7-8-9-10
Diamonds: 5-J-A♥-A-K-Q-10-9-8-7-6-4-3-2
Hearts: 5-J-A-K-Q-10-9-8-7-6-5-4-3-2

Note that A♥ is always the third-highest trump.

❧ **SCORING** Each trick taken is worth 5 points. The first player to score 25 points wins immediately. Games are typically played for a small stake (say, each player contributes 25 cents). If a player scores 25 points and no other player has won a single trick, the stake is usually doubled.

❧ **HOW TO PLAY** Once trump is established, any player holding the ace of trump may exchange *any card* in his hand for the turned-up card.

The player to the left of the dealer leads. Tricks are won by the highest trump played or, if none, by the highest card of the leading suit. Players are generally required to follow suit, though you may play trump at any time. If you cannot follow suit, you may play any card. When trumps are led, however, players must follow suit. The one exception is if you're holding only the top three trump cards—in Twenty-Five you are never forced to play the top three trump cards unless a player has led a higher trump.

VARIATION: FIFTY-FIVE

This variant is less about luck of the draw and more about skillful bidding. The rules are exactly as in the main game, but deal an extra hand at the start. This goes to the player who wins the bidding.

Bidding always starts with the player to the left of the dealer. Players may bid or pass, and once you pass you may not jump back into the bidding. The only valid bids are 10, 15, 20, 25, 60. A dealer may equal the previous bid and win; all other players must increase the previous bid.

The bid winner takes the extra cards into her hand, discards any five cards, and nominates the trump suit. Tricks are still worth 5 points, and whichever player captures the ace of trump earns an extra 5 points.

If the bid winner meets or exceeds her bid, she scores the bid amount and nothing more (though she is eligible for the 5-point high trump bonus). Otherwise, the bid amount is deducted form her score. The first player to score 55 points wins; if the bid winner crosses 55 points first, the round must still be played out to see if she meets her bid or not. If more than one player earns 55 points in the same hand, the player to score it first wins.

OTHER MULTIPLAYER GAME VARIATIONS

Some of the games covered in the *Ultimate Book of Card Games* have multiplayer variations. Here's a complete list:

.08 ~

Betting Games

CHAPTER EIGHT

Betting Games

SOME SAY POKER WAS INVENTED IN CHINA and introduced to the West by Marco Polo. Others claim it's derived from a seventeenth-century Persian game called As Nas. A more likely link is Poque, a French betting game based on a four-suit deck of hearts, spades, diamonds, and clubs. Poque was introduced into the Louisiana territories by French settlers; by the early 1800s, a new game called Poker was all the rage in New Orleans. The rest, as they say, is history.

For most of the twentieth century, Stud Poker (both five- and seven-card) was the most common and popular form of the game. In the 1990s, all this changed with the invention of the in-table television camera. Previously Poker was not a telegenic sport. After the in-table camera came along, millions of home viewers began watching professional players bluff and swagger in real time. And the games in which the most money was at stake, notably No-Limit Texas Hold'em, exploded in popularity.

TIPS FOR POKER VIRGINS

If you're new to poker, the basic concept goes like this: All players are dealt a certain number of cards, with which they attempt to make the best hand according to the rules of the game being played. In each game there is a single *dealer*, who shuffles and distributes cards to all players. Most games may be played with a minimum of three and a maximum of seven or eight players. Dealing is done one card at a time, starting to the left of the dealer and proceeding clockwise. The number of cards dealt depends on the game.

All poker games feature one or more *rounds of betting*, in which players declare how much money they're willing to wager on their cards. To complete the bet, players must put a corresponding number of **chips** into a **pot**. Poker chips are not mandatory, but they're useful if you are not comfortable playing with cash.

The value of the pot changes with each hand, depending on the number of players and the amounts being bet. In almost every hand, one or more players will **fold**, which is a nice way of saying they are out of the hand from that point on.

If a player makes a bet no other player will match, that player wins the pot and is not required to show his or her cards to anyone. Many of these bets are usually **bluffs** (making a bet with bad cards, in hopes that other players will fold). Bluffing requires patience, guts, and the ability to fool other players into thinking you have an unbeatable hand.

Once all players receive the correct amount of cards and complete the required rounds of betting, a winner is decided in a **showdown**. No guns or knives, please; simply show your cards and determine who has the best hand according to the rules of the game. The pot goes to the winner (or winners, in split-pot games).

☞ **HAND RANKINGS** There are fifty-two cards in standard poker decks, plus two jokers that are generally unused. In most poker games, players compete to have the best five-card hand. The definition of "best" varies from game to game. The method of ranking cards, however, is almost always measured against the following list, which is ordered lowest to highest in value:

HIGH CARD The highest card in a hand of unrelated cards (A-J-6-4-3 beats K-Q-5-3-2 because the ace is higher than the king).

ONE PAIR Two cards of the same rank. In a showdown, the higher pair wins (J-J-10-6-3 beats 9-9-A-K-Q).

TWO PAIR Two cards of one rank and two of another. In a showdown, the highest single pair wins (J-J-3-3-2 beats 10-10-9-9-4).

THREE-OF-A-KIND Three cards of matching rank. In a showdown, the highest triplet wins (Q-Q-Q-4-2 beats A-J-J-J-7).

STRAIGHT Any five cards in sequence, regardless of suit. In a showdown, the highest card in sequence determines the winner (K♣-Q♣-J♦-10♥-9♠ beats 6♦-5♣-4♦-3♥-2♠). Note that A-K-Q-J-10 is the highest possible straight, while 5-4-3-2-A is the lowest. Also note that ranking is not *continuous,* so that wrapping around an ace is not allowed (Q-K-A-2-3 is not a valid hand).

FLUSH Any five cards of matching suit. In a showdown, the highest-ranking card determines the winner (K♥-J♥-8♥-5♥-2♥ beats Q♣-J♣-9♣-7♣-5♣ because the king is higher than the queen). If two players have high cards of matching rank, the next-highest card determines the winner.

FULL HOUSE Any three-of-a-kind plus any pair. In a showdown, the highest triplet wins.

FOUR-OF-A-KIND Four cards of matching rank (e.g., J-8-8-8-8).

STRAIGHT FLUSH Five sequential cards of matching suit. This is the Holy Grail of poker, very rare and very beautiful. The highest straight flush, called a royal straight flush, is A-K-Q-J-10, all in the same suit.

☞ **LOW HANDS** In games that include low hands, players compete for the worst possible five-card poker hand. The "best" worst hand is 6-4-3-2-A because these are the lowest possible cards without a pair or straight. (Note: In some casinos, the best low hand is 5-4-3-2-A, which is called the wheel; it is the dealer's choice in home games whether or not to accept this low straight.) After 6-4-3-2-A, the next "best" worst hand is 7-4-3-2-A. Just remember that it's always the lowest *high* card that determines the winner in a showdown.

☞ **WILD CARDS** Some games include standard wild cards. Other games may be spiced up on a whim, if the dealer chooses, by publicly declaring a wild card (or cards!) at the beginning of any poker game, before the cards are dealt.

Wild cards do not change hand rankings, but they may be used to make losing hands into winning ones. For example, if the dealer calls a game where 3s are wild, the hand 7-4-4-3-2 improves from a pair of fours to three-of-a-kind. Because hand rankings are applicable in all situations, wild cards may not be used to create nonstandard hands (unless players agree before any cards are dealt). In other words, there is no such poker hand as "five-of-a-kind." Nice try.

☞ **ANTES & BETTING** Poker games generally start with all players contributing an *ante*, or pre-bet, to the pot. The value of antes is not fixed; some games require large antes, some small antes, some no antes at all. Casinos have standard antes for most games. At home games, a good rule of thumb is that antes should at least equal the value of the game's minimum bet (typically 25 to 50 cents).

After you ante, betting is done in *rounds*, usually after a set number of cards are dealt to all players. When you make a bet, state the cash amount and place the corresponding number of chips into the pot.

Chip values vary from game to game, depending on the ***table stakes*** (how much money you are gambling for). Black, purple, and green chips are typically highest in value, followed by blue, red, and white. In "friendly" home games, chips might be worth something like $5 (black), $1 (blue), 50 cents (red), 25 cents (white).

Betting always proceeds clockwise around the table, usually starting with the player to the left of the dealer. Once all players have called the bet, raised it, or folded (see below), the pot is said to be **neat** and the next card (or round of cards) is dealt.

Most poker games have a preset *betting limit*, such as $2–$5 maximum per bet. Most games also impose a limit on the number of raises allowed per round of betting (three or four is common). For example, in a three-raise game with a $2 betting limit, player one may open the bet up to $2, while players two, three, and four may each raise the opening bet up to the $2 limit. At this point, each player would have to pay a total of $8 into the pot (or fold).

Here are the common betting terms in poker:

OPENING BET   The first bet is typically made by the player showing the highest (sometimes the lowest) cards. In games where no cards are visible, betting is opened by the player to the left of the dealer.

CHECK   A second option for opening is to *check* the bet (passing the decision to the next active player). After a check, if a subsequent player opens the betting, players who previously checked must call or raise the announced bet, or fold, when it's their turn again. If all players check, the round of betting is skipped and the next round of cards is dealt. At some tables, a check may also be called a *knock*, which derives from players rapping their knuckles on the table.

CALL   After a bet is announced, subsequent players may *call* (match) the bet by placing the appropriate number of chips into the pot.

RAISE   When it's their turn, players may raise the announced bet up to a preset limit. Note that nearly all games limit the number of raises to three or four per betting round.

ALL-IN This option is for players who are low on chips and cannot afford to raise a bet or to have their bet raised. By placing all your remaining chips into the pot, it means you may not be forced out of the game by subsequent raises or bets. Instead, all subsequent bets are placed in a *side pot* that you are not eligible to win. At the showdown, there are two possible outcomes: 1) somebody beats the all-in player and takes both the main pot and the side pot, or 2) the all-in player beats everybody at the table and wins the main pot, while the side pot is awarded to the player with the next-best hand.

FOLD Players may *fold* (give up, call it a night, run away) at any point during their turn. After folding, they are out of the hand for good and must forfeit any money already contributed to the pot. When folding, players should turn their cards face down on the table and resist the temptation to complain publicly about their miserable cards.

☞ **POKER ETIQUETTE** Poker has its own etiquette. Here are five of the most important points:

1. Never bet or fold out of turn.

2. Keep your cards in sight at all times—never put your cards under the table or walk away from the table with your cards.

3. Advice—don't give it, don't take it. It's always a bad idea to discuss your cards with other players.

4. Know what's in your hand. Cards may speak for themselves, but it helps if you can correctly interpret what they are saying.

5. Don't walk out with the winnings. If you plan to leave early from a home game, announce it before the game starts. In casinos, the opposite holds true: get out as quickly as possible once you win a large haul.

BACCARAT

| DIFFICULTY *high* | TIME LENGTH *short* | DECKS *multiple* |

When James Bond goes to Monte Carlo, he heads straight for the Baccarat tables. Baccarat has been around since the fifteenth century, and over the years it's developed a reputation for glamour and sophistication.

It's a rare home game that features Baccarat. The game is simply too tedious— the real fun comes from the unique atmosphere of the casino Baccarat room: plush chairs, roped-off tables, discreet staff, and very high stakes. The minimum bet at casinos is rarely less than $50. Often it's more like $200 to $500 per hand. Some casinos are attempting to transform Baccarat into a mainstream game with lower stakes; so far the attempts have not been successful.

Baccarat is a very straightforward game. Once the game starts, there are absolutely no decisions for players to make.

∾ **DEALING THE CARDS** Baccarat tables seat seven to fourteen people. Each seat corresponds to a number on the table, where you place your bets. Traditionally, three dealers service a table, with the middle dealer known as the *croupier*. While some casinos still use three-dealer tables, single-dealer tables are becoming more common.

The dealer starts each game by dealing two cards, face down, to a fictional *player* and a fictional *banker*. Your only role is to wager on which hand will be closest in value to 9 or if they will tie. All bets are made before the cards are dealt.

A typical Baccarat shoe holds six to eight decks of cards. Each player gets a turn to handle the shoe. Note that when handling the shoe, you are expected to bet on the banker. If this seems quaint, or too stressful, you may pass the shoe to the next player.

❧ HAND VALUES   In Baccarat, cards have the following fixed values:

2 to 9 are worth face value

10s and face cards are worth zero

Aces are worth 1

Simply add up the cards to calculate a hand's value. If the value is greater than 9 (that is, if it's two digits, such as 10 or 11), the first digit is dropped. Don't ask why, that's just the way the game is played. For example, the hand 8-4 adds up to 12, so the 1 is dropped and the value becomes 2. The hand A-10 is worth 1 point, while the hand K-10 is worth zero.

❧ DECLARING A WINNER   After the initial deal, if the value of either hand is 8 or 9, it's called a **natural**. In this case both hands *stand*, or stop taking cards, and the scores are compared. The hands tie if they are of equal value. Otherwise, the natural hand wins. If neither hand is natural, the game continues with the player first, followed by the banker, according to the following rules:

If the player's initial cards are valued at 6 or more, the player stands. If the player's initial cards are 5 or less, the player draws one (and only one) card.

If the banker's initial cards are valued at 7 or more, the banker stands. If the banker's initial cards total 0, 1, or 2, the banker draws one card. If the banker's initial cards total 3, 4, 5, or 6, the banker draws one card if:

The banker's hand is worth 3 and the player took no third card, or if the player's third card is worth zero to 7 points or 9 points.

The banker's hand is worth 4 points and the player took no third card, or if the player's third card is worth 2 to 7 points.

The banker's hand is worth 5 points and the player took no third card, or if the player's third card is worth 4 to 7 points.

The banker's hand is worth 6 points and the player's third card is worth 6 or 7 points.

∾ **BETTING** You are gambling on one of three potential outcomes:

The player's hand wins. This generally pays 1:1, so if you bet $50 you win back the $50 plus another $50.

The banker's hand wins. This also pays 1:1, but with a major catch. Nearly every casino charges a 5 percent commission on hands won by the bank. This effectively reduces the payout to .95:1 (you bet $50 to win back your original $50 plus another $47.50).

The hands tie. Casinos generally pay 8:1, so your bet of $50 wins $50 plus another $400.

Once all bets are placed, there's nothing more for you to do. Both hands are simply dealt according to the rules.

∾ **STRATEGY TIPS** There are no effective strategies in Baccarat. All cards are dealt according to fixed rules and there's nothing you can do about it. So what's the point? For many people, the answer is *pattern chasing*, which is a fancy way of saying "betting on an irrational hunch." A typical pattern chaser tallies the number of times the player's or banker's hands win and then bets either with or against the pattern. Statistically speaking, the banker's hand wins slightly more than 50 percent of the time (which is why casinos charge a 5 percent commission when the banker's hand wins).

- -
VARIATION 1: CHEMIN DE FER

Chemin de Fer takes the basic Baccarat game and adds a few twists. First and foremost, there is some decision-making involved for the players. Second, players bet against each other rather than against the fixed player's and banker's hands of basic Baccarat.

In Chemin de Fer, one player acts as both the bank and the dealer. The amount he bets determines how much other players can wager. If the bets of one or two players match this amount, the remaining players may not bet in the round. As in Baccarat, the casino makes its profit by taking a 5 percent commission on all winning banker hands.

The player to the right of the casino's dealer is the first banker and places on the table the amount of chips she is prepared to wager. If you want to bet against the banker, you call out "banco," and place an equal number of chips on the table. If more than one player challenges the bank, precedence is given to the player closest to the casino dealer's right. If the banker is not challenged at all, two or more players may join together to match the banker's wager (the player who contributes the largest amount plays the hand).

As in Baccarat, two cards are dealt face down to the player's and banker's hands. If the player has a natural (8 or 9), the cards are turned over immediately. If the player must take a card, or with a total of 5 chooses to do so, you say "carte," but do not turn over the cards (exposing them gives the dealer an advantage). The third card is always dealt face up for both the player and the banker.

- -
VARIATION 2: MINI-BACCARAT
Casinos have introduced Mini-Baccarat as a way to make the game less intimidating. The rules are identical to the basic game; the only differences being that minimum bets are smaller and the dealer takes on the role of banker, so the players never touch the cards.

BLACKJACK

DIFFICULTY *low*	TIME LENGTH *short*	DECKS 1

There's not much strategy in Blackjack, except when it comes to betting, which makes it an ideal game for novice card players. The casinos know this—and know that novice card players are typically "easy money." That's why Blackjack was one of the first games to be legalized in Las Vegas back in 1931.

It is possible to win money at Blackjack, but it requires a lot of doubling down and splitting. If that puts you off, enjoy a few hands of casino Blackjack and just remember that the odds are heavily stacked in the casino's favor.

> Blackjack evolved from the French game Vingt-et-Un (Twenty-One), part of the Chemin de Fer family. Originally, casinos offered 10:1 or even 100:1 payouts for players dealt A♠ with a black jack.

You do not compete against other players. Instead, your only goal is to beat the house (dealer). You do this by creating a hand that is closer in value to 21, without exceeding it, than the dealer's hand.

∾ **NUMBER OF PLAYERS** Up to 9

∾ **HAND RANKINGS** All face cards are worth 10, aces are worth 1 or 11 (whichever makes the best hand), and all numbered cards are worth their *index value*. The hand K-8, for example, is worth 18. The hand A-5 is worth 6 or 16 (it's up to you).

∾ **BETTING** Players put their bets on the table in a clearly marked spot before any cards are dealt. Minimum and maximum bets are always posted and range from $2 to $100 or more. At home games, the maximum bets are usually $1 or $2. Payouts for winning hands are 1:1, which means if you bet $10 and win, you receive the original $10 plus another $10.

The only exception is when a player scores 21 with two cards (e.g., A-K or A-10). This is called Blackjack and is usually paid at 3:2, which means if you bet $10 and win with Blackjack, you receive the original $10 plus another $15.

∾ **HOW TO PLAY** All players (including the dealer) are dealt two cards, one up and one down. In some casinos, the players (but never the dealer) receive both cards face up. After the initial deal, the game proceeds clockwise, starting with the player to the left of the dealer. If your two cards equal 21, you have Blackjack and are paid immediately. Otherwise, you must hit or stay (you may also double-down or split; more on that later). *Hitting* means taking an extra card in an attempt to score closer to 21. *Staying* means refusing any extra cards.

You may hit as many times as you like, as long as your hand does not exceed 21 points. If it does, your hand *busts* and, tough luck, you're out of the game. When you bust, the dealer immediately removes your cards and your bet from the table.

Once all players have an opportunity to hit or stay, the dealer turns up his or her cards and calculates the total. If the dealer's hand is 17 or more, the dealer *must* stay. If the dealer's hand is less than 17, the dealer *must* continue taking cards until the hand busts or scores 17 or more. When a dealer busts, all active players win!

If the dealer's hand scores between 17 and 21, the dealing is over. The dealer simply pays any hand on the table that is greater in value, and beats all hands of lesser value. If you and the dealer have cards of equal value, it's called a *push*, and no money changes hands.

The only exception is when a dealer's hand adds to 17 points and includes an ace. This is called a *soft* 17 because aces are worth either 1 or 11. In some casinos, a dealer must *hit* when dealt a soft 17. In other casinos, a dealer will *stay* on 17, soft or not.

DOUBLING DOWN Any player with two cards may double down. This betting option allows you to double your initial bet and to receive one—and only one—extra card. For example, if you bet $5 and are dealt 6-5, you have a good hand for doubling down. Your bet is doubled (to $10), and you receive one extra card. If that card is a king, queen, jack, or 10, you're loving life, because this gives you 21. If that card is low, such as 2 or 3, you're loving life much less.

SPLITTING It's a good idea to split your hand (play two hands simultaneously) when you are dealt an initial mid-ranking pair such as 8-8 or 7-7. For example, if you split 8-8, each card becomes part of a separate hand, and you must double your bet. The dealer treats each hand individually, asking you to hit or stay on each one. Remember that the odds of drawing a 10 or face card are good, so instead of standing on a mediocre 8-8, you could end up with two strong hands of 10-8 and Q-8. Of course, you might also end up busting one (or both) of your split pairs. Life is full of risks.

Note that some casinos allow you to split an initial pair only, while others allow you to split any two initial cards. Some casinos also have special rules about splitting aces. Ask the dealer if you're unsure.

☙ **STRATEGY TIPS** Most casinos use a *shoe* that holds up to eight decks of cards. Your odds of winning improve when there are fewer decks in play, so consider searching out the few casinos where single-deck Blackjack is still played.

You should always double down with 6-5 or 5-5. Your odds of reaching 20 or 21 are excellent in these situations. It's wise to stay on hands between 12 and 17 if the dealer is showing a 4, 5, or 6—odds are good that the dealer will be forced to draw an extra card and, hopefully, bust.

Conversely, take an extra card if you're holding between 12 and 17 and the dealer is showing 7, 8, 9, 10, or a face card. You may bust, but if you don't take a card, your low hand is likely to lose to the dealer's 17, 18, 19, or 20.

GUTS

DIFFICULTY *high*	TIME LENGTH *short*	DECKS 2

The Guts family of betting games is aptly named. It takes courage and a take-no-prisoners attitude to win. Not surprisingly, they're popular end-of-the-night games at home poker games, when alcohol- and adrenaline-infused players are all too willing to make big-money bets. Just remember: Friends don't let friends bet the pot on a $100 hand of Psycho Shelby.

All players compete to have the highest three-card hand. Flushes and straights do not count; the highest hand is A-A-A.

☙ **NUMBER OF PLAYERS** Up to 10

☙ **HOW TO PLAY** All players ante and receive three cards face down. Each player must then decide if she is "in" or "out" based on the strength of her hand. All players hold their cards in one hand and then, on a count of three, simultaneously drop or hold them. Players who drop are out of the hand and forfeit their antes to the pot. If all players drop, re-ante and deal new cards.

Assuming more than one player holds, all players show their cards and the highest three-card hand takes the pot. All losing players must also pay *double* the current pot amount into the next pot. If just one player holds, he wins the entire pot and the game is over. Otherwise all players ante and new hands are dealt.

∾ IRREGULARITIES & DISPUTES Players who hesitate at all in the drop—they lag a noticeable second or two behind the group in holding or dropping their cards—are automatically considered "out" for the hand. There is no recourse for players who mistakenly drop when they meant to hold or vice versa. Actions speak louder than words in Guts.

- -

VARIATION 1: BELLY WOUND
This variation is geared to generate large pots. Follow the basic rules, but when all players drop, you play again with the same cards and continue doing so until at least one player holds.

- -

VARIATION 2: BLOODY SEVENS
Follow the basic rules until the drop. All players who stay in receive three additional face-up cards and compete to make the highest five-card poker hands. All face-down 7s are wild; all face-up 7s are force-fold cards (you're out of the hand instantly when dealt one). If you're pushed out of the game with a face-up 7, unlike the other losing players, you are not required to match the pot.

- -

VARIATION 3: HIGH-LOW COJONES
Follow the basic rules until the drop. All players who stay in may draw up to three cards from the deck, paying the ante amount for each card taken. At the showdown, the pot is split 50-50 between the highest and lowest

three-card hands (3-2-A is lowest, A-A-A is highest). All other losing players must match the pot as usual.

This is a favorite go-for-broke variation at late-night home games. Follow the basic rules, but everybody shows their hands when all players drop. The highest hand (which *would* have won) matches the pot as a penalty, all players re-ante, and new cards are dealt.

Shelby is a multiround version of Guts. Normally a player who drops is out of the hand and forfeits his ante. This is not the case in Shelby. A player may drop in one round and then jump back in (by holding his cards) in the following round.

In Round 1 all players receive two cards, face down. In Round 1, the goal is to have the lowest two-card hand (A-2 or A-3; in Shelby, aces play high or low). On a count of three, a player holding a strong hand will challenge other players by holding her cards; players with weak hands will drop. At this point there are three possible outcomes:

If only one player holds, she places a marker (called a *Shelby*) in front of herself. The first player to earn three Shelbys wins the entire pot and ends the game. Otherwise the game proceeds to Round 2.

If more than one player holds, all players holding cards show each other their cards to determine who has the lowest two-card hand. Hands are typically exchanged in a clockwise direction, face down, so that only players who held may see each other's cards. After all hands are returned to their proper owners, each losing player pays the winner the value of the current pot, up to a preset limit (typically $2 to $5). The game then proceeds to Round 2.

If no player holds, all players pick up their cards, re-ante, and proceed to Round 2.

In Round 2, all players receive one face-down card. At the drop, players compete to have the highest three-card hand (A-A-A is the highest possible hand). After dropping, all players who held cards compare and pay the winner as usual.

In Round 3, all players receive another face-down card and compete to have the lowest four-card hand (4-3-2-A is lowest). Another drop, another payout.

In Round 4, all players receive a fifth face-down card and compete to have the highest five-card poker hand. And remember that if a player earns three Shelbys at any point, he wins the entire pot and the game is over. Otherwise, all players re-ante and new hands are dealt.

- -
VARIATION 6: PSYCHO SHELBY
This is no-limit Shelby, with plenty of scope for aggressive betting and humongous pots (and equally humongous challenge payouts!). Unlike the basic Shelby game, there is no preset limit for challenges; the stake for challenges is always the current value of the pot. However, all money added to the pot in the current betting round is not incrementally added to the pot total; the pot total is not recalculated or adjusted until the following round of betting.

In Round 1, all players receive three face-down cards and compete to make the highest hand using only two of three cards (A-A is a guaranteed winner at this point). In Round 2, players receive two more face-down cards and compete to have the lowest hand using only three of five cards (3-2-A is lowest at this point). In Round 3, there is a twist: players receive two additional face-down cards and compete to have the highest five-card poker hand using Baseball rules (meaning all 3s and 9s are wild, and 4s buy an extra card off the deck for a preset amount, typically $1).

- -
VARIATION 7: TENNESSEE GUTS
Aces always and only rank high, and the suits rank (high to low) spades, hearts, diamonds, clubs (e.g., K♠ beats K♥). After an ante, deal one card to each player. After a drop, players that hold must turn up their cards, and the winner places a marker or button in front of himself. The loser(s) pays an agreed-upon amount to the pot. All players re-ante, and new cards are dealt (deal from the existing deck;

do not shuffle until the deck is exhausted). The first player to earn three markers wins the pot and ends the game.

FIVE-CARD DRAW

DIFFICULTY *low*	TIME LENGTH *medium*	DECKS 1

Five-Card Draw emerged in the 1850s and '60s, at the height of the American Gold Rush in California. Its predecessor used a twenty-card deck that limited the number of players and the possible hand combinations. The fifty-two-card deck became standard in the 1850s. This led to the introduction of a draw round, which led to more aggressive betting, which led to the game's raging popularity on the gold fields of California and Alaska.

Players are dealt five cards. After the first bet, players may discard and replace up to four cards. At the showdown, the highest poker hand wins.

∾ **NUMBER OF PLAYERS** Up to 7

∾ **INITIAL DEAL** Each player is dealt five cards, all face down.

∾ **FIRST BET** Player to the left of the dealer opens.

∾ **SECOND DEAL** Player to the left of the dealer may (but is not required to) discard up to four cards, face down. The dealer gives the player an equivalent number of replacement cards, face down, and repeats the draw with each subsequent player.

∾ **SECOND BET** The player who opened the first round of betting opens the second round. If there was no betting in the first round, the player to the left of the dealer starts the betting.

∾ **REST OF GAME** Once the pot is neat, all players must flip their cards face up. The highest hand wins.

∾ **STRATEGY TIPS** If you are dealt an initial pair, the smart move is to discard the three unpaired cards even if they look promising. For example, if you start with A-7-7-5-2, don't even think about keeping that ace. Discard everything except 7-7 and you have a 40 percent chance of drawing either a third seven or a second pair.

VARIATION 1: DEUCES DIABLO
You have been warned: This game is for crazy people only!

RULE CHANGE The initial and second deals are identical to the basic game, but all 2s (deuces) are wild, and any player who folds is out for all subsequent hands and redeals. The "diablo" part comes with the first bet: if you are crazy enough to open, you *must* win the hand. If you do not win, the hand winner takes the pot and the game continues with a twist: all eligible players ante as normal, except the previous hand's losing player, whose ante must match the value of the previous pot!

That's right, if the value of the previous pot was $15, the losing player must ante $15 in addition to the normal ante. It's called a penalty ante, and it really hurts! The pain, and game, continue until a player who opens the bet actually wins the pot.

STRATEGY TIPS You are crazy to open the bet without having one—preferably two—wild cards. Strategy for the remaining players is straightforward: try to improve your hand at the draw, bet big, and never fold (by folding you disqualify yourself from play in the later hands, when the pots typically bulge with penalty antes). A straight rarely wins this game. Two pair? Not a chance in hell.

VARIATION 2: JACKS TO OPEN
Follow the standard Five-Card Draw rules, except you may not open the first round of betting holding less than a pair of jacks. If no player can open the betting, the hand is dead, the pot is carried over to the next hand, players re-ante, and new cards are dealt. Once you fold, you're out of the game for

good, even if new cards are redealt. If all but one player folds, the survivor wins the pot and the game is over.

VARIATION 3: JACKS TO OPEN, TRIPS TO WIN

Follow the rules for Jacks to Open until the showdown. At this point, only players holding three-of-a-kind or better are eligible to win the pot. If nobody meets these requirements, the hand is dead, the pot is carried over, and new cards are dealt.

VARIATION 4: KNOCK POKER

All players ante a single chip (typically worth 50 cents or $1) and receive five cards, face down. The undealt cards (called the stock) are placed on the table. The player to the left of the dealer takes the topmost stock card and then discards (face up) any card from his hand. The next clockwise player takes the topmost stock card or the previous player's discard, and ends her turn by discarding one card.

Any player, after drawing and before discarding, may knock by tapping on the table and discarding. The other players each have one turn to draw and discard (the knocker does not get another draw). After drawing, each player may fold (immediately, paying the knocker one chip) or stay in.

At the showdown, the high poker hand wins. If the knocker is victorious, the other players pay him two chips each. If the knocker loses, he pays two chips to all players who stayed in, and the actual winning hand collects the original antes (minus any that were already paid to the knocker). In case of a tie, the antes are split evenly and no other penalties are paid.

VARIATION 5: SHOTGUN POKER

Play is the same as in a standard five-card game, but before the final betting round, all players stack their cards in a pile, face down. The player who opened the last bet flips one card face up on the table, followed by a round of betting. The next clockwise player must beat the previous hand (keep turning up cards until he does), or fold. There's a round of betting each time the previous hand is beaten. The last player standing wins the pot.

VARIATION 6: SKINNY MINNIE

This is the standard Shotgun Poker game played high-low, with the pot split 50-50 between the players holding the highest and lowest poker hands.

VARIATION 7: SPIT IN THE OCEAN

Deal all players four cards, face down, and deal a single fifth card face up on the table. This card is shared among all players and is wild (so in effect all players have a wild card in their hand). If you're holding other cards of the same rank, they're also wild. After a round of betting, players draw cards from the deck as usual and bet as usual. The high hand wins at the showdown.

VARIATION 8: WHISKEY POKER

Deal five cards face down to all players and five cards (also face down) to a *widow* hand. After a round of betting, the player to the left of the dealer has three choices: pass, exchange, or knock.

The first player to choose the exchange swaps his entire hand for the widow. The replacement widow hand is turned up for all players to see, and each player in turn has the option of exchanging one (or more) face-up widow cards with a card(s) from her hand. If the widow comes around to the dealer untouched—i.e., all players have passed—the dealer turns the widow face up and each player has another turn to exchange cards. Players may pass multiple times and jump back in on a subsequent turn; the only restriction is that you may not pass two turns in a row.

At any point, a player may knock to signal that she likes her hand and will not draw additional cards. After a knock, the remaining players have one final chance to exchange cards with the widow. After a round of betting, the high hand wins the pot and the low hand (worst hand) pays a penalty of 50 percent of the current pot's value into the next pot.

FIVE-CARD STUD

DIFFICULTY *low*	TIME LENGTH *short*	DECKS 1

Five-Card Stud is a classic poker game—that's Classic as in Old West, six-shooters, and whiskey by the pint. Part of the allure, no doubt, is that Five-Card Stud has always been an all-or-nothing game. Then as now, your choices are to play aggressively with a strong hand, bluff the competition with a weak hand, or drop out early to avoid the expensive heartache of getting caught in between.

*All players are dealt five cards (one down, four up). At the **showdown**, the highest poker hand wins.*

∾ **NUMBER OF PLAYERS** Up to 9

∾ **INITIAL DEAL** Each player is dealt one card face down and a second card face up.

∾ **FIRST BET** The player with highest face-up card opens.

∾ **SECOND DEAL** Each player is dealt one card, face up.

∾ **SECOND BET** The player with the highest visible pair (if none, the highest face-up card) opens.

∾ **REST OF GAME** One card is dealt face up to all players, followed by a round of betting. This is repeated until all players have five cards each.

∾ **STRATEGY TIPS** An unpaired ace or A-K combination often wins this game. Keep in mind that the odds of pairing your **hole card** are only 20–25 percent, so don't count on pairing up. Conversely, bet as aggressively as possible if you have a hidden pair.

- -
VARIATION 1: FIVE STUD HIGH-LOW
This is similar to the basic game, except that the pot is split 50-50 between the highest and lowest winning hands.

RULE CHANGE Any player may ask to receive his fifth card face down (this is called a *swap*). When swapping, players turn up their hole card for all to see. They then receive the fifth card face down.

STRATEGY TIPS The fifth card swap can be an important part of your betting strategy. For example, use the swap aggressively (by disclosing a previously hidden pair) or defensively (by disclosing an inside straight or four-card flush, and possibly scaring off the competition).

- -

VARIATION 2: FOUR FLUSH

Use this variation to spice up either the basic stud or high-low games.

RULE CHANGE A "four flush" is any hand with four cards of the same suit. This beats any pair, but loses to any two pair or higher hand. A four flush does not affect low hands. For example, a player with 8♥-6♥-5♥-2♥-7♦ could win the low hand (8 high) and the high hand (four flush).

STRATEGY TIPS Even starting with three cards of the same suit, you have only a 25 percent chance of suiting up on the fourth or fifth cards. These odds are not great.

- -

VARIATION 3: LET IT RIDE

This is a popular casino variation, no doubt because the odds of winning are against you! All players play alone, against the dealer.

RULE CHANGE Each player puts three bets of equal amount in front of them—typically three stacks of $2 or $5 in chips. All players and the dealer each receive three cards face down. The dealer immediately discards one card without looking. All other players look at their three cards and ask for one of their three bets back (by sweeping their cards along the table, as in blackjack) or agree to "let it ride" by doing nothing. The dealer returns any bets requested (leaving some players with three stacks of chips, others with two) and then turns up one card.

All players now use the dealer's upcard, along with their three-card hand, to make a Five-Card Stud hand. The process then repeats—let your second bet ride or take it back (if you let your first bet ride, take back only your second bet, leaving the first on the table). Tuck your cards under your remaining bet(s) to signify you're ready for the third and final round. And don't touch your cards from this point forward.

The dealer turns up her second (and final) card, which becomes the fifth card in each player's hand. You win holding a pair of 10's or better, and are paid for each of your bets left on the table (for all bets you let ride). Payouts vary among casinos. The typical amounts are:

> 10s or better pays 1 to 1
>
> Two pair pays 2 to 1
>
> Three-of-a-kind pays 3 to 1
>
> Straight pays 5 to 1
>
> Flush pays 8 to 1
>
> Full house pays 11 to 1
>
> Four-of-a-kind pays 50 to 1
>
> Straight flush pays 200 to 1
>
> Royal flush pays 1,000 to 1

- -

VARIATION 4: CARIBBEAN STUD

This is another popular casino variation. All players compete against the house (the dealer) and try to make the best five-card poker hand.

RULE CHANGE Before cards are dealt, place an ante on the table (dollar amounts vary among casinos), and decide whether to enter the (optional) progressive jackpot by placing a chip (typically $1) into the marked slot on the table.

Each player receives five cards: all face down to the players, four down and one up to the dealer. If you choose to fold, you lose your ante. If you choose to play, place double the amount of your ante in the betting box (marked on the table). This is your *call* bet.

The dealer turns up his four hole cards. He qualifies (stays in) holding A-K or higher; otherwise all players receive 1 to 1 payouts on their antes and all call bets are a push (neither won nor lost). If the dealer qualifies, each player goes head to head against him and loses both the ante and call bets to the dealer's higher hand. If the player wins, she earns a 1-to-1 payout on her ante, plus a bonus payout for her call bet, depending on her hand:

Pair or less pays 1 to 1

Two pair pays 2 to 1

Three-of-a-kind pays 3 to 1

Straight pays 4 to 1

Flush pays 5 to 1

Full house pays 7 to 1

Four-of-a-kind pays 20 to 1

Straight flush pays 50 to 1

Royal flush pays 100 to 1

If you made the progressive jackpot bet at the start of the game, you are also paid the following (even if you don't beat the dealer—the progressive jackpot is a separate standalone bet):

Flush wins $50

Full house wins $100

Four-of-a-kind wins $500

Straight flush wins 10 percent of total progressive jackpot

Royal flush wins 100 percent of total progressive jackpot

Statistically speaking, the progressive jackpot is a losing proposition. Even so, the progressive jackpot is *the* reason to play Caribbean Stud for many players. The wisdom of the crowd also suggests you should *not* fold holding a low pair or even ace-high. On their own, these hands rarely pay off; however, it's more costly in the long term to fold constantly and lose your ante, rather than waiting for a high-payout hand such as three-of-a-kind or a straight.

SEVEN-CARD STUD

DIFFICULTY *medium*	TIME LENGTH *long*	DECKS 1

Before the current Texas Hold'em craze took hold in the mid-1990s, Seven-Card Stud was the undisputed king of poker. The scope for psychological play and strategic betting is immense. The downside, of course, is that Seven-Card Stud can feel s-l-o-w to new players unfamiliar with the game's subtleties.

*All players are dealt seven cards (two down, four up, one down). At the **showdown,** the highest five-card poker hand wins.*

∾ **NUMBER OF PLAYERS** Up to 7

∾ **INITIAL DEAL** Deal each player two cards face down and one card face up.

∾ **FIRST BET** The player with the lowest face-up card opens the bet.

∾ **SECOND DEAL** Deal each player one card, face up.

∾ **SECOND BET** The player with the highest pair or, if none, the highest face-up card opens the bet. If there's a tie for high card, the card dealt first opens.

∾ **REST OF GAME** One card is dealt face up to all players, followed by a betting round that is opened by the player with the highest visible poker hand. This is repeated until all players have four face-up cards (six cards total).

The seventh (and final) card is dealt face down, followed by a final betting round. At the showdown, the best five-card poker hand wins (each player's two unused cards have no effect on the game's final outcome).

∾ **STRATEGY TIPS** Two strong pairs (or a three-of-a-kind) often win this game. But don't wait for your hand to improve. Fold 'em if you don't have the makings of a winner after four cards. Experienced players often bet aggressively early on, to stop opponents from improving a weak pair to three-of-a-kind, or two weak pairs to a full house.

- -

VARIATION 1: 10-4 GOOD BUDDY

Bust out your CB and trucker's hat; this game honors (if that's the right word) America's eighteen-wheelers with no fewer than eight wild cards: 10s and 4s. Follow all other rules for basic Seven-Card Stud.

- -

VARIATION 2: ANACONDA

This is a popular variation at home games. Not much skill is needed here, just an appetite for betting (there are nine rounds of betting in Anaconda!).

Deal seven cards to each player, face down, followed by a betting round. Each player then passes three cards, face down, to his left. Round of betting. Now players pass two cards to their left. Round of betting. Now one card is passed to the left. Round of betting.

Next, all players select their best five cards and place them face down on the table. On the dealer's signal, all players turn up their top card. Round of betting, led by the player with the highest card showing. This process is repeated until all cards are face up, with a round of betting each time led by the player with the best hand showing. The best poker hand wins.

You may play Anaconda high-low. In some poker circles, the pass is handled differently: three cards to the left, two cards to the right, one card to the left.

- -

VARIATION 3: ANACONDA ROLL 'EM

Play the standard game until the final showdown. At this point, all active players stack their cards on the table, face down. The player to the left of the dealer turns up a card. The next clockwise player must beat the previous hand (keep turning up cards until he does) or fold. There's a round of betting each time the previous hand is beaten. The last player standing wins the pot.

VARIATION 4: HOWDY DOODY

This high-low Anaconda variation adds wild cards into the mix. All **3**s are wild if the hand they're in is played high. All kings are wild if the hand they're in is played low.

VARIATION 5: BASEBALL

People love to hate Baseball. The game is similar to basic Seven-Card Stud, but includes wild cards and match-the-pot betting. Batter up!

In Baseball, all **9**s and any face-down **3**s are wild. In addition, any face-up **3** may be made wild by matching the value of the current pot. For example, if you're dealt a face-up **3** and the pot's current value is $8.25, simply pay $8.25 to the pot to make the card wild. You are not required to make a face-up **3** wild, though it may be tempting to do so—plus it makes the next **3** that much more expensive for an opponent to purchase.

The final curveball is that any player who is dealt a face-up **4** may choose to buy an additional card off the deck (dealt face down) for a preset amount, usually 50 cents to $1. The money goes straight to the pot. That player now has eight cards with which to make a five-card poker hand.

> **STRATEGY TIPS** You will rarely win Baseball with less than a full house. Four-of-a-kinds are more common. With so many wild cards, so are straight flushes. If you are dealt a face-up **3** early in the game, match the pot and make it wild. Even if you don't exactly need a wild card, it's a good defensive move—your pot-matching will double the cost to any opponent who's dealt a subsequent face-up **3**.

VARIATION 6: NO-PEEKIE BASEBALL

If you think Baseball is too wild, prepare yourself for the *no-peekie* version. The rules are essentially the same as Baseball, except that players may not look at *any* of their cards. Once all cards are dealt, the player to the left of the dealer turns up a single card. A round of betting follows. Moving clockwise, the next player turns cards up one at a time until they beat the previous hand. For example, if player one turns up a king, player two must turn up cards until the king is beaten (either by an ace, by a king plus a higher *kicker,* or by a higher poker hand such as a pair). After a round of betting, the next player must turn up cards and try to beat the previous hand, and so on. If any player turns up all his cards and still cannot beat the previous hand, he is out of the game (this is equivalent to a force fold). The game is won by the last player standing. In this game there are no hole cards, so all 3s are considered face up.

- -

VARIATION 7: RAINOUT BASEBALL

This variation adds a little spice to the basic and no-peekie versions. Any time Q♠ is turned face up, the hand is dead, all cards are thrown in, and a new hand is dealt to all players who did not fold in the previous round. Players also should re-ante.

- -

VARIATION 8: BISCUITS & GRAVY

Spice up the basic Seven-Card-Stud game with "biscuit and gravy" wild cards. Biscuits are 3s, and 8s are gravy. It's commonly held, especially in the American South, that biscuits taste best with gravy, so these cards are only wild in combination. For example, nothing is wild in the hand K-J-8-5-2, whereas there are two wild cards in the hand K-8-5-3-2. You need a helping of gravy for each biscuit, and vice versa, so there are only two wild cards in the hand K-8-8-3-2.

- -

VARIATION 9: BLACK MARIAH

To the basic Seven-Card-Stud game, add one simple twist: a hand may be won only by a player with the best five-card poker hand *and* the highest spade dealt in the hole (face down). The game is over—and the pot is captured—by a player who wins both. Otherwise the pot stays, all players re-ante, and a new hand is dealt.

- -

VARIATION 10: BUTCHER BOY

Deal cards one at time to all players. When a card of matching rank is subsequently dealt (e.g., player three is dealt 5♣, then player four is dealt 5♥), the card is given to the previous player (the 5♥ is given to player three), followed by a betting round starting with the player who received the card in question. The deal starts again at the player who was stripped of the card, and continues until a player has four-of-a-kind. The pot is then split 50-50 between that player and the player holding the lowest hand. If a player has five or more cards, she may choose which five to use. If a player has fewer than five cards, the voids are considered unbeatable low cards. For example, the hand 6-5-3 is considered 6-5-3-0-0 and beats a natural 6-5-3-2-A.

- -
VARIATION 11: BETWEEN THE SHEETS

This is a great end-of-the-night game, when players are willing to make large bets on the flimsiest of hunches. Start with an ante (typically 50 cents to $1), and deal two cards face up, with room for a third card in between. The player to the left of the dealer bets (ante minimum, pot maximum) whether the next card will be "in between" the two face-up cards. If the face-up cards are 4 and 8, for example, in-between cards are the 5, 6, or 7.

The dealer turns up the next card and, if the player bet correctly, he takes that amount from the pot. Otherwise his ante is thrown in, and the next clockwise player is dealt two more face-up cards and the process continues. If a player bets and wins the pot before all players have a turn, all players re-ante and the game continues. Otherwise, the game ends when a player bets and then wins the pot.

Aces are always high; however, if a player's *first* face-up card is an ace, he chooses whether it ranks high or low.

If the in-between card "hits the goalposts" (matches the rank of either face-up card), the player loses his turn and contributes double his ante to the pot. For example, if the turn-up cards are 4 and 8, and the in-between card is 8, the player loses his turn and pays double his ante to the pot.

- -
VARIATION 12: ACEY DEUCY

This is a gentler version of Between the Sheets. The first time around, table players may wager only up to half the pot total. Thereafter, the game ends when someone wins the entire pot. And if a player hits the goalposts, there is no double-ante penalty. She simply loses her turn and forfeits the original ante.

- -
VARIATION 13: SHEEP SHAGGER

If Acey Deucy is the gentle version, Sheep Shagger is the evil one. Follow the standard rules, but add a third "upcard," plus room for a second in between card. For example: upcard–in-between card–upcard–in-between card–upcard.

The first "up–between–up–x–x" grouping is played exactly like Between the Sheets. The second "x–x–up–between–up" grouping requires its own bet (ante minimum, pot maximum), and the penalty for hitting the goalposts increases to a triple-ante penalty. So, if you bet $5 on the second grouping and hit the goal-posts, you owe $15 to the pot.

- -
VARIATION 14: CHICAGO

Does the game have anything to do with the Windy City? Who knows. It's exactly like standard Seven-Card Stud, except that the pot is split 50-50 between the player holding the best five-card poker hand and the player holding the highest spade in the *hole.*

- -
VARIATION 15: CINCINNATI

Deal five cards to each player, face down, plus five communal cards on the table, also face down. After a betting round, turn up the communal cards one at a time, followed by a betting round. At the showdown, players may use any combination of community and hole cards to create the highest five-card poker hand. Ties split the pot evenly.

- -
VARIATION 16: CINCINNATI LOW BALL

One of the most common variations of Cincinnati is low ball, played exactly like the standard game except that the lowest five-card hand wins the pot.

VARIATION 17: CINCINNATI LIZ

This is standard Cincinnati with a single wild card—namely, the lowest community card (aces are low in lowball games, otherwise 2s are low). That card is also wild for all players holding a card of matching rank.

VARIATION 18: CINCO DE MAYO

This game honors not Mexican Independence (that's September 16), but the day that Mexican armies beat the French at the Battle of Puebla on May 5, 1862. As a result all red 5s are wild—it's as simple as that. Viva la Revolución!

VARIATION 19: COWPIE

This is basically Pai Gow (see p. 349) without all the frills. After the last round of betting in a normal Seven-Card-Stud hand, all players create a five-card hand and a two-card hand. The five-card hand must beat the two-card hand, and the latter must contain at least one hole card. There's a final betting round, followed by the showdown. The winner of each splits the pot 50-50; if there are multiple winners, the 50 percent share is split evenly among them.

VARIATION 20: DAKOTA

Each player's high hole-card is wild. Start by dealing three cards face down to each player. All players then turn up one card, followed by a betting round. Continue dealing cards face down and one at a time—with players turning up a card followed by a betting round—until each player has six cards. At this point, all players choose to receive a seventh card either face up (for free) or face-down (for the maximum bet amount). At the showdown, the highest five-card poker hand wins.

VARIATION 21: DIRTY SCHULTZ

It's another "just like Seven-Card Stud" game, with a single twist: whenever a player is dealt a natural face-up pair, the next card dealt face up is wild for all players holding that card. There may only be one wild card, so if a subsequent natural pair is dealt face up, the new wild card replaces the previous one.

There are no wild cards if the second card of a natural pair is the last upcard in the round.

- -

VARIATION 22: EIGHT-CARD STUD

At the end of a normal Seven-Card-Stud hand, deal an eighth card face down to all players. After a round of betting, players make their best five-card poker hands.

- -

VARIATION 23: ENGLISH STUD

In English Stud, all players are dealt six cards total and compete to make the best five-card hands. Follow the basic Seven-Card-Stud game until all players have five cards. Before dealing the sixth, all players may pay (typically $1) to draw a single card from the deck, replacing an upcard with an upcard or a downcard with a downcard. After a round of betting, a sixth card is dealt to all players, followed by a final round of betting and the showdown.

- -

VARIATION 24: FOLLOW THE QUEEN

It's Seven Card Stud, with queens always wild. And when a queen is dealt face up, the next card dealt face up is wild for all players, too. If another queen is dealt face up, the next face-up card replaces the previous wild card. If a queen is the last upcard, only queens are wild.

- -

VARIATION 25: FOLLOW THE WHORE

Politically correct this game is not. It's identical to Follow the Queen, except that queens are never wild. Only the card following a queen is wild. If a queen is the last upcard, no cards are wild.

- -

VARIATION 26: FOOTBALL

No doubt this game was invented by hardcore fans of Baseball who wanted American football to have its own poker variant. The game follows the rules of Baseball, except that 7s (think: touchdown) are always wild, face-down 3s (think: field goal) are wild, and face-up 3s may be made wild by matching the pot. Face-up 10s (think: first down) allow you to purchase a new card off the deck for a preset amount (typically 50 cents to $1).

VARIATION 27: GOLF

Another sports-inspired game played just like Baseball, with the following exceptions. All 8s (think: snowman) are *dead* cards, which means they are useless for the entire game. Dead, too, is the card immediately following your 8 (think: shank on the next tee box). This penalty only applies to your own hand; it does not carry over to the next player in rotation.

VARIATION 28: GHOST

Six or fewer may play Ghost. Follow the basic Seven-Card-Stud rules, but deal an extra card face down in each round to a "ghost hand." At the showdown, the player with the highest five-card poker hand must also beat the ghost hand. If this happens, that player wins the pot, and the game is over. Otherwise, there is no winner and the entire pot is carried over to the next hand.

VARIATION 29: THE GOOD, THE BAD & THE UGLY

This is similar to the basic game, with the addition of a single wild card (good), a single *dead* card (bad), and a single *force-fold* card (ugly). After the initial Seven-Card-Stud basic deal, the dealer takes three cards off the deck and places them face down on the table. The dealer nominates which card is good, which is bad, and which is ugly.

The game continues as normal until all players have a full seven-card hand. At that point, the dealer turns over the "good" card. If any player has a matching card(s) anywhere in his hand, his matching card(s) becomes wild. After a round of betting (initiated by the player with the highest visible hand), the dealer turns up the "bad" card. If any player has a matching card(s) anywhere in his hand, the card(s) becomes useless and must be thrown face-up on the table. Players who lose a card play at a disadvantage. After another round of betting, the dealer turns up the "ugly" card. If any player has a matching card(s), that player must immediately fold. End of story. A final betting round follows.

VARIATION 30: HOT DANG!

Follow the rules of the Good, the Bad & the Ugly, but with two modifications. After the initial Seven-Card-Stud basic deal, the dealer takes five cards off the deck and places them face down on the table, nominating good, bad, and ugly cards as usual, plus first and second *auction* cards.

Once all players have a full seven-card hand, but before the good, bad, and ugly cards are turned, the dealer turns up the first auction card for all players to bid on. The card is won by the player who bids highest. The auction winner pays the bid amount to the pot, takes the auction card, and replaces it with a card from her hand. This card is now up for auction. The process continues until nobody bids on a card, at which point the first auction ends and the second auction card is turned up, and the entire process is repeated. Once both auctions are over and after a round of betting, the "good" is turned and the game proceeds as normal.

VARIATION 31: H-BOMB

Play a standard Seven-Card-Stud hand until the showdown. At this point, the player to the left of the dealer may match the pot and thereby force-fold the player to his left. Moving clockwise around the table, the next active player may match the pot and force-fold the player to her left. The pot is won by the best five-card poker hand.

VARIATION 32: HAVE A HEART

Play the normal Seven-Card-Stud game, but each time a player is dealt a face-up heart, they take any card (face up or down) from any other player. The card taken is not replaced, and the victim plays at a disadvantage.

VARIATION 33: HEINZ

Think: ketchup. It's the standard Seven-Card-Stud game, with all 5s and 7s wild. When a wild card is dealt face up to any player, that player must match the pot or fold.

VARIATION 34: HENWAY

Deal ten cards to each player. Next, split your ten cards into two hands of five cards each, one competing for high and one competing for low. All players then place their cards face down on the table, high hands to the left and low hands to the right. After a betting round, all players turn up one card from each of their two hands, followed by a betting round. At the showdown, the pot is split 50-50 between the high and low hands.

VARIATION 35: HIGH-LOW/8

High-Low Split 8 or Better—more commonly abbreviated as High-Low/8—is the most common variation of Seven-Card Stud, especially in casinos. It's similar to the basic game, except the pot is split 50-50 between the highest five-card hand and the lowest five-card hand containing no cards above an 8. In standard high-low games it does not matter how low the low hand is. In this variation, a hand qualifies for low only if it contains no card higher than 8. For example, 8-5-3-2-A qualifies as low, while 9-5-3-2-A does not. If there are no qualifying low hands at the showdown, the high hand takes 100 percent of the pot.

It's possible for the same player to win both low and high using his seven cards to make two different hands. For example, if you hold 7-7-7-4-3-2-A, you have both an excellent high hand (7-7-7-A-4) and a hand that qualifies for low (7-4-3-2-A).

VARIATION 36: INDIAN POKER

Oh, the silliness. All players ante (typically $1), and receive one card face down, which they then place on their foreheads with one hand, so all other players except themselves can *see* it. If a player ever sees his own card, he is out of the hand and forfeits his ante to the pot.

The highest card wins the pot (ties split the pot evenly). Starting with the player to the left of the dealer, players decide whether to stay in the game based on (a blind guess) whether their card is higher or lower than the other players' cards. Throw in your ante if you're in; otherwise fold and take your ante back. The deal moves clockwise, using the remaining cards from the deck (do not reshuffle). The game ends once the deck is exhausted.

- -

VARIATION 37: IRON CROSS

Deal four cards to each player, face down. Next, deal five communal cards, face down, in the shape of a cross. The cross's center card is wild. After a betting round, turn up a cross card one at a time, followed by a betting round. At the showdown, players create the best five-card poker hands using four hole cards plus *either* the vertical or horizontal row of community cards.

- -

VARIATION 38: LOWBALL

This is the quintessential low-hand poker game. It follows the normal Seven-Card-Stud rules, except all players are competing for the lowest five-card poker hand (as opposed to the highest). The traditional *lowest* low hand is 5-4-3-2-A (called "the wheel"). In this version of the game, aces may be played high or low, and straights and flushes do not count.

- -

VARIATION 39: ACE-SIX LOWBALL

Players who cannot stomach, abide by, or otherwise accept the wheel play this variant, where the lowest low hand is 6-4-3-2-A, and straights and flushes count as high hands.

- -

VARIATION 40: DEUCE-SEVEN LOWBALL

Aces are always high in this Lowball variant—so the lowest low hand is 7-5-4-3-2. Straights and flushes count as high hands.

- -

VARIATION 41: LOW-OF-A-KIND

Follow the normal Seven-Card-Stud rules, but at the end of the game, the pot is split 50-50 between the player with the highest four-of-a-kind and the player with the *lowest* five-card poker hand. If no player has four-of-a-kind, the low-hand winner takes half the pot, and the other half is carried over to the next hand's pot. The game ends when 100 percent of the pot is won in a single hand.

VARIATION 42: MERRY-GO-ROUND

Deal all players one card, face down. The player to the left of the dealer may pay $1 to swap cards with the player to his left. After a round of betting, deal a second card to all players. The player sitting two spots from the dealer may now pay $2 to swap her hand with the player to her left. After a round of betting, deal a third card, then a fourth, etc., each time allowing the next active player in rotation the option to swap hands with the player to his left for $3, $4, $5, etc. Continue until all players have seven cards. At the showdown, the pot is split 50-50 between the highest and lowest five-card poker hands.

VARIATION 43: MEXICAN STUD

This is basically No-Peekie Baseball without the wild cards. All players are dealt seven cards face down. The most important rule is also the simplest: Do not look at your cards! The player to the left of the dealer turns up one card, followed by a round of betting. The next player turns up a card (or cards) until the previous hand is beaten. For example, if the previous hand is K♥, the next player must continue turning up her cards until K♥ is beaten by a pair, an ace, or a king with a high *kicker*. If you cannot beat the previous hand, it's a force fold, and the turn rotates clockwise. Each time the previous hand is beaten, a betting round follows. The process is repeated until every player but one has force folded.

VARIATION 44: MEXICAN SWEAT

This is the same as Mexican Stud, but with a good, bad & ugly twist. After all players have seven face-down cards, there's an initial round of betting, followed by the dealer turning up three cards from the deck. The first is good (wild for all players), the second is bad (a dead card; it has no value for all players holding it), and the third is ugly (a force-fold; all players holding this card must fold immediately). The game proceeds as normal. If all players fold in the same hand, the pot is carried over and a new hand is dealt.

VARIATION 45: MISSISSIPPI STUD

Follow the standard Seven-Card-Stud rules until all players have two down cards and one upcard. Next, deal all players two face-down cards (not the usual one card), followed by a betting round. Deal the remaining three cards *face up*, one at a time, each card followed by a betting round. All players thus end the game with two cards in the hole and five cards face up on the table.

VARIATION 46: ONE-EYED JACKS & SUICIDE KING

The one-eyed jacks (seen in profile on most decks of cards) are the J♠ and J♥; the suicide king (pictured with a sword through his head) is the K♥. Add some or all of these as wild cards to a standard Seven-Card-Stud game for variety.

VARIATION 47: PAI GOW

This is a common Seven-Card-Stud variation in casinos, although you can also play at home. Up to seven players compete against the dealer for the best five-card poker hand and the best two-card hand.

To a fifty-two-card deck, add a single joker, which may be used only as an ace or to complete a straight, flush, or straight flush. Otherwise the joker has no value.

Each player places a single bet on the table (there is no other ante; the minimum and maximum bet values vary in casinos; in at-home games, the range is typically $1 to $5). Deal each player (including the dealer) seven cards. Players may look at their cards; the dealer may not.

Players organize their seven cards into a five-card hand and a two-card hand. Follow standard poker rankings for the five-card hand, but note that 5-4-3-2-A is *always* the second-highest straight or straight flush, beating K-Q-J-10-9 but losing to A-K-Q-J-10. The best two-card hand is A-A. The final restriction: Your five-card hand must beat your two-card hand.

All players place their two hands face down on the table. When all players are ready, the dealer's seven cards are turned face up. From this point on, the players may not touch their cards. The dealer creates two hands (following the same rules as the other players) and then reconciles with each player as follows:

If the player wins both hands, the dealer pays the amount of the player's original bet.

If the dealer wins one hand and the player wins the other, no money changes hands.

If the dealer wins both hands, the dealer wins the player's original bet. Ties are awarded to the dealer—which is a major advantage. So, if the dealer wins one hand while the other is tied, or if both hands are tied, the dealer wins. If one hand is tied and the player wins the other, no money changes hands. Given the dealer's advantage in Pai Gow, it's important to rotate the deal frequently in home games.

- -
VARIATION 48: PASS THE TRASH
At the very end of a standard Seven-Card-Stud hand, just before the showdown, all active players pass three unwanted cards—the "trash"—to their left. After a final round of betting, it's time for a showdown. The high poker-hand wins. (In some circles, Pass the Trash starts with seven cards dealt face down to all players, followed by a round of betting. Players then pass their trash, followed by a final round of betting and the showdown.)

- -
VARIATION 49: PEG LEG
It's unclear whether this is a better drinking or gambling game—and as always, it's dangerous to confuse the two! Play a standard Seven-Card-Stud hand, but place all antes and bets in a single stack. (It's important to wait your proper turn before adding chips to the stack.) The player who knocks over the stack in the course of adding chips to it is automatically out for the round. At this point, the game proceeds as normal, with no further peg-leg action. If the stack does not fall prior to the showdown, the highest five-card hand takes the pot, and each of the active players pays the winner a penalty of $1.

VARIATION 50: POLISH

Deal each player two cards face down. Use a **button** to keep track of the draw; the button starts one player to the left of the dealer. The dealer turns up a card from the deck, and the player on the button may either accept or pass. If passed, the card is offered to the next player, who may also accept or pass. If passed a second time, the next player *must* take the card. The process continues (skipping players who've taken a card in the current round) until all players have taken a card. After a betting round, the button rotates one player to the left, and the draw starts again. The entire process continues until all players have six cards. The seventh card is dealt face down to all players. At the showdown, the pot is split 50-50 between the high and low five-card poker hands.

VARIATION 51: THE PRICE IS RIGHT

After the initial Seven-Card-Stud deal (all players should have two cards face down, one card face up), deal two face-down cards from the deck. Nominate one of these cards as "Door 1," the other as "Door 2." The top card on the deck is "Door 3." The player to the left of the dealer is up first: he or she may purchase Door 1 for 25 cents, Door 2 for 50 cents, or Door 3 for $1 (adjust the amounts as desired), or pass.

If the card behind Door 1 is purchased, the Door 2 card is moved into the Door 1 slot, and the Door 3 card is moved into the Door 2 slot. The same repeats if the card behind Door 2 is purchased.

Repeat until all players have bought a card or folded. After a round of betting, start the process once again, until all players are holding seven cards or have folded. The high poker hand wins.

VARIATION 52: RAZZ

In Razz, the lowest hand wins. Aces are always low. Unlike some low-hand variations, flushes and straights have no effect on rankings, which means the best possible low hand is 6-4-3-2-A (or 5-4-3-2-A if you play the wheel).

VARIATION 53: RAZZMATAZZ

This is identical to the main game, except there's a progressive Follow-the-Queen-style wild card element. At the start of the game, all aces are wild, and they stay wild unless a 2 is dealt face up. Once this happens, all 2s are wild (replacing aces) and stay wild unless a 3 is dealt face up, in which case 3s replace 2s as the wild card, etc.

VARIATION 54: SCREW YOUR NEIGHBOR

All players start with an equal number of chips (typically three, each worth $1 or $2). All players are dealt a single face-down card. Use a **button** to keep track of the turn; the button starts with the dealer and rotates one player to the left after each deal.

The player to the left of the button may keep her card, or swap with the player on her left—unless that player is holding a king (called a *stopper*). The player holding a stopper turns it face up and keeps it for the remainder of the game. In this case, the original player is stuck with his card. The dealer (playing last) keeps her original card, or receives the top card off the deck—unless that card is a king, in which case she must keep her original card.

At the end of the round, the player holding the lowest card forfeits one chip to the pot. In case of a tie, both players forfeit their chips to the pot. The game ends when all players but one run out of chips. The winner takes the pot.

VARIATION 55: SIX-CARD STUD

This is one of the few Seven-Card-Stud games suitable for eight players. That magical feat is performed by dealing cards two down, three up, one down to all players for a total of six cards (not the usual seven). Follow all other rules.

VARIATION 56: ST. VALENTINE'S DAY MASSACRE

This is a split-pot game. The player holding the highest-ranking heart—A♥ is always high—in the hole splits the pot 50-50 with the high five-card poker hand.

VARIATION 57: UP THE RIVER, DOWN THE RIVER

Up to six may play this variation. After the initial Seven-Card-Stud deal, deal two face-down rows of five cards each (ten cards total). Nominate one row as "up the river" and the other as "down the river." Play the standard game until just before the showdown. At that point, the dealer turns up one upriver card (wild for all players holding a card of matching rank) and one downriver card (dead and of no use for players holding a card of matching rank).

After a round of betting, turn up the next set of river cards and repeat. If you end the game with fewer than four cards, you play at a disadvantage. At the showdown, the highest poker hand wins.

If the standard game has too many betting rounds for comfort, deal the first seven cards face down to all players, followed by a single round of betting, before turning up cards from the river.

In some circles, this game is played as a five-card-stud variation (not seven-card).

VARIATION 58: WOOLWORTH

Players of a certain age will remember the Woolworth's chain of "five and dime" drug stores. This game pays its respects by making all 5s and 10s wild. The catch? Take the value of your game's most expensive chip (a quarter, in games of nickel, dime, quarter) and multiply it by five. That's how much you pay to stay in the game when you're dealt a face-up 5. Multiply the amount by ten if you're dealt a face-up 10. You must immediately fold if you don't pay. In all other respects the game follows the standard rules.

Texas Hold'em

Back in the 1970s and '80s, the professional poker world was dominated by Seven-Card Stud. The game is a masterpiece of strategy and subtlety—unless you're watching from the sidelines, in which case the game moves slower than frozen molasses. Not so with Texas Hold'em. It's a frenzied game that rewards guts, luck, and intelligence in that precise order.

> **If you've watched the World Series of Poker or similar events on television, Texas Hold'em is the game they always play. As a result, Texas Hold'em now rules the airwaves, the casino gaming rooms, and most home games.**

The genius of Texas Hold'em is that any player may win any hand. Few hands actually make it to a showdown. Instead, hands are settled based on bluffs, counter-bluffs, and gutsy bets. In Hold'em games, it all comes down to how smart you play. Your cards don't really matter that much.

All players are dealt two cards, face down. All other cards are held in common (shared by all players) and are dealt face up in the following way: three cards (called the *flop*), followed by a betting round; one card (the **turn**), followed by a betting round; and a final card (the **river**), followed by a betting round.

∾ **NUMBER OF PLAYERS** 9 is best, but up to 12 may play

∾ **ANTE** Before any cards are dealt, the first two players to the left of the **button** make forced blind bets, which function like antes. No other players ante. The first blind bet (called the *little blind*) is typically half the value of the maximum bet. The second blind (the *big blind*) typically equals the maximum bet. Since so many players fold early in Texas Hold'em, forced bets are used to generate larger pots for players who stay in the game.

∽ **INITIAL DEAL** Deal each player two cards face down (called *pocket* or *hole* cards), always starting with the player to the left of the *button* (bottle caps are handy), which is placed in front of the dealer. In subsequent rounds, the button rotates clockwise to the next player.

∽ **FIRST BET** The two blind bettors are automatically in, so betting in the first round starts with the third player from the button. That player (and all subsequent players, including the little blind) must call the big blind, raise it, or fold. There is no checking in the first round of Texas Hold'em. If no player raises the big blind, that player is allowed to raise her own bet. If any player raises the bet, she may not raise again unless she is re-raised (as opposed to called). Raises and re-raises are typically limited to the value of the maximum bet, and in most games there's a limit of four raises and re-raises per round. The betting stops when all players have either folded or called the last raise.

∽ **SECOND DEAL** The dealer *burns a card*, and then deals three communal cards, face up. This is the flop.

∽ **SECOND BET** Betting starts at the little blind, then continues clockwise. Checking is allowed in this and all subsequent betting rounds.

∽ **REST OF GAME** The dealer burns a card and then deals one communal card (the turn) face up, followed by a betting round, starting with the little blind. The final communal card (the river) is dealt face up, followed by a last round of betting, again starting with the little blind.

At the showdown, the player who made the final bet (whose last bet was called) shows cards first. The best five-card hand—using any combination of the player's two hole cards and five communal cards—wins the pot. Ties split the pot evenly.

STRATEGY TIPS It's generally worth paying to see the flop—you get to see 71 percent of your cards at this point. Since five of your seven cards are communal, it's also important to start with a strong two-card pocket hand. The best starts are A-A, A-K, A-Q, K-K, and Q-Q. You're off to an equally strong start if your first two cards are sequential (e.g., 8-7 or Q-J) or are suited (the same suit). In general, you should not play past the flop without a strong pair, four suited cards, or an open straight.

Where you sit is an important factor. The dealer has the best position, as being "on the button" means you always act last and can decide to fold, raise, or re-raise based on how your opponents play. Conversely, the worst seats at the table are the so-called "early positions"—the first three players left of the button, who must act without knowing anything about the other players' hands.

Finally, a piece of advice for first-time players: the best Texas Hold'em players either raise bets or fold; they almost never call a bet.

> **It is wholly appropriate—not to mention a smart play—to "muck" your cards (discard without showing them to anyone) if you win a pot because all other players folded.**

VARIATION 1: POT LIMIT TEXAS HOLD'EM
This is played exactly like the standard game except that raises and re-raises are limited to the current value of the pot. So if the pot holds $15.25 at the start of a betting round, the maximum bet, raise, and re-raise is $15.25. All money added to the pot in the same betting round is not incrementally added to the pot total; the pot total is not recalculated or adjusted until the following round of betting.

VARIATION 2: NO LIMIT TEXAS HOLD'EM
This is the game you see played on late-night television. It's the most gutsy and dramatic way of playing Texas Hold'em because any player may—at any time—declare himself *all-in* and bet everything he has on the table (you may

not buy in or use money not already on the table). In some cases, an all-in bet is less than the current pot's total. If this happens, create a *side pot* that the all-in player cannot win.

- -
VARIATION 3: OMAHA

Omaha is Texas Hold'em with more cards, more action, and more betting. On the initial deal, all players receive four cards, face down. The game proceeds as normal until the showdown, during which the winning hand must use *exactly* two hole cards and three community cards.

Flushes and straights are common in Omaha, so it's important to have a high card in the hole to gain an edge. It's also a good idea to bet hard if you have a strong opening hand—your opponents likely will improve their hands if you let them stay in the game. Like all Texas Hold'em variations, you may play Omaha with a limit, pot limit, or no limit.

- -
VARIATION 4: BUSH LEAGUE

Follow the general rules of Omaha, but deal the communal cards face down. These are turned up one at a time, followed by a betting round. All 3s and 9s are wild, and when a communal 4 is turned up, all players receive an extra hole card from the deck. As in Omaha, the winning hand must use exactly two hole cards and three community cards.

- -
VARIATION 5: PINEAPPLE

This game is essentially basic Texas Hold'em with one nasty little twist. On the initial deal, all players receive three cards face down (instead of two). Continue play as normal. After the flop and a round of betting, each player must throw out one hole card, face down. This card is useless for the remainder of the game. So, even if you're dealt A-A-A and the flop contains A-K-Q, you must discard one of your pocket aces. The remainder of the game continues as normal.

VARIATION 6: BAGUDI

This is lowball Texas Hold'em played with draw cards. Follow the standard Hold'em rules, but deal each player four hole cards instead of two. After a betting round, the small blind may draw zero to four cards from the deck; then the draw moves clockwise around the table. Reshuffle the discards when the stock is low. Once all players have drawn cards, a betting round is followed by a second draw, a bet, a third draw, and a final bet. Aces are always low in Bagudi, so the best low hand is **4-3-2-A**. Ties split the pot evenly.

DIFFICULTY *medium*	TIME LENGTH *long*	DECKS 1

Look no further if you're searching for a serious pot-building game. 7–27 is one of those games that infuriates some players because the betting never seems to stop, at least not until every last player has exactly the cards they want. The upshot? Pots in 7–27 grow quickly.

The goal is to collect cards as close as possible in value to 7 or 27. The pot is split 50-50 between the player closest to 7 and the player closest to 27.

Use a standard fifty-two-card deck. When calculating hand values, all face cards are worth ½ point, and aces are worth either 1 or 11 points (your choice). All other cards are worth their **index value**. Aces may be played both high and low in the same hand—for example, the best possible hand is 5-A-A because it totals to both 7 and 27.

∾ **NUMBER OF PLAYERS** 4 to 10

∾ **INITIAL DEAL** All players ante and receive one card face down, one card face up.

∾ **FIRST BET** The player to the left of the dealer opens the betting. The betting ends as soon as all players pass the bet.

∾ **REST OF GAME** All players (starting with the player to the left of the dealer) either draw a single face-up card or stay. It's perfectly acceptable to stay one round and jump back in the next. The player to the left of the dealer opens the betting after each drawing round.

There's an immediate showdown when no players want an extra card. The pot is split 50-50 between the two players closest to 7 and 27. In case of an exact tie (two players both have 27 exactly) they split 50-50 the 50 percent share of the pot awarded for holding 27. In case of non-exact ties (one player holds 26½ and a second holds 27½), the player below the target wins outright (the player holding 26½ wins the entire 50 percent share of the pot awarded for holding 27). It's also possible for a single player to win both 7 and 27, in which case they capture 100 percent of the pot.

- -

VARIATION: 31

Instead of splitting the pot 50-50 between two players, the entire pot is awarded to the player closest to 31. All face cards are worth 10 points, aces are worth 1 or 11, and all other cards are worth their *index value.* After an ante, all players receive one card face up and one card face down. There's a round of betting, followed by a third (and final) card dealt face up to all players. After a final betting round, the player closest to 31 wins the pot. Ties split the pot evenly.

THREE-CARD BRAG

DIFFICULTY *medium*	TIME LENGTH *short*	DECKS 1

This game is hugely popular throughout the United Kingdom and its former colonies, and for good reason. It's a superb betting game that blends skill and luck in just the right amounts. The betting process can confuse seven-card-stud poker players. Don't let that stop you from introducing Three-Card Brag and its variants at your next home game.

∾ **NUMBER OF PLAYERS** 4 to 8

∾ **HOW TO DEAL** Use a standard fifty-two-card deck. The rank of cards is standard, with aces always high. The hand rankings in Three-Card Brag (low to high) are:

HIGH CARD In a showdown, the highest-ranking card wins, so A-5-6 beats K-Q-10.

PAIR In a showdown, the higher pair wins (A-A-5 beats K-K-Q). When the pairs are of equal rank, the highest *kicker* card wins (Q-Q-10 beats Q-Q-4).

FLUSH Three cards of matching suit. In a showdown, the flush with the highest-ranking card wins, so A♥-5♥-4♥ beats K♥-Q♥-9♥.

RUN Three cards in sequence, in mixed suits. The highest run is A-3-2, followed by A-K-Q, K-Q-J, etc.

RUNNING FLUSH Three cards in sequence, in matching suit. The highest running flush is A-3-2, followed by A-K-Q, K-Q-J, Q-J-10, etc.

PRIAL Any three cards of matching rank. The highest prial is 3-3-3, followed by A-A-A, K-K-K, Q-Q-Q, etc.

❧ HOW TO PLAY All players ante and receive three face-down cards. Players either look at their cards or play blind (see below). The player to the left of the dealer opens the bet or passes. Once the bet is opened, all subsequent players must match the bet of the preceding player or fold. Unlike poker, the pot is never truly "neat" because subsequent players are required to match the bet of only the previous player and not *all* previous players.

If player one bets $1, for example, player two may fold, bet $1, or raise the bet (up to a predetermined maximum). If the bet is raised, say, to $3, player three may fold, bet $3, or raise the bet—but player three is not required to match player one's original $1 bet. If player three then bets $3 and player four follows with $3, player one must bet $3 to stay in the game (even though player one has already bet $1).

When just two players remain, you may also *see* a player by doubling the previous player's bet and proceeding straight to a showdown. If you paid to see a player, your opponent exposes his cards first. If you have a better hand, turn your cards face up and take the pot. If you have a worse hand, concede the pot, but do not expose your cards. You're allowed to ***muck*** in this case. If the two hands are equal, the player who paid to see loses the hand.

As players fold, their cards are added to the bottom of the deck. After each game, the deal rotates clockwise, but cards are not reshuffled *unless* the previous hand was "see a player" and won by a prial.

If you decide to *play blind*, do not look at your cards. On your next betting turn, you may fold or bet half the required amount (this is the blind bonus). So if the bet is $10, you may pay $5 to the pot. In a showdown, you're entitled to win 100 percent of the pot even though you've contributed at a 50 percent level. Blind players may look at their cards at any point, but once they do, they must start paying the full betting amounts to the pot. You cannot "see a player" when someone is playing blind.

If all players fold except a blind player, the pot is carried over to the next hand along with the blind player's cards. The blind player receives a new three-card hand (and therefore has two hands on the table). If you look at either hand, you must choose between playing it (in which case you fold the other hand without looking at it) or folding it (in which case you play the other hand as blind, or look at it; it's up to you). If you look at neither, play both hands blind until you eventually decide to look at one, in which case you follow the procedure above.

- -
VARIATION 1: FOUR-CARD BRAG
Follow the rules of Three-Card Brag, but deal each player four cards face down. You may play blind or not; either way, the moment you look at your four-card hand, you must discard one card face down on the table. The goal is to create the best three-card Brag hand. Ties are broken by the highest discarded card.

- -
VARIATION 2: FIVE-CARD BRAG
This is exactly like Four-Card Brag, but this time all players are dealt five cards. And as soon as you look at your cards, you must discard two in order to create the best Three-Card-Brag hand.

- -
VARIATION 3: TEEN PATHI
Three-Card Brag is known as Teen Pathi in India. The rules are virtually identical, with the following changes. If you are playing blind, you must bet the current bet or double it—you may not bet any other amount. If you play an open hand

(you are not playing blind), you must bet a minimum of *twice* the current bet and a maximum of *four times* the current bet—you may not bet any other amount.

If all players but one fold, that player wins the pot—even if he was playing blind. As long as no players are playing blind, on your turn you may make the minimum bet and then ask the preceding player for a *compromise*. The preceding player is free to accept or decline your compromise. If accepted, look at each other's cards and the player with the lower hand must fold (in case of a tie, the player requesting the compromise folds). If declined, the game continues as normal.

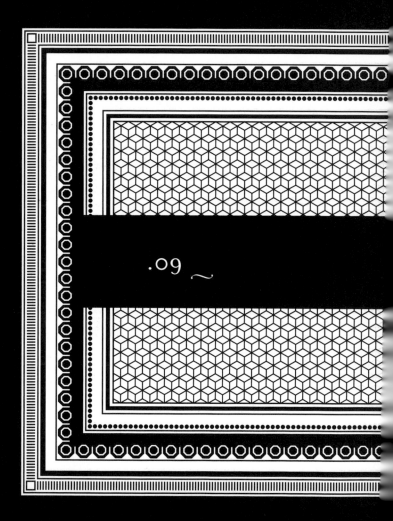

.09 ~

Games for Kids

CHAPTER NINE

Games for Kids

KIDS GENERALLY LOVE CARD GAMES, as long as you follow a few simple rules. First off, make sure everybody understands the game. Spend a few minutes reviewing the rules and strategies. It also may help to play a practice hand or two.

It's also important to switch up the games and the dealers. Make sure everybody has a chance to play his or her favorite game, and everybody should get a turn at shuffling, dealing, and acting as the game's official referee.

On the flip side, remember that card games are not a chore—so don't make them one! If your kids don't want to keep score, don't make them. If your kids don't want to play a certain game, don't force them.

Finally, don't be too competitive. Remember that there's a fine line between spirited competition (which is healthy) and getting an ego boost from crushing a ten-year-old opponent (which is definitely not OK).

AUTHORS

DIFFICULTY *low*	TIME LENGTH *short*	DECKS 1

Authors is an excellent choice when your children are ready to graduate from Go Fish! (p. 374). The two games are almost identical. The main differences are that Authors requires more concentration (because cards are exchanged one at a time rather than in sets) and that Authors has no stock pile (instead, all cards are dealt at the start of the game).

Authors has a noble legacy. The game was one of the first widely available card games, published by Parker Brothers in the 1890s. The title comes from the game's original cards, which featured illustrations of popular authors and philosophers.

∾ **NUMBER OF PLAYERS** 3 to 8

∾ **HOW TO DEAL** Start with a fifty-two-card deck, and deal all players cards until none remain. It's OK if some players have one or two fewer cards.

∾ **WINNING** The player who collects the most four-of-a-kinds wins the game. In case of a tie, shake hands and congratulate your opponent on a well-played and evenly matched game.

∾ **HOW TO PLAY** The player to the left of the dealer starts by asking any other player for a single card. The only restriction is that you must already have at least one card of matching rank in your hand. For example, you may ask any player for the 7♦ as long as your hand already contains a 7. You get another turn if your request is successful. Otherwise, the turn moves one player to the left.

If you are the player being asked for cards, you must hand over the matching card. If you don't (intentionally or not), you lose the game if your error is discovered.

At the start of your turn, play any four-of-a-kinds in your hand. Simply show the set of four to the other players and place the cards face down in front of you.

Once you run out of cards, your turn is skipped in all subsequent rounds. The game ends as soon as all players but one run out of cards.

BEGGAR YOUR NEIGHBOR

DIFFICULTY *low*	TIME LENGTH *medium*	DECKS 1

Try Beggar Your Neighbor whenever your games of Egyptian Ratscrew (p. 372) get out of hand. The games are very similar, minus the hand slapping.

∾ **NUMBER OF PLAYERS** 2

∾ **HOW TO DEAL** Divide a fifty-two-card deck roughly in half, and place the halves face down in front of each player.

∾ **WINNING** The goal is to avoid running out of cards. The first player to do so loses the game.

∾ **HOW TO PLAY** The game starts with one player turning up the top card of his face-down pile, and placing the card face-up in the center of a table. The other player then does the same.

There are two kinds of cards: **honors** (A, K, Q, J) and *ordinary* (10 through 2). The game continues until one player turns up an honors card. When this happens, the opponent pays a penalty by turning over cards from her stack to the center pile: four cards for an ace, three cards for a king, two cards for a queen, one card for a jack. After the penalty is paid, the original player takes the face-up pile of cards from the table and places them face down at the bottom of his own personal stack of cards.

You're in luck if you happen to turn up an honors card when paying a penalty. The roles immediately switch, and your opponent must now pay you the appropriate penalty.

BOODLE

DIFFICULTY *medium*	TIME LENGTH *medium*	DECKS 1

Whether you know it as Michigan, Newmarket, or Boodle, this game is heaps of fun for kids who grasp the basic elements of cards and are looking for a little extra challenge. While gambling is not a requirement, if you decide against money stakes, you should nominate a prize ahead of time for the winner. A good incentive—and the healthy competition that comes with trying to win it—is what makes Boodle so much fun.

☙ **NUMBER OF PLAYERS** 3 to 8

☙ **HOW TO DEAL** Start with a fifty-two-card deck, and deal each player cards one at a time until none remain. It's OK if some players have one or two fewer cards. The dealer also deals a ***widow*** or "extra" hand (in a game with five players, six total hands are dealt) that is not used. Card rankings are standard, with aces always high.

Each player should start with an equal number of markers, or chips; 15 or 20 per player is a reasonable amount. (Toothpicks are a good household stand-in for chips.)

☙ **WINNING** The game ends when any player runs out of markers, and whichever player collects the most markers is the winner. Typically each marker is worth a token amount of money. Otherwise, a small prize is awarded to the overall winner.

☙ **HOW TO PLAY** Before dealing, remove the following four cards from a second deck and place them face up on the table: A♥-K♣-Q♦-J♣. These are the Boodle cards. Next, each player places one marker on each Boodle card (the dealer places two markers on each card).

The player to the left of the dealer starts by leading his lowest card in any suit. Whichever player holds the next highest card in the very same suit must play it. For example, if 4♣ is the first card played, then whoever has the 5♣ must play it. The process continues until the highest card is played (A♣ in this example), or until there's a gap in the cards (nobody has the required card because it's already been played or is buried in the widow hand). When this happens, whichever player played the last card starts all over again, playing her lowest card in any suit.

Whenever a Boodle card is played in rotation, that lucky player captures all the markers on the corresponding Boodle card. The hand ends as soon as any player runs out of cards. The remaining players forfeit one marker for each card in their hand to the winning player. Any markers left on the Boodle cards are carried over to the next hand. The deal rotates clockwise and new cards are dealt.

- -

VARIATION: AUCTION BOODLE

This is identical to the basic game except that the dealer may decide to swap her hand with the widow prior to the start of play. And no, the dealer is never allowed to look at the widow hand before deciding to swap!

CONCENTRATION

DIFFICULTY low	TIME LENGTH medium	DECKS 1

Even younger kids enjoy Concentration. The only skill required is, well, a little concentration. You need to remember which cards are where on the table so you can turn up a matching pair.

☙ **NUMBER OF PLAYERS** 1 to 6

☙ **HOW TO DEAL** Deal an entire fifty-two-card deck face down in a pattern of your own choosing: four rows of thirteen cards, a pyramid, two squares— it doesn't really matter as long as all cards are face down.

WINNING Collect the most sets of paired cards to win the game.

HOW TO PLAY Pick a player to start (traditionally the youngest goes first, then the second youngest, etc.). He turns over two cards and keeps them if they match in rank—two 7s, for example, or two 10s. Otherwise, he turns both cards face down again and the turn rotates. The game ends when no cards are left on the table.

CRAZY EIGHTS

DIFFICULTY *low*	TIME LENGTH *short*	DECKS 1

Kids love Crazy Eights, especially when you add in family "house rules"—for example, whoever plays the 10♥ must jump up and down three times, or play ing A♠ means the order of turns is reversed from clockwise to counterclockwise. The number of variations is infinite, and there's really no such thing as a "bad" variation. To each his own variations, both in life and in Crazy Eights.

The traditional basic game is covered below, though few play it exactly as described. Like we said, Crazy Eights is all about homemade special rules and variations.

NUMBER OF PLAYERS 2 to 12

HOW TO DEAL You need one fifty-two-card deck for up to six players; two decks for up to twelve players. Deal everybody five cards (seven cards if only two are playing) and place the remaining cards face down on the table (this is your stock pile). The top card of the stock is turned face up and placed beside the stock (this is your discard pile).

WINNING The first player to run out of cards earns 50 points. All other players score penalty points according to the cards they are left holding: -50 points for each 8, -10 points for each face card or ace, -5 points for all other cards.

❧ **HOW TO PLAY**   The game starts with the player to the left of the dealer. He may play a card that matches either the suit or rank of the top card in the discard pile (e.g., if 10♣ is the top discard, he may play another 10 or any club). If he cannot play, he must take a card from the stock.

Eights are wild. When you play an 8, give it a suit for the next player to match. For example, you play an 8 and declare it "hearts." The next player must play a heart (or another 8), or else take a card from the stock. The game ends when one player runs out of cards.

EGYPTIAN RATSCREW

DIFFICULTY *low*	TIME LENGTH *medium*	DECKS 1

The name? Nobody really knows. The game has been around in some form or another since the 1890s. It borrows heavily from games such as Slapjack and Beggar Your Neighbor, but adds a few unique twists of its own. Kids love the game—or more accurately, kids love to slap the heck out of their friends and family. Try it at your next family reunion or teenager's birthday party.

❧ **NUMBER OF PLAYERS**   Best for 4 to 8

❧ **HOW TO DEAL**   Start with a fifty-two-card deck. Deal the entire deck to all players, face down, and don't worry if a few players have an extra card or two.

❧ **WINNING**   The player who collects all fifty-two cards wins.

❧ **HOW TO PLAY**   Players should organize their cards in a single face-down pile. The player to the left of the dealer starts by turning up the top card in his pile. In the interest of fairness (and self preservation), turn the card so that all players can see it at roughly the same moment, drop it on the table, and move your hand out of harm's way as quickly as possible.

If the card is a numbered card, the next player turns up a card from her pile. This continues until a face card is turned up—now the fun begins!

If player two turns up, say, an ace, player three now has a fixed number of chances to turn up another face card. In the case of aces, you get four chances; for kings, three; for queens, two; and just one for jacks.

If player three fails to turn up another face card in the allotted time, player two takes the entire pile of cards from the table and places it at the bottom of his stack of cards. If player three succeeds, however, player four must now turn up another face card within the allotted number of turns.

> In Egyptian Ratscrew, when we say "slap" we mean slap—be it a blow, smack, spank, strike, or whomp! It's your call to set slap guidelines. We heartily recommend the Golden Rule: Slap Unto Others as You Would Have Others Slap Unto You.

During any point in the game, a player may slap—yes, slap!—the communal card pile if any of the following sequences are visible: pairs, triplets, or runs of three or more cards (*continuous ranking* is permitted, and aces play both high and low). The player who slaps the pile first takes all cards into her own pile and leads the next card.

Players are (temporarily) out of the game when they run out of cards. They may sit the game out, or they may remain as observers—and if they happen to properly slap a pile, they are allowed back in the game.

∾ **IRREGULARITIES & DISPUTES** In disputes over who slapped first, an impartial judge comes in handy. Failing that, if a dispute cannot be settled, then neither player wins the cards. The game continues as if no slapping had occurred. And whether intentionally or not, slapping a pile that does not contain a pair, triplet, or run has the following consequence: the pile is awarded to the player who led the card immediately prior to the erroneous slap. When players slap in error, penalties must be paid!

GO FISH!

DIFFICULTY *low*	TIME LENGTH *short*	DECKS 1

This is the quintessential kids' game. The rules are simple, the game play is quick, and—perhaps most important of all—kids are allowed to tell their parents (emphatically and in no uncertain terms) to GO FISH!

∾ **NUMBER OF PLAYERS** 3 to 6

∾ **HOW TO DEAL** Start with a fifty-two-card deck, and deal each player five cards.

∾ **WINNING** The player who collects the most four-of-a-kind sets wins the game.

∾ **HOW TO PLAY** The player to the left of the dealer starts by asking any other player for a specific rank of card. The only restriction is that you must already have at least one card of matching rank in your hand. If you're holding a 9, for example, you may ask a player for his or her 9s. If the player has any, you get *all* of them.

Otherwise, the person says "Go Fish," which means you draw a card from the stock and your turn is over. That is, unless you happen to draw the card you were just asking for (in this case, a 9), in which case you show it to everybody and get another turn.

At the start of your turn, play any four-of-a-kinds in your hand. Simply show the set of four to the other players and place the cards face down in front of you. The game ends as soon as one player runs out of cards, or the stock pile runs out of cards.

OLD MAID

DIFFICULTY *low*	TIME LENGTH *short*	DECKS 1

Have you played the game Hot Potato? If so, you'll instantly get the gist of Old Maid—don't be the last player holding the queen! If so, you lose. It's as simple—and fun—as that.

∾ **NUMBER OF PLAYERS** 2 to 8

∾ **HOW TO DEAL** Start with a fifty-two-card deck, and remove three queens from the deck. The remaining queen is the *old maid*. Shuffle and deal the deck to all players, as evenly as possible (it's OK if some players have a few extra cards).

∾ **WINNING** At the end of the game, the player holding the old maid loses.

∾ **HOW TO PLAY** Start by discarding all pairs from your hand. If you have three of a kind, remove a pair and keep the third card in your hand. Once all players have discarded their pairs, the dealer starts by offering her hand (face down) to the next clockwise player. This player takes a random card from the dealer's hand and either keeps it or pairs it with a card in his own hand (make sure to discard this new pair!). The player to the left of the dealer then offers his hand to the player on his left. The cycle repeats until the only remaining card is the old maid.

Pig

For kids of a certain age (usually around age ten or eleven), Pig is the ultimate cool game. It features playing cards, funny faces, and competitive group dynamics. Preteens love this game almost as much as teenagers hate it. Go figure.

❧ NUMBER OF PLAYERS 3 to 13

❧ HOW TO DEAL Start with a fifty-two-card deck. You need one four-of-a-kind set for each player in the game (the rank of the set does not matter). So, with four players, for example, your starting deck might consist of these sixteen cards: 4-4-4-4, 7-7-7-7, Q-Q-Q-Q, K-K-K-K. With five players, you start with twenty cards (add a fifth four-card set); with six players you start with twenty-four cards (add a sixth four-card set); etc.

Once the deck is sorted, shuffle and deal the entire deck.

❧ WINNING The last two surviving players are the game's co-winners.

❧ HOW TO PLAY The goal is to collect four cards of equal rank (e.g., 4-4-4-4) by passing cards one at a time to the left while receiving cards from the player to your right. Everybody starts by placing a single unwanted card face down on the table, to each player's left. Each player picks up the card to his right, and then discards another unwanted card to his left. Keep in mind that you may not have more than four cards in your hand at any time, and that you may not look at the card passed to you (coming from the right) until you have passed a card (going to your left).

This cycle continues until one player has four of a kind, at which point she quietly touches her finger to her nose. As soon as the other players notice, they, too, immediately place a finger on their noses. The last player to follow suit loses and is out of the game.

Remove one four-of-a-kind set from the deck (because now there is one less player), shuffle the cards, and deal a new hand. The game ends when only two players—the co-winners—remain.

- -
VARIATION 1: PIGGLY WIGGLY

It's just like Pig, but with an entire deck (or two decks, if more than twelve are playing). Start by dealing each player four cards, face down. The remaining cards are the stock. The dealer draws cards from the stock, and passes discards to his left. The player to the dealer's left either takes the dealer's discard and passes one of her own, or takes a card from the stock and passes a discard. Play continues around the table until the player on the dealer's right receives cards from the player on his right, and discards face up on the table. Reshuffle the discard pile to form a new stock, once the original stock is exhausted.

- -
VARIATION 2: SPOONS

Spoons is a great all-around game. You may play it Pig-style or Piggly Wiggly–style (with or without a stock pile). The only difference is that instead of touching noses, the first player to collect four of a kind grabs a spoon from the center of the table (be sure to start with one fewer spoon than the total number of players; for example, start with four spoons in a five-player game). As quickly as possible, all other players follow suit. The player who is unable to grab a spoon fast enough is out. Remove sets of cards and one spoon from circulation, as appropriate, and then deal another hand. The last two players are declared co-winners.

POUNCE

DIFFICULTY *high*	TIME LENGTH *long*	DECKS *multiple*

Do you or your kids like Solitaire? If so, you will really enjoy Pounce. Each player in this Solitaire-inspired game uses her own deck of cards to build communal foundation piles—at speed, in a jumble, each player trying to outthink and out-maneuver the other.

NUMBER OF PLAYERS 2 to 6

HOW TO DEAL Each player needs a fifty-two-card deck (each deck should have a different design so you can tell them apart). Each player deals his own Klondike-style tableau (see Klondike, p. 71) like so: Starting to your left, deal one card to the first pile, two cards to the second pile, three cards to the third pile, etc., until you have five piles. All cards are dealt face down, except for the top card in each pile, which is turned up.

Next, deal a sixth "Pounce" pile by taking the top card off your deck and placing it face down, followed by the next card off your deck, etc., until there are nine cards in the Pounce pile. Now turn the entire Pounce pile face up. The remaining cards are your stock.

WINNING The goal is to play all your Pounce cards. Each player earns -2 points for each of their remaining Pounce cards and +1 point for every card built on the foundations (different card backings make it easy to assign points to the correct player). Games are typically played to 100 points.

HOW TO PLAY Nominate a scorekeeper before dealing. Once each player has created a five-pile tableau plus a Pounce pile, the scorekeeper says "go!"

Each player starts by moving aces to the foundations, which are shared among all players. Start building on the foundations—any foundation—by suit in ascending rank (on 4♥ you may build 5♥, on J♠ you may build Q♠, etc.). The game is cutthroat, so if you and an opponent can both build on the same foundation, the first player to lay down the card prevails.

On your own tableau, you may build in descending rank by alternating color (e.g., on 4♥ you may build 3♣ or 3♠, on J♠ you may build 10♦ or 10♥, etc.). After you play the topmost card in a tableau pile, turn up the card below. Fill voids in your tableau with a king or the topmost card in your Pounce pile. At any point, you may also use Pounce cards to build on the communal foundations (but never on your tableau piles).

If you get stuck at any point, play cards from your stock to your tableau (never to the foundations) by turning over cards in groups of three. The first player to empty their Pounce pile declares "stop!," and points are scored.

PRESIDENT & POND SCUM

DIFFICULTY *low*	TIME LENGTH *medium*	DECKS 1

This is an easy game for kids to master, and there's just enough head-to-head competition to keep everybody fully focused on the game. After all, nobody likes being called Pond Scum.

∾ **NUMBER OF PLAYERS** 4 to 7

∾ **HOW TO DEAL** Use a fifty-two-card deck, and deal cards clockwise, one at a time, to all players. It's OK if some players have an extra card or two. Card rankings are standard, with aces always high.

∾ **WINNING** The goal is to get rid of your cards. The last player holding cards loses the game—and all players are entitled, for just a minute, to heap abuse and insults on the losing player. A game of President & Pond Scum, much like life itself, is tough going sometimes.

∾ **HOW TO PLAY** The player to the left of the dealer starts. If that's you, lead any single card or multiple cards of equal rank (5-5, 3-3-3, etc.) face up on the table. The next clockwise player either passes or plays an equal number of higher-ranking cards. You're never required to play higher cards, even if you have them—it's always OK to pass. The last person to play wins the lead, when all other players pass. He or she starts from the beginning by playing any card or set of matching cards. A typical round looks like this:

Player 1	Player 2	Player 3	Player 4	Player 5
4-4	Pass	6-6	Pass	Pass
Pass	K-K	Pass	Pass	Pass
Pass				

Player two may now lead any card or set of matching cards, since all the other players passed in sequence. The only exception is when hands of equal rank are played—for example when 5-5 is played on 5-5. In this case, the next clockwise player loses a turn.

The first player to run out of cards is known as President; the next player to run out of cards is the Vice President, followed by Janitor, Garbage Collector, Fish Cleaner, Pond Scum, etc. Or try inventing your own titles—maybe King of the Universe all the way down to Low Life. The point is to create truly awful job titles for the last few positions. On the next hand, all players should sit in order of their new job titles (high to low)—the President, of course, should also get the best chair. Cards are dealt by Pond Scum (or whichever player came in last on the previous hand).

RIDE THE BUS

DIFFICULTY *high*	TIME LENGTH *medium*	DECKS 1

This is a kid-friendly version of the betting game Screw Your Neighbor. While it's not necessary to wager anything but pride in Ride the Bus, it's common to play for something—maybe a chore swap, or an extended bedtime, that sort of thing.

∾ **NUMBER OF PLAYERS** 2 to 8

∾ **HOW TO DEAL** Use a fifty-two-card deck. Deal cards clockwise, one at a time, until all players have three cards. The remaining cards are the stock. Card rankings are standard, with aces always high. Face cards are worth 10 points, aces are worth 11, and all other cards are worth their ***index value***.

∾ **WINNING** All players start with three markers or chips. In each hand, the goal is to score as close to 31 points as possible, using cards of the same suit. The player with the lowest (worst) score loses one marker. Eventually, all players but one will run out of markers; that last player with a marker wins the game.

∾ **HOW TO PLAY** Turn over the topmost stock card to create a discard pile. The player to the left of the dealer now either draws the face-up discard or the topmost stock card, and then ends his turn by playing a card from his hand, face up, on the discard pile. The only caveat: If you draw a card from the stock, you may not discard it in the very same turn.

Your goal is to create a hand worth 31 points, using only cards of the same suit. For example, the hand 5♦-7♦-9♣ is worth 12 points (diamonds) or 9 points (clubs), while the hand 8♥-J♥-A♥ is worth 29 points.

You may ***knock*** at the start of your turn if you think your hand is good enough *not to lose*. Once you knock, all other players are allowed one more chance to draw a card. Once this is done, everybody turns their cards face up, and the player with the lowest score loses a life. If you're lucky enough to hold 31 points (e.g., an ace plus two face cards in any suit), declare it immediately by turning over your cards—in this case all players (except you!) lose one marker.

The deal rotates left at the end of the hand. You're out of the game when you run out of markers.

SLAPJACK

DIFFICULTY *low*	TIME LENGTH *medium*	DECKS 1

Warning! Danger! Attention! This game can lead to swollen knuckles and sore hands. Slapjack is the quintessential "slap the table" game, where you try to capture cards by slapping (not metaphorical slaps—we mean literal smacks) each jack and pair turned up on the table.

∾ **NUMBER OF PLAYERS** 3 to 10

∾ **HOW TO DEAL** Use a fifty-two-card deck, and deal the entire deck (it's OK if one or two players have an extra card).

∾ **WINNING** The goal is to capture every card in the deck. If you do this, you win the game.

∾ **HOW TO PLAY** The player to the left of the dealer turns up a single card and places it in the center of the table, within equal reach of all players. It's very important *how* this card is turned up. First off, turn it over quickly— it's not fair to flip cards slowly, since you'll see them before your opponents. Similarly, flip cards so that all players can see them at roughly the same moment (this usually means flipping cards from the side, rather than away from you off the deck).

The next clockwise player turns up the top card on her pile and places it, face up, on the table. The process continues until either a jack is turned up or a card of matching rank is turned up (e.g., 5 on a 5, 10 on a 10, etc.). When either happens, all players rush to physically slap the card on the table—this is called a slapjack.

The slapjack is won by the first player to slap the proper card on the table. The fun part begins when more than one player slaps the cards. Chaos ensues, along with some very sore hands. The rule of thumb here is that if your hand is lowest in the pile, you win! When you win a slapjack, add all cards on the table to your existing pile and then shuffle your pile.

If a player mistakenly slaps at any card, he gives one card from his pile to the player whose turn it is. You're not necessarily out of the game when you run out of cards; instead, you are allowed one final chance to win cards, at the next slapjack. If you don't win cards on the next slapjack, you are out of the game.

- -

VARIATION: SNAP!

This is a similar but gentler game—no physical slapping is involved. Cards are not played to a central pile on the table. Instead, each player turns up the top card of her individual piles and plays it directly in front of her. Whenever the cards in front of two players match, the first player to shout "Snap!" wins both piles and places the newly captured cards face-down in his own pile. If two players declare "Snap!" at the *exact* same moment, take both piles and move them to the center of the table—this is called a Snap Pot. When a matching card eventually is turned up, the first player to declare "Snap Pot!" wins the Snap Pot cards. The game ends when one player captures all fifty-two cards.

WAR

DIFFICULTY *low*	TIME LENGTH *long*	DECKS 1

Card games do not get much simpler than this. War requires no strategy or special skills, which makes it the perfect introduction to cards for first-time players.

∾ **NUMBER OF PLAYERS** 2

∾ **HOW TO DEAL** Use a fifty-two-card deck, and deal each player twenty-six cards. Card rankings are standard, with aces always high.

∾ **WINNING** The goal is to capture every card in the deck. If you do this, you win the game.

∾ **HOW TO PLAY** Don't look at your cards! Leave them in a face-down pile in front of you. Next, you and your opponent simultaneously turn up a single card. Whoever turns up the higher card wins both; the winner places the two cards face down at the bottom of her pile.

War is declared when the two turn-up cards are of matching rank. When this happens, leave the matching cards on the table. Both players now deal one card (face down) and one card (face up) on the table. The higher face-up card wins the war (and captures all six cards). If there's another tie, another set of face-down and face-up cards are dealt, and the process is repeated.

The game ends when either one player captures all fifty-two cards, or if a player runs out of cards at any point.

- -

VARIATION: MULTIPLAYER WAR

You may also play War with three players (deal seventeen cards each) or four players (deal thirteen cards each). The only difference is that, in case of a War, all players compete—not just the two with matching cards.

AUTHOR'S PICKS

✎ MOST UNDERRATED GAMES FOR 4 PLAYERS

✎ MOST UNDERRATED MULTIPLAYER GAMES

✎ MOST UNDERRATED BETTING GAMES

✎ BETTING GAMES THAT GENERATE THE LARGEST POTS

✎ SILLIEST BETTING GAMES

✎ DRINKING GAMES

✎ GAMES TO CUT YOUR TEETH ON

GLOSSARY OF CARD TERMS

ALL-IN: Betting all of your remaining chips.

ANTE: An obligatory amount bet by all players at the start of a game, before cards are dealt.

AUCTION: Bidding to determine the trump suit and winning contract in Bridge and similar team-based games; selling undisclosed card(s) to the highest bidder in Poker games.

BID: The number of tricks (sometimes also a trump suit) an individual player or team commits to winning during a hand.

BLIND BET: A forced ante by one player (sometimes two) before the start of a game, or a bet made by any player who has not yet seen any of their own cards.

BLUFFING: Making a bet with bad cards, in the hope that other players fold.

BOARD: Refers to a layout of cards—usually face up—on a table or other playing surface, used by all players for building or melding depending on the game. In Solitaire, the board refers to the tableau.

BOAT: A full house in Poker games. Sometimes called a "full boat."

BUILD: Ordering cards in sequence either up or down in rank, sometimes also by suit and/or alternating color.

BULLETS: A pair of aces in Poker games.

BURNING CARDS: The act of setting aside the topmost card from the deck before dealing a hand, especially common in games of Texas Hold'em.

BUTTON: Typically a marker placed in front of a player to indicate where the dealing should start. In some betting games, buttons are used to track the number of "lives" a player has remaining.

BUY-IN: In Poker it's the amount of money all players should start with, as in the game's buy-in is $20.

CALL: A betting term for matching the bet made by a previous player.

CHECK: A betting term for passing the decision to the next active player while simultaneously reserving your right to call whatever bet is eventually made.

CHASE: To stay in the game with a worthless or low-value hand, hoping to draw a valuable card(s).

CHIP: A counter used in Poker in lieu of actual money.

CONTINUOUS RANKING: Refers to a sequence of cards that wraps around an ace from low to high or high to low, as in 3-2-A-K-Q. In many games ranking is not continuous, in which case 3-2-A-K-Q is not a valid sequence. *See also Rank.*

CONTRACT: *See Bid.*

COWBOYS: A pair of kings in Poker games.

CUT: A shuffling term, meaning to lift the top part of a shuffled deck and place it beneath the lower half in order to obscure the bottom card of the deck.

CUTTHROAT: A game played without teams; every player for themselves.

DEAD: When referring to a single card, it means the card cannot be used, scored or counted in the current hand. When referring to a player's hand of cards, it means the hand itself cannot be used, scored, or counted.

DEAL: To distribute cards to players according to the rules of the game being played.

DEALS: *See Hand.*

DECLARE: To announce the contract in Bridge games, or to announce the number of tricks to be taken, the trump suit, etc., before the start of a hand.

DECLARER: The player who makes the highest (winning) bid.

DEUCES: A pair of twos in Poker games.

DOUBLETON: Mostly a Bridge term, when a player holds exactly two cards of the same suit.

DOWN & DIRTY: Refers to the last card dealt (face down) in Seven-Card Stud Poker games.

DRAW: To take a card(s) from the deck, the stock, or a waste pile.

DUMMY: A Bridge term referring to the declarer's partner, who lays down his or her hand on the table, face up, for the active partner to play from.

DUMMY HAND: Any hand dealt to the table that is subsequently turned up and played by the declarer.

ELDER HAND: The player who must make the opening bid or play the first card, often by virtue of having been dealt the first card and/or by sitting one seat left of the dealer.

FACE VALUE: *See Index Value.*

FAN: A Solitaire term for cards arranged face up, with the edges overlapping slightly so that the index value of all cards in the fan is visible.

FIFTH STREET: The fifth card dealt in Seven-Card Stud games.

FINESSE: Usually limited to Bridge and similar games; refers to playing the weaker of two cards in the hopes of winning an extra trick.

FLOP: The three communal cards dealt face up in Texas Hold'em.

FLUSH: A five-card Poker hand where all cards are of matching suit regardless of rank, as in Q♦-8♦-5♦-3♦-2♦.

FOLD: A Poker term for bowing out of the current hand. After folding players are out of the hand for good and must forfeit any money already contributed to the pot.

FORCE-FOLD: A general term for being forced to quit a hand under certain conditions—for example when you draw, or are dealt, a certain card.

FOUNDATION: A Solitaire term for the starting card or cards upon which all subsequent cards are built upon.

FOUR-OF-A-KIND: Any four cards of matching rank, as in 3-3-3-3.

FOURTH STREET: The fourth card dealt in Seven-Card Stud games.

FULL HOUSE: Refers to a five-card Poker hand consisting of three-of-a-kind plus a pair, as in J-J-J-5-5.

GO OUT: To play the last card in your hand, often in order to win the hand or game.

HAIL SATAN: Three sixes; at pagan poker tables this is considered the highest possible hand.

HAND: Most games are composed of individual hands (sometimes called deals), in which all players compete.

HIDDEN PAIR: Any pair that cannot be seen by other players because one or more cards are in the hole.

HOLE CARDS: Refers to any cards dealt face down in Poker games.

HONORS: Refers to groupings of royalty cards (ace, king, queen, jack) that earn bonus points when held or captured by the same player or team.

HUSTY: To spill liquid (usually beer) on a poker chip. Similarly, when two poker chips stick together, they have been *hustied*.

INDEX VALUE: The intrinsic value of a card, represented by its rank number—e.g., the 7♦ has an index value of seven, the 9♥ has an index value of nine, etc. The index value of face cards is typically 10, though this varies from game to game.

INSIDE STRAIGHT: A Poker term for four cards requiring an additional card in the middle to make a straight, as in 6-5-3-2.

KICKER: Refers to a high card *not* part of the original hand, but used to determine a pot winner in case of ties. For example, Q-Q-10 beats Q-Q-4 because the 10 is a higher kicker card.

KITTY: *See Pot.*

KNOCK: In Rummy and similar games, players knock when they feel their hand is good enough to win. Knocking typically means all competing players have one final chance to draw a card, discard, meld cards, etc.

MARKER: *See Button.*

MARRIAGE: The king and queen of matching suits in Rummy and similar games; in Solitaire it refers to any two cards in matching suit and/or sequence (depending on the requirements of the individual game).

MELD: A combination of matching cards according to the rules of the individual game. Players are said to make or form melds by disclosing such a combination.

MUCK: To discard a hand without showing your cards to anyone. This usually happens when all players but one fold. In that case, the winner is not required to show their "winning" hand to any other player.

NATURAL: Refers to a nonwild card or nonwild hand. For example, a natural full house does not contain any wild cards.

NEAT: Refers to the pot after all bets have been announced and all chips are in.

NO-PEEKIE: Any game where players are not allowed to look at some (or all) of their cards prior to betting, bidding, or playing a card.

ONE-EYED JACK: The J♥ or J♠, shown in profile.

OPEN STRAIGHT: Four cards requiring an additional card at either end to make a straight, as in 6-5-4-3.

OVERCALL: Any bid higher than the previous announced bid.

OVERTRICK: In bidding games, any trick above and beyond what's needed to win the contract.

PAIR: Any two cards of matching rank, as in 5-5.

PARTNERSHIP: When two or more players play together for a common goal. Partnerships are either permanent (lasting multiple hands) or temporary (lasting just one hand).

POT: In Poker games it's the amount of money, represented by chips, at the center of the table. The pot is eventually awarded to the winner(s) of the hand.

POT LIMIT: Any gambling game where the maximum bet is the current value of the pot.

PRIAL: An old-fashioned term that means 'pair royal' and refers to three cards of matching rank, as in 7-7-7. *See also Trips*.

PUSH: When two or more players win a game with identical cards or equal points, it's called a "push." In most games, no money changes hands when players push.

RANK: The value of a card. Standard card rankings (high to low) are A-K-Q-J-10-9-8-7-6-5-4-3-2.

RE-ANTE: Refers to when all active players are forced to contribute an additional ante to the pot, typically because all players passed or failed to act in the previous round.

RESERVE: A Solitaire term for cards that can be used under special circumstances to build on the tableau or the foundations.

RIVER: The final card dealt in Texas Hold'em.

ROUND: A single hand of cards is typically broken into rounds, in which each active player is required to perform some action (play a card, discard, make a bet, etc.).

RUBBER: A Bridge term, referring to the number of games needed for a team to win. A team winning two out of three games typically wins the rubber.

RUFF: In trick-taking games it refers to playing a trump on a non-trump lead, and thereby winning the trick.

ROYALTY: Refers to the ace, king, queen, and jack of any suit.

SEQUENCE: Any run or combination of cards in ordered rank or numerical sequence with no gaps, as in 7-6-5 or K♥-Q♥-J♥ depending on the game played.

SET: As in "to be set," means the bid winner failed to achieve his or her bid and suffers a scoring penalty depending on the game.

SHOE: A device used in casinos to hold multiple decks of cards for the purposes of speeding up the dealing.

SHOWDOWN: The point at which all active Poker players compare hands to determine a pot winner.

SINGLETON: Mostly a Bridge term, when a player holds only one card of a suit.

SPLIT-POT: Any gambling game where the pot is automatically split between two or more winners.

STAKES: *See Buy-in.*

STARTER CARD: A face-up card(s) played at the start of a hand, generally used as a foundation card (in Solitaire) or as a card to be swapped, traded, or matched depending on the game played.

STOCK PILE: Any cards not initially dealt, but used later in the hand or game.

STOPPER: Refers to any high-ranking card in a suit that is guaranteed to win a trick. For example, A♠ is a stopper in spades. If you hold K♦ and another diamond, for example, the K♦ is considered a weak stopper, since K♦ is highly likely to win at least one trick in diamonds.

STRAIGHT: Refers to a five-card Poker hand where all cards are in sequence, as in 7-6-5-4-3.

STRAIGHT FLUSH: Refers to a five-card Poker hand where all cards are in sequence and matching suit, as in 7♥-6♥-5♥-4♥-3♥. The highest straight flush, called a "Royal Straight Flush," is A-K-Q-J-10 of matching suit.

SUICIDE KING: The K♥, with a sword through his head.

SUITS: Refers to cards of a matching type, usually indicated by the symbols ♥ (hearts), ♠ (spades), ♣ (clubs), ♦ (diamonds).

TABLE STAKES: *See Buy-In.*

TABLE TALK: Refers to players or spectators of a game discussing any aspect of the current hand or game, its strategy, what has been discarded, who's bluffing, etc. Table talk is not allowed in most games.

TABLEAU: A Solitaire term for the starting layout of a game, typically including piles of cards organized in a specific pattern or order.

THIRD STREET: The third card dealt in Seven-Card Stud Poker games.

THREE-OF-A-KIND: Any three cards of matching rank, as in 8-8-8.

TRICK: A complete round, with all active players contributing a card in succession to a shared pool of cards on the table. Tricks are typically won by the highest card in the leading suit, or by the highest trump.

TRIPS: Three-of-a-kind, as in "trip 7s" or "trip 10s."

TRUMP: Any suit that has been elevated temporarily (as in Bridge) or permanently (as in Spades) to superior status above the other three suits.

TURN: Within individual hands of a game, each active player has his own specific turn to perform an action (e.g., make a bet, fold, etc.). In Texas Hold'em the 'turn' refers to the fourth common card dealt.

TURN-UP CARD: A card exposed off the top of the deck at the start of some games, used to determine trump suit for the hand.

UNDERTRICK: In bidding games, any trick less than what's needed to win the contract.

UPCARD: Any card turned face-up.

VOID: Refers to a suit that is completely absent from a hand.

VULNERABLE: A Bridge term for the team that has won one game in a rubber, and thereby attracts additional scores or penalties in the next game.

WASTE PILE: Refers to discarded cards, which often can be replayed or reused later in the hand when certain conditions are met.

WHEEL: Refers to the hand 5-4-3-2-A, which is sometimes considered a winning low hand *and* a strong high hand.

WIDOW: A hand dealt to the table and not to any specific player. In some games players exchange cards with the widow hand; in gambling games players must often beat all active players as well as the widow hand in order to claim the pot.

WILD CARD: Any card that is temporarily or permanently used to represent another card in the deck.

YOUNGER HAND: The last player to bid or play a card, often the dealer.

ALPHABETICAL LIST OF GAMES

SCOTT MCNEELY is the author of *Poker Night: All You Need to Bet, Bluff & Win* and *Casino Night: All You Need to Bring the Tables Home* (both from Chronicle Books). His writing has appeared in numerous magazines, Web sites, and travel guidebooks. He lives in Portland, Oregon.

ARTHUR MOUNT is an illustrator whose work has appeared in publications around the world. His clients include *The New York Times*, *Sunset Magazine*, and Google. He lives in Portland, Oregon.

The girl decided to set her brothers free, no matter what it
cost her. She went out into the wood and climbed a tree and slept
there. The next morning, she set to work. She gathered nettles and
began sewing them together, not minding the stings. She had no
reason to laugh and there was no one to speak to.

A long time passed. One day some huntsmen saw the girl in the
tree. 'Who are you?' they called out. But she did not answer.

'Come down!' they cried. 'We won't hurt you.' But she shook
her head. The huntsmen climbed the tree, carried her down and
brought her to the King of this foreign land.

The King asked kindly, 'Who are you? What were you doing
in the tree?'

But she didn't answer.

The King spoke to her in all the languages he knew, but she remained silent. However, the King felt a great love for her. She saw he was very kind and liked him very much. After a few days they were married.

The King had a wicked stepmother who was unhappy with the marriage. 'Who knows where this girl is from?' she asked. 'She doesn't speak a word! She is not worthy of a King!'

After a year had passed, the young Queen had her first child. The King's stepmother stole it away and told the King that his wife had killed it. The King didn't believe her and ordered that no one should harm his wife. All the while, the young Queen went on quietly sewing the nettle shirts.

Some time later, another baby was born. The King's wicked stepmother once again stole the baby and blamed the young Queen, but the King would still not believe her.

When the young Queen had a third baby, the stepmother again stole it away. She accused the young Queen and this time the court forced the King to bring her to justice. She was sentenced to death by fire.

The day she was due to die was the last one of the six years of toil. In that time she had neither spoken nor laughed to free her dear brothers from the evil spell. The six shirts were ready, except one that was missing the right sleeve. The young Queen was led to the pile of wood, carrying the six shirts with her. As the fire was about to be lit, she suddenly shouted out. There were six swans flying towards her and her heart burst with joy.

The swans landed around her and stooped so that she could throw the shirts over them. Her brothers stood before her safe and sound. As one shirt was missing the right sleeve, the youngest brother had a swan's wing instead of a left arm.

The young Queen said to the astonished King, 'Dearest husband, now I can speak and tell you that I am innocent.' She told him of the treachery of his stepmother. To their parents' great joy, the three children were found and the wicked stepmother was punished.

The father of the six brothers and young Queen, whose evil wife had died, was brought to them and they celebrated for many days.

The King and young Queen lived many years and grew older with her six brothers in peace and joy.

THE THREE
BILLY GOATS
GRUFF

Once upon a time there lived on a hillside three billy goats whose name was Gruff.

Winter had passed and the lean, hungry billy goats wanted to go to the green meadow on the other side of the valley so they could eat the juicy, tasty grass and grow fat over the summer. At the bottom of the valley was a cascading stream that they had to cross. Over the stream was a bridge, but under the bridge there lived a great, ugly Troll, with eyes like big, round saucers and a nose as long as a poker.

First of all went the youngest and smallest Billy Goat Gruff.

'Trip, trip, trip, trip!' went the wooden bridge as the billy goat's hoofs danced across it.

'Who's that tripping over my bridge?' roared the Troll from underneath the bridge.

'It's me, the tiniest Billy Goat Gruff,' said the billy goat in a tiny voice. 'I am going up the hillside to eat some juicy, tasty grass so I can grow fat!'

'No you're not!' roared the Troll. 'I am coming to gobble you up!'

'Oh, please don't eat me! I'm too little, I am,' said the youngest Billy Goat Gruff. 'If you wait a little while longer, the second Billy Goat Gruff will come along. He's much bigger than me.'

'Bigger, is he?' asked the hungry Troll. 'Well, be off with you then!'

And the youngest Billy Goat Gruff tripped lightly across the bridge to the meadow.

After a little while, the second Billy Goat Gruff came along to cross the bridge. He was a medium-sized billy goat.

'Trap, trap, trap, trap!' went the wooden bridge as the second billy goat made his way across.

'Who's that trapping over my bridge?' roared the Troll from underneath the bridge.

'It's me, the second Billy Goat Gruff,' said the billy goat in a medium-sized voice. 'I am going up the hillside to eat some juicy, tasty grass so I can grow fat!'

'No you're not!' roared the Troll. 'I am coming to gobble you up!'

'Oh, please don't eat me! I'm only medium-sized, I am,' said the second Billy Goat Gruff. 'If you wait a little while longer, the third Billy Goat Gruff will come along. He's much bigger than me.'

'Bigger, is he?' asked the hungry Troll. 'Well, be off with you then!'

And the second Billy Goat Gruff trapped across the bridge to the meadow.

Then the third Billy Goat Gruff came along to cross the bridge. He was a very large billy goat.

'Tramp, tramp, tramp, tramp!' went the wooden bridge as the third billy goat stomped across it.

'Who's that tramping over my bridge?' roared the Troll from underneath the bridge.

'It's me, the third Billy Goat Gruff!' roared the billy goat in a very loud voice. I am going up the hillside to eat some juicy, tasty grass so I can grow fat!'

'No you're not!' roared the Troll, jumping up on to the bridge.
'I am coming to gobble you up!'

'Well, come along then!' said the third Billy Goat Gruff.
He lowered his head and pointed his horns at the Troll. Then
he charged!

The Troll bounced into the air and landed on the bridge. The big billy goat jumped on to the troll and stomped him with his big hoofs. Then he kicked out his hind legs and tossed the Troll into the rapids below. The Troll floated away, black and blue, and that was the last anyone ever saw of him.

The three Billy Goats Gruff went up the hillside to the green meadow. There they ate some juicy, tasty grass until they were so fat that they could scarcely walk home again. And after that day, they went to the meadow on the opposite side of the valley whenever they wished.

THE END

NOTES FOR THE READER

THE THREE LITTLE PIGS

Shakespeare scholar James Halliwell-Phillipps first recorded this crowd-pleaser in his *Popular Rhymes and Nursery Tales* in 1849, but it more famously featured in Australian-born folklorist Joseph Jacobs' *English Fairy Tales* (1890). Walt Disney won an Academy Award for his animated short film *Three Little Pigs* (1933), in which the three were given the names Practical Pig, Fiddler Pig and Fifer Pig.

DICK WHITTINGTON AND HIS CAT

The real Richard Whittington (c. 1350–1423) was a wealthy merchant who served as Lord Mayor of London four times. Though Whittington inspired the British folk tale, first recorded in the early 1600s, there is no evidence that he owned a champion rat-catcher. For centuries British audiences have watched this tale performed as a pantomime, a tradition that continues today.

GOLDILOCKS AND THE THREE BEARS

British poet Robert Southey first published *The Story of the Three Bears* in 1837, but it was a popular tale well before then. Originally, the character of the intruder was an ugly old woman, but over time she morphed into the pretty yet delinquent, little girl known as Goldilocks.

THE STEADFAST TIN SOLDIER

Hans Christian Andersen included this tale of romance between a tin soldier and a paper ballerina in his 1838 *tales, Told for Children. New Collection. First Booklet*. With a pirouetting central character, it is not surprising that *The Steadfast Tin Soldier* has been embraced by ballet companies around the world. The tale also features in Disney's animated *Fantasia* sequel, *Fantasia 2000*.

RUMPELSTILTSKIN

There are countless versions of this cautionary tale about the dangers of boasting, and every country seems to have its own name for the mischievous dwarf: Trit-a-Trot, Tom Tit Tot, Ricdin-Ricdon, Whuppity Stoorie. The best-known version, the German *Rumpelstiltskin*, featured in the Grimm Brothers' *Children's and Household Tales* (1812).

THE WOLF AND THE SEVEN LITTLE KIDS

Jacob and Wilhelm Grimm included this popular story in their 1812 collection *Children's and Household Tales,* and it has since been adapted and reproduced countless times.

In 2009, a new German game called *Nicht zu Fassen* (The Uncatchables) was produced. Marketed as a hide-and-seek game for 'clever little goats', it is based on this popular fairytale.

THE LITTLE RED HEN

A traditional folk tale that highlights the importance of hard work, *The Little Red Hen* was made into a 1934 Silly Symphonies cartoon called *The Wise Little Hen* by Walt Disney. Donald Duck made his debut in this cartoon.

THE PRINCESS AND THE PEA

In 1835, Danish author Hans Christian Andersen published *The Princess and the Pea* in *Tales, Told for Children. First Collection. First Booklet,* adapting a folk tale he had known since childhood. Andersen's fairytales are believed to be among the most frequently translated works in all literary history.

THE GINGERBREAD MAN

Various oral versions of this tale were known in Europe and stories of an escapee pancake were published in the mid-19th century. The popular tale of a gingerbread man first appeared in print as *The Gingerbread Boy* in the American *St Nicholas Magazine* in 1875, while more modern stories of fugitive food can be found in *The Runaway Rice Cake* and *The Runaway Tortilla*.

LITTLE RED RIDING HOOD

Little Red Riding Hood comes to a sticky end in Frenchman Charles Perrault's *Tales of Mother Goose*, published in 1697, which featured the first printed version of this tale. Many happier adaptations were to come, notably *Little Red Cap* by the Brothers Grimm, included in their 1812 collection *Children's and Household Tales*.

THE THREE WISHES

Joseph Jacobs popularised this colourful story in his second collection of fairytales, *More English Fairy Tales* (1894). Earlier versions include French author Charles Perrault's *The Ridiculous Wishes*, published in the late 17th century, and *The Woodman's Three Wishes*, which appears in Thomas Sternberg's *The Dialect & Folk-lore of Northamptonshire* (1851).

RAPUNZEL

Rapunzel features in the Grimm Brothers' 1812 collection *Children's and Household Tales*, but similar 'Maiden in the Tower' stories had been popular in Italy and France for generations. The heroine in the Italian version, *Petrosinella*, was named after the herb parsley rather than the rapunzel lettuce. The story was published as early as 1634 in Giambattista Basile's *Pentamerone*.

THE LITTLE MATCH GIRL

Danish author Hans Christian Andersen gleaned the original tale of *The Little Match Girl* from his mother's experiences as a child beggar. First published in 1845, it has since been adapted around the world into countless books, movies, TV shows and songs, many of which vary from the original by saving the freezing girl from death at the story's end.

THE ELVES AND THE SHOEMAKER

This is the most popular of three tales about elves included in the Grimm Brothers' *Children's and Household Tales* (1812). Part of the tale describes the complicated relationship that elves have with clothing, a common theme in European folklore. A more recent example can be seen with Dobby the house-elf in JK Rowling's *Harry Potter* series of books.

THUMBELINA

Danish author Hans Christian Andersen first published Thumbelina (*Tommelise* in Danish) in his 1835 publication *Tales, Told For Children. First Collection. Second Booklet*. Earlier petite characters who may have inspired the tale include the French *Hop o' My Thumb*, the British folk hero *Tom Thumb* and the teeny Lilliputians in Jonathan Swift's *Gulliver's Travels*.

THE SHEPHERDESS AND THE CHIMNEY SWEEP

The Shepherdess and the Chimney Sweep is one of several Hans Christian Andersen stories that anthropomorphise inanimate objects. This rather odd fairytale, in which two china figurines fall in love, was published in 1845 in Andersen's collection *New Tales. Third Instalment,* and later inspired the French animated film *Le Roi et l'oiseau* (The King and the Mockingbird).

THE WILD SWANS

The Wild Swans was first published in 1838 in Hans Christian Andersen's *Tales, Told for Children. New Collection. First Booklet.* Similar tales abound, but a notable version is *The Six Swans*, published in 1812 by the Brothers Grimm. In 2009, the Danish film version, *De Vilde Svaner*, was released, with HM Queen Margrethe II of Denmark contributing the script and production design.

THE THREE BILLY GOATS GRUFF

This Scandinavian favourite was published in *Norske Folkeeventyr*, by Norwegian authors Peter Christen Asbjørnsen and Jørgen Moe, in 1845. Trolls originated in Scandinavian folklore. In German folklore a similar tale, *How the Goats Came to Hessen*, includes a greedy wolf instead of a troll.